I0147156

Other books by Hugh Drummond Fulcher:

Emotional Mind Modeling (1995)

The Clear Mind Procedure (2007)

Bipolar Blessings & Mind Expansion (2008)

God, the Universe, & You! (2008)

Bipolar Blessings & Mind Expansion, 2nd Edition (2009)

"This book is for those wishing to glimpse into the 'troubled mind and spirit,' like Job (tested by the Lord.) In the author's darkness, a juncture of desperation and inspiration motivated the next discoveries and revelations."

Reverend George Jones,
Rational Emotive Therapist

"The author may be ahead of his time in recognizing he is a child of God by connecting science and Christianity. Struggles include communication challenges with his fellow man and God. Mr. Fulcher has made progress in adjusting his inner thoughts and spiritual processes. His writings reveal a remarkable person."

Rev., Dr. Joe T. Lindsoe

Cover: A Small Glimpse of God's Creation

GOD,
the Universe, & You!

SECOND EDITION

SECOND EDITION

Can we understand God?

Hugh Drummond Fulcher

Published
By
H Fulcher Publishers

INTEGRATING SCIENCE AND SPIRITUAL MODELS

Disclaimer: Neither the author nor the publisher is responsible for consequences experienced or not experienced if practicing the author's mental healing and spiritual models. Models are to be used at readers' discretions. Models have been extremely beneficial to the author but not scientifically proven.

Published by: H Fulcher Publishers, Forest, VA.
Printed in the United States of America

First printing: 2009
ISBN: 0-9790710-5-4
ISBN13: 9780979071058

Visit **www.booksurge.com** to order additional copies.

Vita

Hugh Drummond Fulcher resides in Forest, Va. He has two children: Dr. Keston Hugh Fulcher, Kara Fulcher Hawkins, MD, (and her husband, Andrew Hawkins, MD, and son, Jack.)

The author graduated from VA Tech - BS degree in Physics (math minor) and MS degree in Nuclear Engineering. His thesis was on nuclear reactor modeling and design. He was licensed by the Nuclear Regulatory Commission as an operator of the experimental nuclear reactor at Virginia Tech and studied at Argonne National Laboratory.

He taught University physics, engineering, and computer courses at the VA Tech branch in Danville, VA, and at Danville Community College. He worked in nuclear and computer industries for twenty-five years in management, reactor core modeling and design, nuclear software systems, and nuclear safety analysis (and modeling.) He has worked for nuclear reactor design companies, nuclear utilities, consulting companies, and on design of the New Production Reactor. He has written design and operation manuals, and given presentations on nuclear physics and nuclear software to nuclear societies.

Conversations on neurosurgery with Dr. O. Hugh Fulcher (an uncle, deceased) former Head of the Georgetown University Neurosurgery Department and experience in modeling complex nuclear systems, gave the author confidence in modeling the brain and mind for understanding, and healing bipolar disorder.

Mr. Fulcher's books are written to understand and heal the mind, cure bipolar disorder, and integrate science and Christianity for spiritual understanding. He has given talks, and television and radio interviews. Simple physics models cross boundaries into metaphysical treatments of the mind and God. An unusual spiritual message demanded dedication. Mind healing and spiritual technologies were developed over a thirty year period.

In 2005, Mr. Fulcher established a financial company, Wide Acceptance Financial, Inc., in Forest, VA. He is a member of *Who's Who in the South and Southwest* and a member of *Who's Who in America.*

Table of Contents

List of Illustrations

(1) Holusion™ Art ("Holusion™ Art is a trademark of NVision Grafix, Inc.")

Acknowledgements

I am eternally grateful to my parents, Lewis Page Fulcher, Sr. and Frances Drummond Fulcher (both deceased) for their love and guidance. They were the love beneath my wings.

I wish to thank:

My Savior, Jesus Christ, integrated within God, and God for sharing so many ideas.

P. Joanne Bryant for her editing the entire manuscript,

Dr. Keston Fulcher, Kara Fulcher Hawkins, MD, and Professor Carole Mac Clanahan for their comments and editing of several chapters of the manuscript,

Professor Reverend George Jones for his insight and comments on *The Clear Mind Procedure* that have helped focus and presentation,

Computer builders and software developers for their organizational tools that have made writing and editing easier,

And to others who have added to this effort.

Dedications

God, the Universe, & You! 2nd Edition is dedicated to:

1. My parents, Frances Drummond Fulcher (deceased) for her patience, and Lewis Page Fulcher, Sr. (deceased) for his wisdom, and both for their love;

2. My Uncle, O. Hugh Fulcher, MD (deceased), former Head of the Georgetown University Neurosurgery Department, who gave confidence to reason about the brain and mind;

3. My friend, P. Joanne Bryant, who has been so kind in editing the manuscript;

4. My children, Dr. Keston Hugh Fulcher, Kara Brenn Fulcher Hawkins, MD, and son-in-law Andrew Hawkins, MD;

5. My grandson, Jack Henry Hawkins, and future grandchildren;

6. My double first cousin, Barbara Fulcher Mays, and her husband, Carlton, for having cared for my aged parents, and are still caring for my childhood church, Ivy Hill United Methodist Church;

7. All ancestors in heaven and all future descendents;

8. All readers who need healing from stress disorders or who support afflicted loved-ones;

9. All who wish to learn about God for spiritually uniting the universe;

10. Everyone who loves, cares for, and shares with, others.

Purpose

Writers have been inspired by unusual messages, visions, dreams, and feelings for centuries. Humans learn through normal and inner senses. In different ways, writers have attempted to understand and describe purposes of inner messages and lives.

The author does so by integrating religion, spiritual messages, and science. To understand great writers or architects, we study their work. We must explore and study the universe to understand God.

The purpose of the brain and body is the foundation of the mind. The brain creates the mind and recursively the mind controls the brain, and body. The brain is physical; the mind is, or can be, spiritual.

Parents learn about themselves as they reflect and respond to their children. God learns about Himself as He reflects and responds to free wills of human minds. Human purpose is to share free will praises and reflections with God, and surrender to God at times.

The purpose of the universe is God's foundation. The universe creates God, and recursively, He controls the universe. God's purpose is for existence, awareness of existence, and perfect spiritual guidance for continuing existence and building relationships within existence.

Creation?

Assuming an established science uncertainty principle was true at the beginning of physical time, God's Word created God, and His Inventive Abilities and Power created the universe. His Word was the architect of the Big Bang in spiritual time before physical time!

Human purpose is to advance knowledge, and love one another, the world, the universe, and God. Believing in Jesus, integrated within God, promotes inner peace, spiritual blessings, and is good psychiatry. Jesus was the liberal spiritual teacher on earth and is now integrated eternally within God.

The origin of, and everything in, the universe was and is based upon uncertainty. Otherwise, there would no need for man's or God's decisions. God integrates awareness of all past uncertainties and the entire history of the universe into spiritual certainty, makes long-range predictions, but does not know the entire future of the universe. If He did He could not make decisions, or answer prayers, and would be only a recorder of events in the universe. God is greater than that.

CHAPTER 1

Introduction

"Do not conform any longer to the pattern of this world,
But be transformed by the renewing of your mind"

Romans 12:2, New International Version – Disciple's Bible (1)

You may never think the same about your mind, and even God, after reading this book. With science and inner spiritual study, we can learn to reason about the brain, mind, universe, and God. The author and other manic-depressives receive spiritual messages but sometimes lose normal mental control. A <u>cured</u> manic-depressive uses simple physics, not chemistry, to understand and cure his disorder.

Amazingly, spiritual themes received by manic-depressives are quite similar. However, words used to describe spiritual experiences are different depending upon life experiences and vocabulary. There was and still is a compelling interest to communicate with and understand God with very different manic mental processing.

Manic-depressives and the mental health community should work to analyze and benefit from spiritual messages. If prepared, we all can receive the same spiritual message.

Manic-depressives the author has met have experienced uncertainties and received messages from God during extreme manic episodes. Spiritual messages often become so exciting and rapid that manic minds lose earthly reason.

Family and observers do not believe messages are from God. This book was written to change that misperception. As with any challenging endeavor, bipolar disorder thinking can create the highest accomplishments or devastating defeats. Manic spiritual messages are too common and similar not to have spiritual truth. Was Jesus manic when He received spiritual messages and blessings?

Family, supporters, ministers, and psychiatrists work to end bipolar mania and do not attempt to nurture or understand spiritual messages. The medical community and families need to nurture spiritual messages on the creative edge of sanity while maintaining patient and overall safety and productive levels of behavior.

Usually, we do not think about or learn things in depth unless inspired by teachers, parents, mentors, or traumatic events. We can break the chains of childhood indoctrination and traumas to expand current mental limits for understanding the universe and God.

Bipolar Blessings & Mind Expansion, 2nd Edition,[(2)] also by the author, includes an in-depth description of events that led to his bipolar disorder and includes processes for its cure. A condensed description of bipolar disorder healing is given in the first part of this book to support spiritual models.

This work is to communicate with and understand God using science, traditional religions, and personal messages from God. We must have an understanding of the brain and mind before constructing models for understanding God and man's spiritual purpose.

The author has had two near-death experiences. The first was an expected-death near car accident, which was avoided by a "flash of emotional events." The second near-death experience was the result of severe depression and devastating side effects from a psychiatric drug. After the second near-death occurrence, the author became sensitive to spiritual feelings and words. Feeling life escaping with no tomorrow dramatically affects thinking and inner healing sensations.

Those of us who are science and religion oriented often have conflict. Tradition religions sometimes conflict with science discoveries. Prayer communication must be very different from sound and electromagnetic communications.

Traditional religions and their recorded miracles have saved and destroyed lives. We do not understand miracles even with today's scientific technology. In the next one thousand years, advanced descendents will still know only a very small portion of God's great designs and truths. Man crawls along using the knowledge his forefathers have passed along and that which he has learned.

This book is dedicated to visionaries who have experienced near-death beyond physical awareness and felt spiritual joy hidden within manic insanities.

Humans know very little of reality. We see through limited electromagnetic spectra – light. God "sees" with all electromagnetic spectra and all field forces. His "vision" focuses into elementary or atomic particles and holistically senses the entire universe.

We need to purge stress and trauma effects from the brain to improve spiritual communication. The author developed creative models and unique physical exercises to understand and heal the mind. Our complex minds heal slowly. Exercise heals depression more effectively than current antidepressants. [3, 4]

This work presents astonishing new background ideas for healing bipolar disorder and assisting scientists in modeling the brain, mind, and God. If understanding God's work, His universe, scientists will understand God's creative structure. Studying famous work, gives understanding of the creator's genius. Inventive minds iterate between uncertainty and certainty to discover the wonders of God's Truth through science. What could be more profound than understanding more of God's Truth in our moment of time? It is our duty!

To lesser or greater extent, everyone needs healing from childhood and adult repressed memories caused by stress and trauma. Many develop stress disorders and think and act irrationally at times. In trauma, the brain processes differently at emotional limits. At limits, normal mental processing is interrupted, and the mind momentarily blacks out. A trauma scar is ingrained within a localized neural network.

Being afraid of making mistakes and of what others think has suppressed so many brilliant ideas. Fantastic mental adventures may create mind models that inspire advanced models later. One goal is to inspire the physics community to develop models of the mind and God, and ultimately, the relationship between the two. Models may help the human race construct physical and spiritual synergy.

Mind and spiritual models use established science and imaginative steps for spiritual discovery. Inner analyses are performed to integrate science and religion, mostly Christianity.

After surviving depression and mania, there is joy and inner awareness of the mind and God. The author's healing processes were quite unusual so they were kept secret to avoid negative comments until mental goals were assured and spiritual channels reopened. Short-term trials and errors were not disclosed. As society experiences the benefits, mental reconstruction processes and practices may be performed more openly.

The subconscious mind integrates daily events and thoughts with historical memories. Sleeping is the time for self-focus and recursive reflections to and from God for His guidance. Relaxing the mind before sleep enhances long-range right-brained thinking processes. The mind is no longer constrained to worries of the day and can dream creatively.

Since the author's first manic episode in 1977, he has often wondered why God saved him from death when he was too depressed to be angry, mentally void, in pain, and experiencing the feeling and smell of death. He felt certain of never recovering.

Death was welcomed. God, his children and parents, became reasons for transforming expected death into hope and wonder.

Hardships in childhood and marriage, stresses, severe manic depression, and inspiration from unexpected spiritual communications, have developed a new perspective in life. The mind is good at thinking of outward events, but requires training and culturing to become aware of, and improve, subconscious processes. Modeling has increased inner awareness and inner abilities. In the beginning, psychiatric and spiritual exploration was bold and daring, but after years of practice, became routine.

In near-death and severe depression experiences only God matters. Experiencing near-death became a driving force for writing this book. Uncertainties during mania reduce worldly reason but strengthen spiritual communication. The author developed spiritual rebirth and purpose.

Immediate awareness of a "certain-death" car crash presented a "flash" of the author's emotional scenarios that saved his life. It contained a hundred scenarios spliced together and running fast-forward at nearly one million times life speed. Inner mental processes had time to select and edit scenarios in this spiritual, life-saving flash!

Survival is genetically programmed deep within human souls. From this experience, the soul may produce important scenarios of life for God to judge a person's character. Almost subconsciously the author's arm jerked the steering wheel and saved his life.

"Flashes" occur during abrupt life-threatening crises. Everyone will experience "a flash" at the moment of death. If we learn more about subconscious processes, we may be able to construct "flashes" with better content for God's Judgment.

Babies are born with few physical skills; instead, they are born with perfect spiritual skills. Babies and young children need parents' acceptance. As children grow, parents gloat at every bit of physical control they gain. Parents guide children toward taking care of themselves. Children grow to be independent and loving or only caring about self. Life-cycles usually continue for generations.

Due to traumas and self-centered parental training many children become less spiritual as they gain control over their environments. After gaining confidence toward independence, older children arrive at tipping points in their lives.

They continue to gain control of their lives and environments or surrender to God. Concepts of being saved, surrendering to God, and letting Him or Jesus take control of lives needs definition. We add to that definition throughout this book.

If socially sound, parents' adjust to reasonable relationships with adult children. As we age, we reflect back more on our lives and God. We should review our histories at times to improve goals. Many of us have worshipped, and surrendered our emotional wills to, God for purposeful lives.

Spiritual lives are cuddled by God. Upon physical death, humans are reborn as spiritual babies in heaven eager to learn heavenly ways. Heavenly spirits learn to make decisions in heaven for divine purposes.

We may surrender to God or true spiritual leaders. If so, God influences our emotional holistic processing right brains. With free will, humans retain control of left-brain mental processes for everyday tasks.

God is Light or Electromagnetic Waves and Resonances. Through electromagnetic frequencies and resonances below and above free-will frequencies, God influences emotional direction, long-range decisions, and reduces guilt from traumas and failure.

Upon weakening or aging, many people become more spiritual. At the beginning and end of life, God has total control. During most of life, man possesses mental free will, physical strength, and can live independently of God's guidance. With life's choices, we die of sin or live eternally.

Philip Yancey includes a quotation Dr. Martin Luther King, Jr. made in private to Dr. Robert Coles, in *Soul Survivor, How Thirteen*

Unlikely Mentors Helped My Faith Survive the Church. (5) Dr. King understood that many people were suffering spiritually more than many African-Americans. His genius awakened spirituality in people of all faiths and races. It is a human defect for those lacking spirituality to exert superiority over others. Dr. King's statement below is a meaningful account of human nature:

> "I have begun to realize how hard it is for a lot of people to think of living without someone to look down upon, really look down upon. It is not just that they will feel cheated out of someone to hate; it is that they will be compelled to look more closely at what they don't like in themselves." (5, p108)

Looking down on others is not simply racial. Egotistical, deranged families, spouses, siblings, cousins, and neighbors act superior, look down on, and degrade even those close to them.

Dr. King realized America needed guidance for a new normal. Each individual has personal guidelines for being "normal." This work concentrates on the abnormal for "new" ways of thinking about and analyzing the mind, the soul, the universe, heaven, and God. With practice over time, the abnormal becomes the normal.

Models of the mind and God are developed on quasi-scientific and metaphysical bases. Philosophical and heuristic ideas are the forerunners of scientific discovery. Heuristic refers to best guesses, which are deeply believed to be true.

Intelligent guesses and models are precursors to science experimentation and evaluation of results. Scientific discoveries prove laws or consistencies in nature, and, in the future, may cross boundaries to reveal the connection between the universe and God. Hopefully, models and processes given in this book will help readers construct their own healing and spiritual processes.

Our minds are integrations of all brain, and to some extent body, cell activities. Each brain cell constructs a small fraction of one's awareness and thought. In spiritual models, God is the integrated awareness of all atoms, light, and field forces throughout the universe.

It is difficult to believe mental healing sensations or spiritual communications unless having experienced them personally. Normal people usually think others are similar to themselves unless someone has built a noted reputation. This is not true for those having been overstressed or near death. In depression one knows his thinking is severely less than normal. After recovery, thinking can become more creative than normal.

Exploring inner uncertainties develops spiritual certainty. Beyond normal mental limits, the mind integrates uncertainties and insanities into spiritual reality. Modeling God improves spiritual communication, direction, and healing. Only the adventurous will choose this yellow brick road of mental healing and spiritual development.

We were perfectly spiritual upon conception. There is no spiritual superiority. Some traditional religions claim spiritual superiority and the only path to heaven. This causes sins of pride and degradation of other religions and their believers. Adults may reduce spiritual uncertainties but never regain the spiritual level at conception during life.

Humans and living beings have no reason to live without uncertainty. Life would be predestined. However, God integrates all physical uncertainties within the universe into spiritual wholeness or certainty. Humans have their part in mentally integrating uncertainties into spiritual certainty. By developing and practicing one's own spiritual science, each of us can become messengers of God. The author strives to be a small part of the spiritual generation.

Science strives to understand brains, minds, and the universe. Spiritual science can be cultivated for understanding God and many paths to heaven.

After the author had modeled the brain and mind, modeling heaven and God flowed logically. Modeling forces in-depth analysis. Engineers and architects make drawings and models to guide construction. Scientists use detailed plans and models to guide experiments for understanding and proving physical laws. Modeling is not easy but may help the understanding of spiritual communication and an "infinite" God. We really have no understanding of infinity.

Bipolar disorder disrupts everyday behaviors, but uncovers hidden mental and spiritual abilities. Mania reduces inhibitions and expands creative thinking limits beyond earlier mental processing boundaries. Extreme emotions and uncertainties have motivated inner analyses toward certainty in God. Persistent imagination crosses scientific boundaries for amazing models of God. When humans construct artificial thinking boundaries, minds become limited.

When extremely manic, the author had an intense desire to communicate with, and understand, God. Shattering spiritual words were more believable than those received from all words heard or read. Spiritual words demanded dedication and guided focus for the author's writing. He began organized spiritual writing in 1994. Mental healing extended into spiritual healing.

The author's belief in truthfulness of deep-structure English language helped develop spiritual models. Deep-structure language reflects the inner self and has assisted with break-through healing discoveries and integration of science and religion.

God communicates with us personally, especially, when facing death and only He can save our lives. God's message is as strong, constant, and complete today as in traditional spiritual times. Believers must respond to spiritual messages quickly or opportunities are often lost similarly to remembering dreams.

Science cannot yet prove inner messages are from God. However, the author cannot believe he has had so many creative ideas on his own.

Wouldn't it be wonderful for our generations to "heal" abuse, mental isolation, and depression? We must dream of, and culture kinder, rewarding spiritual futures.

Worshipping God is a right-brain process promoting feelings of completeness. The right brain perceives God holistically beyond details as continuously infinite. At times, humans are able to vaguely describe continuous, spiritual feelings with fragile discrete words.

All, who destroy minds whether recognized by victims or not, are the truly mentally ill. Without love, guidance, and discipline in childhood, mental illness extends through generations.

Having lived through depression gives a richer, more spiritual perspective of life. Patience, love, and dedication can heal the sick and depressed, and are among life's highest virtues. Learning through science requires dedication.

Studying cosmology helps develop spiritual reasoning. God created the universe and its laws with perfect reason. We study science to understand the physical nature of the universe and religion to understand God's spiritual or paranormal nature beyond science. As science knowledge and spiritual wisdom increase, human minds will iterate and then converge more as a holistic spiritual existence.

Bipolar patients experience inner sensations beyond the normal senses. Psychiatrists do not acknowledge that patients are receiving spiritual communications and drug sensations away to calm behaviors. They refer to unusual messages as "psychotic hallucinations" without trying to understand them. Unusual voices heard through the ears are referred to as "auditory hallucinations." Unusual inner voices are referred to as "thought intrusions." Doctors will not help patients understand unusual sensations and spiritual communications.

Non-Christians may think Moses and Jesus only had thought intrusions or psychotic hallucinations. God uses these spiritual channels to speak to us today. Cultivation of inner spiritual channels allows reception of deeper spiritual meaning. If advanced spiritual skills were easy, everyone would be prophets.

If normal people worship in church and feel God's presence, they are respectable church goers. If manic-depressives receive spiritual messages in words, ministers and psychiatrists label them as "psychotic" without helping them develop spiritual skills. Psychiatric medications dull the mind and destroy spiritual feelings and communications. Manic-depressives must maintain humbleness and sanity around others but continue spiritual work.

Models of the brain, mind, soul, heaven, God, and biological life are developed within similar frameworks. Integrating mental and spiritual processes attracts feelings and words from God. This work constructs mental holograms for understanding the clear mind, freed of trauma scars and effects.

Spiritual models are presented and refined later at times. No human model or book can represent the complete truth of God's physical and spiritual creations. Knowledge will continue to improve with models from creative individuals. Scientific discoveries begin as educated guesses or theories. Theories suggest models and experiments to prove or disprove ideas. Today's abilities and quality of life are based upon yesterday's struggles, ideas and dreams.

The author's work reduces conflict between science, Intelligent Design, and Creationism. Evolution is simply "slow" creation. Mind healing and integration of science and spirituality are breakthrough efforts to improve quality of life and more correct beliefs. As life becomes more meaningful, our highest goals are to communicate with, understand, and obey God. With limited minds, we separate and categorize events and ideas for understanding. God integrates understanding of all things in the universe into continuous spiritual wholeness.

The brain is physical. The mind is spiritual. Remembered and imagined events are not constrained to physical space and time. They are imaginary with only spiritual existence in the mind. Mental holograms, as seen in dreams, are virtual or spiritual building blocks for thoughts. (Holograms are discussed in chapter 3.)

Guidance for this work is from inner spiritual feelings, science, and, mostly, the Christian religion. Work is meant to promote research. Briefly extending inner processes to mental limits initiates creative thinking.

Adults, when beginning to receive spiritual messages, are similar to babies learning language. It takes time to learn an exciting new inner spiritual language and remain earthly conversant. Centuries ago, Plato warned of distinguishing between intellectuals experiencing spiritual communication and the shallow minded.

Hundreds and thousands of years ago, spiritual leaders and writers did not have today's scientific background and could only write simply about God and His perfection. The author encourages readers to analyze models given here and construct their own spiritual models. Readers should be open-minded in judging new, carefully thought-out, spiritual ideas as science and language progress for understanding the universe and God.

A goal is to develop spiritual science and technology for discovering God's purposes. Understanding probability and science laws, one becomes more able to assist God's purposes with His human experiment.

The author believes physical and spiritual science apply equally throughout the universe. With spiritual technology and science, there will be less opportunity for power-hungry ministers to abuse followers. Teaching about God will become more reasonable and logical. Knowledge has come a long way over the last few thousand years. With modern language and science, religious precepts will be more precise and not need to be taught through parables.

Believers will communicate with and worship God in a more logical and proven way. A modern religion will be more scientific and not rely on one person's interpretations of critical excerpts from God's infinite, continuous message. Ministers will need more logical interpretations with less opportunity for emotional, materialistic, and spiritual corruption. Ministers must be more definitive in nurturing psychological and spiritual needs. Traditional religious dogma may be proven or disproven with brain scans of believers. Traditional spiritual passages affect believers and skeptics differently.

As a physicist and former manic-depressive, the author thinks more holistic at times. For healing his bipolar disorder, he extended thinking beyond the physical universe for models of *nothing* before time with sufficient properties to create heaven, God, and the universe.

If anyone believes current spiritual books provide a complete understanding of an "infinite" God, their minds are limited and have been brainwashed. God's understanding is infinite relative to human minds. A billion books could not fully describe God.

Humans have only a meager understanding of the word, "infinite." Free-will and spiritual thoughts coexist within blended borders in the brain and mind. There is no discrete cutoff between the two. Historically, scientists and religious leaders have constructed barriers between the two disciplines.

We must learn our individual purposes from God. Recursively, He learns from humans; otherwise, we would have no need to pray. Parents learn about themselves as they raise their children. God learns about man similarly and reflects our thoughts throughout the universe. Humans and God learn and make judgments. Making decisions causes change. Man and God make decisions, are not predestined, and have purpose.

God's time is different or relativistic relative to physical time. God has infinite spiritual time relative to man's time for His purposes. God is aware of our subconscious processes for conscious ideas before we know our own ideas. He does not control free will thinking but provides guidance above and below free will resonances.

God's predictions of the physical universe are beyond man's imaginations. Prophets have predicted the future for Man's benefit. Throughout history, spiritual writers have either done their best to translate God's flowing language truthfully into words or have twisted spiritual communications for their own selfish purposes.

If electromagnetic, chemical, and possibly field force activities in the brain develop human intelligence, then nuclear, electromagnetic, chemical, and possibly other field force activities throughout the universe develop a higher intelligence.

The author's goals in this book are:

1. Cure bipolar and stress-related disorders;
2. Use the right brain to imagine beyond the physical world and expand emotional thinking processes to receive spiritual guidance, purpose, and completeness;
3. Build confidence in thinking for spiritual awakening and inner joy;
4. Entice the physics community into modeling the human brain for improving mental and spiritual abilities. This task might be of the same difficulty as integrating quantum mechanics and general relativity with "String Theory" models;
5. Suggest the National Institutes of Mental Health promote physics methodologies and clinical studies to prove this physics cure for bipolar disorder.

The author is grateful to be a cured manic-depressive and enjoying God's blessings. His disorder has allowed an extraordinary analysis of his own brain, mind, soul, and the universe, heaven, and God. With normal thinking and mental healing, humans are fortunate. With spiritual healing, humans are most fortunate. Life has not been easy. Blessings flow easier after surviving a long and difficult mental and spiritual journey.

Nothing develops longer-lasting or overall excitement than receiving spiritual words from God. In contrast, evil thoughts and actions bring only brief excitement that fades quickly.

The author often talks of his mind healing and spiritual endeavors, and was once asked about spiritual references. The answer was that the author needed only one spiritual reference. Jesus needed only one spiritual reference. The Bible does not mention Jesus' expertise in studying huge academic volumes about God.

Individuals may study spiritual accounts and works by others. However, important spiritual understanding comes directly from God through minds and hearts.

Many spiritual discoveries will come from manic-depressives who have suffered near-death experiences and surrendered their lives to God's Will. Other discoveries will be made through science.

Psychiatrists seem interested only in preventing uncontrollable behavior. They prescribe drugs that slow down fast manic thinking and end spiritual communications. The energy level of the brain is reduced, and spiritual communication is lost. Manic-depressives must slow thinking down on their own, and control spiritual excitement to benefit from, and record, spiritual experiences.

We should not dismiss, but learn from, spiritual experiences in normal times, and while striving to maintain control in manic times. Spiritual experiences and models have formed traditional religions and promoted mental health for generations.

Is our religion imprisoning our minds and souls or setting them free? Are we trying to think like someone else? We have distinct DNA to build our unique souls as presents to God.

Can you reason beyond ingrained childhood thinking limits or simply believe what others tell you? Do you reason about everyday and spiritual beliefs! This work assists reasoning about inner healing based upon science, spiritual feelings, and God's presence. We strengthen beliefs by surviving at mental limits.

We have been indoctrinated by our parents, religious leaders, and schools with ideas accepted as facts. Our beliefs are only opinions from fragile perceptions. We must think positively of others and ourselves for spiritual blessings.

Religions are major causes of distrust and hatred in the world. No one likes to feel inferior or spiritually inferior. If indoctrinated in early life, people will continue their beliefs without reason defying scientific proof.

Traditional religions have lost touch with God's completeness or holiness. They have succumbed to shortsighted superiority.

For expanding spiritual reasoning, an *epilogue* requests reader feedback and words received from God. We can develop spiritual reasoning together.

Appendix A: *Dark Energy and Matter,* discusses experimental confirmation of the theoretically predicted existence of dark energy and matter which may eventually prove characteristics of God.

REFERENCES:

(1) *The Holy Bible - New International Version - Disciples' Study Bible,* 1984, Holman Bible Publishers, Nashville, Tennessee.

(2) Fulcher, Hugh D., *Bipolar Blessings and Mind Expansion,* 2008, H Fulcher Publishers, a Division of Wide Acceptance Financial, Inc., Lynchburg, VA.

(3) Blumenthal, James A., et al., *Effects of Exercise Training on Older Patients with Major Depression,* October 25, 1999, Archives of Internal Medicine.

(4) Babyak, Michael, et al., *Exercise Treatment for Major Depression: Maintenance of Therapeutic Benefit at 10 Months,* September/October 2000, *Psychosomatic Medicine.*

(5) Philip Yancey, 2003, *Soul Survivor, How Thirteen Unlikely Mentors Helped My Faith Survive the Church,* A Galilee Book, published by Doubleday, a division of Random House, Inc., New York, NY.

CHAPTER 2

A Spiritual Dream: Princess Karalla

Only inner thoughts build lasting happiness.

Hugh D. Fulcher

Of everything you wear, your expression is the most important.

Unknown

An imaginative dream becomes spiritual for the author. I dream a pleasant dream of my deceased parents being the parents of my children with love and success in their lives. I am only a displaced observer in this dream that brings out intense personal emotions. I share the joy of loved ones while only observing. Sharing the joy of others without personal benefit develops spiritual emotions.

A Fairy Tale for Our Times

Once upon a time, a young man, Lewis, set out to seek his fortune. He had heard tales of a land of riches and gold. One night during his journey, he stopped in a small village, Gidsville. There was sorrow in this village. Robbers and thieves came often to steal and plunder. There was a great need for someone brave to organize the people of this poor village. Lewis listened to the villager's stories about the greedy raiders. He was eager to reach his destination, but felt it necessary to help people in need.

The first thing Lewis did was to cheer up the villagers and give them confidence that they could protect themselves. He taught the villagers to fight with swords and shoot straight with arrows. Upon completion of training, there was a big celebration with many games involving shooting arrows, fencing, horseback riding, and other games showing preparation for self-defense. The word spread widely that this village was prepared to defend itself.

Something amazing happened. Not one robber or thief ever came to this land again since it became known that the villagers were prepared to defend their village. Lewis was ready to seek his fortune.

The celebration was on the eve before Lewis' departure. The villagers were sad Lewis was leaving. The village elders had been scheming. One of the prettiest young maidens, Frances, had been away at school. Many in the village were hoping that Lewis and Frances would meet, fall in love, marry, and remain in Gidsville.

The party was lively. Everyone was thanking Lewis for teaching them to defend their village. Lewis was always laughing and telling jokes. The entire community was joyful and managed a bountiful feast. At the very time the music started, Frances entered in a beautiful white dress. She looked radiant. Her mother had died when Frances was very young. Her older sisters, Elsie and Annie, had taught her to be a proper lady.

Frances lived with her sister, Annie, and her husband John. Frances had heard of Lewis but had never seen him. Lewis had not heard of Frances since she lived out in the country and had been away at school. Lewis was talking to friends. Frances and a girlfriend were exchanging compliments on dresses.

It happened! A "magic moment" happened. It just took one glance. Time stood still. Lewis glanced at Frances. She noticed Lewis looking at her. She then realized that she had been looking at him too long. She felt embarrassed and blushed. She felt unladylike for letting her emotions show. A proper lady should not glance too long at a gentleman she does not know. Frances ran weeping from the ballroom.

Lewis was perplexed as to why she ran away. He did not realize how shy she was. The dancing began. Lewis danced with many lovely ladies. Friends wondered about Frances. Her sisters, Elsie and Annie, went to find her. They found Frances sitting in the corner of a bedroom weeping. She was weeping because she had feared that she had not been a proper lady. Annie and Elsie were good at cheering her up. Annie said she wanted Frances to dance with John.

The sisters returned to the dance floor. John was a farmer. This was the first time that he had been to the village for a long while. John was a good dancer and asked Frances to dance. They were enjoying dancing together. As they danced, Lewis by chance danced close to them. Lewis recognized that John was his long lost brother. Lewis was surprised to see John and more surprised to see him dancing with Frances. Emotions ran high.

As the dance ended, Lewis excused himself and rushed to embrace John. There was great rejoicing. They had found one another. Lewis glanced at Frances. John introduced her as his sister-in-law. The music started just then. Lewis swiftly grasped Frances' hand and gently pulled her to the dance floor. They danced beautifully together. Their feet barely touched the floor. Whenever their eyes met, time seemed to stand still and their hearts pounded. The crowd seemed to disappear, and only they mattered to each other. Without speaking a word they both knew they would spend the rest of their lives together. The whole village was delighted to see Lewis and Frances dancing. Love and closeness grew in the village that night.

Lewis married Frances and stayed in Gidsville. Life was filled with love and happiness. Lewis was good at communicating, formed trade agreements with other villages, and improved the roads.

Gidsville and the surrounding lands became prosperous through trading and sharing. The whole area prospered. The people of the valley loved Lewis and the gentle Frances. Both were good at encouraging everyone especially those who were old or sick. Frances especially loved to teach the little children.

Unknown to Lewis and Frances, the people of this valley community discussed their good fortunes and decided to proclaim Lewis and Frances, king and queen. Lewis and Frances thanked everyone very much, but protested that it was not necessary to have a king and queen. However, after much coaxing they accepted.

The community pitched together and built a castle, modest in comparison to nearby castles. The King and Queen worked hard every day to make everyone feel wanted and important. They made visitors and travelers feel welcome. This small kingdom was simple, kind, and loving.

King Lewis and Queen Frances were Christians and worshiped every Sunday and encouraged everyone in their Kingdom to worship. They both taught Sunday school. This Kingdom was a spiritual place.

The Kingdom rejoiced when King Lewis and Queen Frances had a son, Prince Kest, and again two years later when they had a daughter, Princess Karalla. As they grew, Prince Kest and Princess Karalla worked hard at duties around the castle. They knew the importance of studying and learned always to be pleasant to everyone they met. They laughed with each other, and they liked to be funny and entertain the people of the village.

King Lewis and Queen Frances always loved to hug each other. Prince Kest and Princess Karalla grew up loving to hug. As a matter of fact the whole family hugged each member of the Kingdom when appropriate to do so. Everyone in the Kingdom felt loved. The Royal Family showed love and dignity to all and superiority to none. Prince Kest and Princess Karalla lived in a fairyland.

Prince Kest learned the art of defending the kingdom and the refined ways of a prince. Princess Karalla liked to paint pleasant sketches of her visitors. She listened to, and sang to, the birds. They often sang together. Prince Kest and Princess Karalla loved music and loved to sing and dance to entertain the people of the kingdom.

They learned to make people feel at ease, for they knew people think more genuinely and creatively when at ease. King Lewis and Queen Frances wanted to bring out the best in each and every person in the Kingdom. Everyone loved the lively Prince and Princess. The Princess would marry before the Prince would marry.

When Princess Karalla had finished her education, King Lewis decided it was time for her to marry. He sent invitations to kingdoms far and near that there would be a Ball for his daughter to celebrate completing her education. A Ball meant a princess was ready to marry.

All the eligible princes were eager to marry Princess Karalla. Many of the princes had danced with Princess Karalla at other balls. Others had heard of her beauty and charm and how graciously she laughed. Many princes remembered sketches Princess Karalla had made of them and how much fun they had had with her.

The castle was decorated. The dress was made. On the night of the ball, fine coaches began to arrive. Many finely dressed princes and princesses arrived at the palace. Each prince brought a lovely gift for Princess Karalla. She gave each a personalized gift that showed the love and respect she had for them and their families.

Princess Karalla had helped King Lewis fill out her dance card. It was scary for her to think about marrying and moving away from her mother, father, and brother. She loved them and the community so much. But it was time for her to start a family of her own.

Princess Karalla danced with many handsome princes from rich kingdoms. Many princes were bold and valiant knights, but none seemed right to Princess Karalla. She felt she could not be herself with the wealthy princes with whom she had danced. Princess Karalla was becoming afraid that her father would choose someone she did not want to marry. She had come to the last prince on her dance card. Her father had placed him last. Princess Karalla did not recognize this prince's name. She had not yet seen this prince.

The music began, and the main doors of the ballroom opened. The last prince entered the ballroom. Princess Karalla could not believe her eyes. Her childhood playmate, Andrew, was a prince. He was two years older than she and had left the kingdom when she was only eight years old. The prince's royal name was new to her.

It happened. A magic moment happened. It took just one glance. Time stood still. Eyes locked together, and hearts pounded. She had loved Andrew deeply throughout her childhood. She felt embarrassed for a moment. She blushed. His smile was so warm and reassuring that she suddenly felt as if he had left only yesterday.

He reached into his pockets and pulled out a crystal slipper with each hand. Prince Andrew kneeled and placed each shoe onto Princess Karalla's pretty, small feet. He had always told Princess Karalla how pretty she was and how pretty her feet were. They danced beautifully together. Princess Karalla felt like a fairy tale princess. No one was sure whether their feet actually touched the marble floor, but there was an accent to the music as the crystal slippers touched the floor in perfect rhythm. The sound was as pure and clear as a crystal bell, and it seemed to ring out love to all who watched them dance.

Whenever their eyes met, time stood still and hearts pounded. The crowd seemed to disappear and they mattered only to each other. Two hearts beat as one on the marble dance floor that night. Without speaking a word they both knew that they would spend the rest of their lives together. The entire crowd marveled at this magic moment. Tales would be told of this night for years to come.

Princess Karalla and Prince Andrew had shared drawing, games, and learning until his family moved away. Not known to Princess

Karalla, King Lewis sent Prince Andrew's father to a distant land to save a poor community from being plundered. This brave knight taught a distant community to defend themselves. Later, this knight was proclaimed king by the people he saved. In the tradition of Gidsville, this new kingdom had become a loving and peaceful kingdom.

Princess Karalla remembered how she and Prince Andrew talked about keeping the land and the country beautiful. Everyone was delighted to see Princess Karalla and Prince Andrew beaming together. Their faces shone. Heaven embraced two pure hearts as they became one on that magic night. Many toasts were proposed to Princess Karalla and Prince Andrew. As a matter of fact, by the end of the night, toasts had been proposed to everyone in the land. Nine months after their wedding, Princess Karalla and Prince Andrew had Prince Jack and lived happily ever after.

Prince Kest left the day after the ball to save a troubled land.

Epilogue

This fairy tale recalls wonderful memories of my parents and children. It becomes therapeutic and magic when I reread it. I used my parent's names and names similar to those of my children to remember the love we share. This fairy tale strengthens the love between my parents in heaven and my children on earth. Writing (and reading) this fairy tale brought (brings) my parents alive.

This fairy tale is simple emotional writing for spiritual healing. Humbly feeling the joy of others refines emotions. Dream characters were given characteristics of my parents and children. I cry a tear each time I read this dream. Use your imagination to share the joy of loved ones. I encourage readers to write their own fairy tales with a touch of truth to experience deep emotions each time they read it. Set your mind free with creative dreams for spiritual healing.

CHAPTER 3

Foundations of Creative Models

Through the wonders of our brains,
Our experiences are deposited
As imprints on fragile membranes,
To find a virtual universe within.

When working within our disciplines, we
Construct boundaries limiting our thinking.

H. Fulcher

We must extend thinking beyond everyday experiences to be creative. God is intertwined within all creative and efficient processes. We must re-experience our spiritual foundations to re-open creative right brain processes and spiritual channels. Some definition and structure is presented as foundation for mind and spiritual models.

Definition

The author defines his use of the pronouns, "we," "us," and "our." These pronouns refer to the author and readers. It is inferred that readers need healing of, or are interested in helping those with, stress related disorders. Further, it is assumed that readers are interested in improving spiritual communications, thinking about God, or making models to strengthen their own diverse beliefs.

Self

In today's lifestyles, many are so busy listening to music, watching television, or communicating with friends, work, and school that they do not take time to know or even sense themselves. Spiritual leaders can only direct us toward our inner truths. Humans attain heaven and immortality only by understanding their own inner truths. Frequent communications between individuals often add little value to either.

Pain

Severe pain, such as persistent back pain, causes focus on injured areas extending beyond free-will energies. God is aware of our pain. I am uncertain as to how suffering is beneficial to God. However, Jesus suffered on the cross to benefit man and God. He saved mankind from their sins allowing access to eternal life in heaven. Attaining eternal life is beneficial to those saved and must also be so for God.

From my experiences and inner sensations, pain activates mental reconstruction, possibly, for good and bad. Childhood trauma scar releases become more active, but new trauma scars may also be ingrained within localized neural networks.

Mental Health Model

Mental health is feeling good about abilities, accomplishments, and earthly relationships, and accepting current situations and health.

Trauma Scar Model

In normal experiences, the neuron symphony of activations throughout the brain develops reasonable thoughts for appropriate reactions and solutions. Experiencing traumas cause severe mental reactions. Senses are extremely activated by trauma. Nerves generate fast-acting high-energy signals to the brain. These energetic signals produce high-energy electromagnetic frequencies.

Incoming high-energy momentarily freezes or blacks out normal brain functions. A fast-reacting localized neural network with a resonance receptive to the high-energy frequency accepts the entire trauma energy and becomes a localized trauma scar.

This high-energy over-stressed traumatized network no longer fires in symphony with normal neural networks. Its sporadic firings degrade the normal symphony within the brain. The more trauma scars we receive, the more limited our brains and minds become. Creative thinking is affected the most by trauma scars.

The author's unique psychiatric exercises and models purge trauma scars and restore creativity. A long-term goal is to rid the brain of all disruptive trauma effects, expand the mind to genetic limits, and reopen spiritual channels we all had upon conception.

Healing Sensations

During a manic episode in 1995, the author felt snaps, crackles, and pops, or SCAPS, when exercising his neck. Sensations were in the neck, throat, brainstem, and to a small extent in the upper brain. Sensations were modeled as energy releases from trauma memories within localized traumatized networks. These sensations were not unpleasant. Results have supported this theory.

The author's mental energy release theory is much like Freud's psychotherapy for releasing trauma energy from the brain. Similarly to Freud's work, the author's theories will also take time and additional experimentation to be accepted.

Additionally, there were also two very high-energy releases. They are referred to as the metallic sound and the "mental nuclear explosion." These two later powerful sensations caused brief loss of control but no permanent effects. Sensations have caused unusual feelings within a now very different mind.

Gifts

"We have different gifts, according to the grace given us. If a man's gift is prophesying, let him use it in proportion to his faith. If it is serving, let him serve; if it is teaching, let him teach; if it is encouraging, let him encourage, if it is contributing to the needs of others, let him contribute generously, if it is leadership, let him govern diligently; if it is showing mercy, let him do it cheerfully."

Romans 12:6-8 (1)

Spiritual Model of Mental Health

My personal spiritual model of mental health is feeling that struggles and pain have spiritual significance, having confidence in spiritual, mental, and physical abilities to meet expected challenges in life, and being certain of attaining an eternal life beyond imagination. This model includes predicting positive outcomes, fitting in, and feeling comfortable when sharing physical, social, and spiritual environments. Spiritual health is belief in benefits of spiritual communication and feeling God, or a higher power, is concerned for, loves, and helps us through important decisions and circumstances. [Readers are free to make their own models.]

God and Man

The Bible tells us God made man in His image. From a science standpoint this is difficult to understand. However, I think this description is quite good. Prophets and writers thousands of years ago did not have the science understanding we have today. They had to write the way they understood things.

However, from a science standpoint, believing man's mind is made in God's image is very credible. The electromagnetic and field forces that create the mind, its images, and abilities could certainly also create God's infinite awareness, images, and abilities. Science helps us make relationships between similar and dissimilar things.

Resonances

A property of each elementary particle, atom, compound, or structure (a bridge, a radio, or our brains), is its natural resonance frequency. Things absorb more energy at their natural frequencies. Incoming wave energy is reflected back and forth, as resonates, within a structure depositing energy between reflections. Other frequencies simply pass through the structure depositing little energy.

If vibrations, or mechanical frequencies, caused by wind, cars, and trucks produce resonating vibrations, the entire bridge could absorb energy with increasing vibrations and collapse.

At its natural frequency, electronic equipment accepts much more electromagnetic energy than at other frequencies. Let's look at radio stations and radios. At radio stations, an alternating current generator feeds current to an antenna that creates radio waves at a specific frequency allowed and licensed by the federal government.

We want to receive one radio station and receive that station loud and clear. Radios have tuners that allow us to receive different radio stations. Essentially, we can change properties, capacitance, of our radio receivers to change the natural resonance frequencies of our radios to receive that one station we wish to listen to and block out all other stations. Our radio amplifies the radio signal we want to listen to and lets all other radio signals simply pass through.

Water absorbs little energy from most microwave frequencies but many times more energy from its resonant frequency used in microwave ovens. Traveling neutrons have characteristic matter waves. Neutrons have much higher probability of being absorbed by uranium nuclei and causing fissions when traveling slower at uranium nuclei resonance energies. Slowing down or moderating neutron speeds adds control in operating nuclear reactors.

Mental Resonances

Synchronized neuron activations create subconscious electromagnetic resonances. The brain's complex shapes and details support many complex resonances. Subconscious resonances construct inner processes within mental holograms. If subconscious resonances vibrate long enough, they develop consciousness.

Commercial Holograms

Let's ensure we understand mechanisms of constructing commercial holograms. They are made with coherent laser beams. This means all light waves in the laser beam have the same phase angle. A commercial laser beam is focused onto a half silvered mirror at a forty five degree angle. Half the beam is transmitted through the mirror and the other half is reflected. Both beams are reflected again and then magnified.

The magnified transmitted, reference, beam is directed to a photographic plate, and the originally reflected beam is directed toward an object to be photographed. Some light is reflected from the object onto the photographic plate. The laser light striking the photographic plate has taken two distinct paths.

The split coherent laser beams have traveled different paths and lengths. The phase angles between the two split beams are now different but have been kept constant. The reference and image beams interfere with each other as they are absorbed in the holographic photo film. The surface of the film acts as a diffraction grating.

A diffraction grating is a tool for splitting light sources into thin beams for measuring wavelengths. It consists of a large number of small, equally spaced parallel grooves on a glass plate. A single light beam entering perpendicular to a diffraction grating is split into multiple thin light beams which are diffracted at different angles depending upon wavelengths and grating spacing.

A diffraction grating separates light into bands, lines, and fringes of colors at deflected angles depending upon wavelengths. Some light waves with identical wavelengths, but 180 degrees out of phase cancel each other and cause dark bands at some angles.

A hologram photo film surface diffracts light and it is absorbed at different angles within the film. Object and reference light beams interfere with each other as they are absorbed at different angles and depths within the thin photo film producing detailed three-dimensional images.

The two light beams having the same wavelength but different phase angles develop precise resonances in the photographic film at different locations and depths. The film absorbs light energy each time light is reflected between front and back surfaces at widening angles to produce the texture of three-dimensional images. When light meets light in film, there is stored awareness that we can view many times.

Mental Holograms

Dreams and memories are stored in a similar manner to that of commercial holograms. Models of the mind and God depend on understanding holograms. Mental and spiritual hologram models are constructed for understanding the mind and God. The mental hologram is the basic subconscious tool for thought and memory. Dreams support this concept.

Our brains consist of from 50 to 100 billion neurons. We cannot determine which neurons activate for constructing thoughts, but, from experience, we are usually sure of consistent thoughts at reasonable speeds and energy levels for normal conversations and activities.

Each neuron fires about every one tenth of a second. A symphony of neuron activations creates low-energy electromagnetic resonances within the brain for creating thought. Each neuron has a different activation profile and creates a characteristic electromagnetic and a chemical impulse. As a physicist, I am most interested in understanding the light or electromagnetic activity within the brain.

Neuron membranes split impending light or electromagnetic radiation (emr) into smaller beams with widening angles. Brain holograms are much more detailed than commercial holograms. With so much emr reflecting throughout the brain, some coherent light converges on neuron membranes. Neuron membranes reflect, diffract, and absorb light or emr. Neuron and brain structure cells, glia, membranes have awareness or memory storage abilities similar to holographic film.

Stored holographic memories on brain cell membranes can also be recalled many times. Emr, from neuron activities, is absorbed by, and cultures brain cell membranes for awareness and consciousness. These concepts are needed to understand mind and spiritual models.

Spiritual Holograms

If our minds can be constructed by electromagnetic resonances within the brain, God is constructed by all electromagnetic resonances throughout the universe. God is Light or Electromagnetic radiation traveling at the speed of light. God's existence is relativistic to our own existence. Relative to our environments, God's heavenly environment at the speed of light is very different from ours.

God is a perfect recorder of physical uncertainties throughout the universe and integrates all uncertainties into perfect spiritual certainty. Physical, mental, and spiritual processes are iterative. There are no fixed solutions in the universe or heaven. Our thoughts iterate as we search for purpose and direction in things we do. God continually iterates records of physical activities in time to converge to, and update, spiritual truth and completeness in heaven at unbelievable rates.

If we work toward understanding God, our spiritual holograms become more defined and clearer. Not doing spiritual things darkens mental holograms. Our quest for clear holograms and minds lasts until the ends of our lives.

Background

The brain creates the mind, and, recursively, the mind controls the brain. Models help us think in-depth about the mind. The brain consists of a complex structure of various types of atoms. The mind consists of resonating electromagnetic radiation (and field forces), created by a symphony of neuron activities, reflecting throughout the brain at the speed of light. Note: The speed of light in the brain and matter is slower than the speed of light in vacuum.

God travels much faster than the speed of light in spiritual or relativistic time. He travels beyond time in the vacuum of outer space but slows down to exchange time and energy within matter including within human brains. Spiritual and physical energy are exchanged through resonances.

Electromagnetic radiation, from firings of all body cells with their different perspectives, creates an integrated "spiritual shadow hologram" of the entire physical body within the brain.

We must recognize that electromagnetic radiation, from firings of all body cells with their different spatial perspectives, creates an integrated "spiritual shadow hologram" of man's entire physical body.

What is the difference between mental holograms and God, the Infinite Hologram? They coexist in the same spiritual space, but God's Infinite Hologram is 10^{100} times more detailed or dense in spiritual space than man's mental holograms. The soul and God existing in the same spiritual space have constant communication. Our minds must learn to interact spiritually with our own souls. God wants us to understand and learn from Him as our earthly fathers want us to understand and learn from them.

With science we learn about God by studying His universe. In traditional spiritual times, words received and interpreted by prophets led followers to understand and worship God. Words were so limited in those times for understanding a complex universe. People could only write simply about God. For those backward times, their words and understanding were amazing. As good as traditional spiritual books are they describe only a small part of God's love and abilities.

We must continue to learn about God in everyway we can. With current language, spiritual communications, and abilities we can expand the frontiers of spiritual wisdom beyond historical levels.

Naturally, spiritual writers aggrandized their spiritual leaders, and some proclaimed their writings were the "complete" truth about God and that their works could not be added to or subtracted from. These erroneous ideas have held the world back spiritually for hundreds of years. Believing ancient books contain the whole spiritual truth, and every thing we need to know about an infinite God is insane.

Humans are self-centered. We write to give our leaders and ourselves importance. Even, the most conservative religions expand their messages to adjust to today's lives and increase their own importance. Look at the strategies of large churches and televangelists.

Look at dictators and corrupt spiritual leaders, with run-away power, to witness the control and "spiritual" importance they force on oppressed societies and followers. An important thing about science is that discoveries must be repeated and proven by independent researchers. Without checks and balances, power corrupts scientists, politicians and spiritual leaders.

With limited understanding and words, historical prophets could only translate God's characteristics from His flowing, complete language as omnipotent, omnipresent, and omniscient.

With analysis today, this does not appear to be true. From science and relativity, we and God observe the universe from very different perspectives. We must continue to learn God's perspective. This difference in perspective may help us understand why we sometimes think God allows bad things or catastrophes to happen to those "we" consider as good people.

Often science models are updated or replaced. Spiritual models also need to be analyzed and updated or replaced with reason and not continued with perpetuated emotions. God gave us minds to explore and think. However, there is much reason in traditional religions.

Languages two-thousand years ago were not as defined as today's languages. Language became precise with science and mathematics. Man first learned language to communicate involved thoughts about the outside world, and eventually, about the inner spiritual world. Language and ideas advance. Today, language scholars continue to interpret and change meanings of traditional spiritual writings.

Physics for Scientists and Engineers (2) by Paul A. Tipler was the reference for science presented here and in later chapters.

REFERENCES:

(1) *The Holy Bible - New International Version - Disciples' Study Bible,* 1984, Holman Bible Publishers, Nashville, Tennessee.

(2) Tipler, Paul A., 1991. *Physics for Scientists and Engineers,* Worth Publishers, New York, NY.

CHAPTER 4

Bipolar Disorder, Mania, and Insanity

Paradise Lost (Excerpt)

"The mind is its own place, and in itself
Can make a Heaven of Hell, a Hell of Heaven. . . ."

John Milton

Love, hate, read, write, live, and die; I see heaven in the sky!

Hugh D. Fulcher

Mania!

It is easier to agree than disagree. If we disagree, we may expose our ignorance. For mental health, we must learn to disagree wisely.

An abbreviated presentation of the author's bipolar disorder, mania, and insanity from *Bipolar Blessing & Mind Expansion, 2nd Edition* is given as background for spiritual chapters.

Welcome to my inner world of mania with its insanities, dreams, and faith. Experience a path less traveled. Hardships and abuse in childhood and marriage caused severe manic depression and unusual spiritual communications. An unusual perspective of the mind and God has evolved. Science extends into metaphysics to heal the author's bipolar disorder and possibly heal others afflicted with stress disorders. Suggestions are given for mental health research.

Depression is caused by loss of self-esteem, health, a loved one, or exposure to persistent physical or mental abuse. Life seems hopeless and sometimes degrades into a meager existence. Thinking becomes circular without normal resolutions to problems.

In 1977, insane and locked in a cell in a psychiatric ward, the author felt compelled to record his mental excitement and difficulties to begin the healing of his manic depression.

Everyone needs healing from childhood and adult stresses and traumas to lesser or greater extents. For some of us, repressed trauma memories and persistent stress have caused disorganized thinking and mental disorders. With persistent experimentation, exercises, and inner analysis, suppressed traumatic experiences can be recalled and purged to recover childhood creative thinking. Surviving severe trauma or sickness broadens importance of life.

In searching for a cure using his physics background, the author became aware of sharp snap, crackle, and pop, or SCAP, energy releases when exercising his neck. The author uses a physics and engineering approach for understanding and healing the mind.

Energy releases within the neck are similar to the pop and snap energy releases experienced during chiropractic adjustments. If there is pressure on nerves in the neck or spinal column, affected nerves become dysfunctional and produce pain. Similarly, if trauma scars add pressure within neural networks, these networks become dysfunctional and contribute to mental pain. Releasing repressed energy or "mental pressure" allows mental reconstruction healing.

Thoughts and feeling during manic episodes are discussed to help the afflicted heal and families assist. Manic ideas are not as rational as normal ideas but are more fascinating. Subconscious processing limits normally censor extreme or "dream" ideas from consciousness. Emotional conscious ideas are normally limited by trauma scarred network reactions. However, dreaming is not affected by waking mental limits.

Manic thoughts forcefully barge though ruptured "trauma scar" censorship. At the beginning of mania, ideas produce creative solutions with spiritual qualities that should be acted upon. The mind processes faster than normal with feelings of increased confidence. Eventually, as ideas become faster and fantastic, mental confidence is lost. We must analyze these creative thoughts and carefully channel them into structured, useful ideas. Hopefully, this book is an example of a useful channeling process. When mental energy levels become high enough to activate trauma scar networks, mania begins.

In 1993 when working in the Washington, DC, area, strange and exciting inner sensations occurred within the neck. Manic thoughts were fast and exciting at the time. The author became compelled to exercise the neck to increase these apparent energy release sensations which felt slightly pleasant.

Psychophysiotherapy is the author's term for healing the mind through physical exercises and models. During exercises, manic ideas become exciting but can go out of control. With medication, the mind sometimes regains normal control and becomes less sensitive to SCAPS. Receiving spiritual ideas usually ceases.

We do not understand or appreciate sanity until we have experienced insanity. Insanity can create an awakening into a higher level of consciousness. Do not worry when others makes fun of you if preoccupied. You may be experiencing higher levels of spiritual communication. However, we must periodically become aware of the normal life to eat, sleep, and take care of mind and body.

Over time, adult thinking usually becomes restricted to adhere to mores and customs. However, the manic mind becomes so excited with unexpected spiritual ideas it loses sight of normal behavior. Manic ideas are creative, but evolve so fast and forceful that actions cannot be completed before another strong idea dominates. The best advice is to tell manic-depressives to slow down and write ideas for later organization.

As in dreams, a full-blown manic-depressive does not question or judge manic ideas. He becomes a displaced observer. Just as dreams come from deep within the subconscious mind, so do manic ideas. It becomes difficult to determine the difference between spiritual and worldly sanity.

Dream distortions occur since waking reason is no longer needed during sleeping. Distortion is due to subconsciously comparing "uncertain" remembered events to "certain" genetic and spiritual truths. Genetic truths were formed by extensive repeated successful experiences throughout generations. Spiritual truths are formed by all successful events over all time throughout the universe.

We should understand our inner selves to be truly responsive to loved ones and God. We must organize ideas to make sense to ourselves before communicating normal or spiritual ideas with others.

Manic ideas become so pleasant, strong, and confident that a manic-depressive is often reluctant to return to his normal state. Mania is as intoxicating as alcohol. Alcohol eventually degrades and deceives. Mania enhances logical, emotional, and spiritual processes at first, but often degrades into insanity.

Computers and subconscious processes can be reprogrammed. If we stimulate the subconscious mind with simple models, it can understand and reprogram itself.

After releasing repressed emotional energy, traumatized neural networks and their memories can resynchronize with normal brain processes for a more efficient brain. Essentially, psychiatric exercises initiate significant emotional events that promote neural network reprogramming.

Spiritual communications affect large areas of the brain equally or holistically. We can only translate God's continuous message only into discrete words and analogies that relate to our earthly experiences. Our minds are very limited. Low-energy spiritual messages are received as smooth, continuous, or analog processes. If we sense spiritual feelings, then we must translate those feelings into earthly analogies. Jesus used parables to simplify His teachings.

God's message is constant or the same everywhere. With diverse experiences, each of us may interpret His message differently. God's complete message is always up-to-date. Updates during our lifetimes are very small compared to God's 15 billion year history.

In my wonderfully weird manic experiences in October of 1994, I had fun running through my beautiful fields communicating with God in an unusual way. In this brief time I received simple communication in words. God and I became buddies during those days of my worldly insanities. I would romp in my fields and think of something funny to say to God and then clear my mind of all thoughts.

I would wait and God would answer as in the distant thunder. I was so happy when God responded. His answers were deep yet funny. There was a delay but God always answered. His answers seemed to be funnier than my questions. Surrendering to God while not caring about worldly things, the manic mind invited spiritual communication.

Manic, spiritual thoughts are like dreams and rather difficult to recall. Here are a few communications recalled from that sunny day:

H. "Why is the grass green?"
G. "Had you rather have it blue?"

H. "Why do trees exist?"
G. "Trees?"

H. "Why do ducks quack?"
G. "Should they quake?"

H. "Why is the sky blue?"
G. "Physics."

H. "Why can't I see you?"
G. "You can't?"

H. "You neglect me."
G. "Who are you?"

H. "You make me laugh."
G. [The earth shook with laughter as I fell in the grass.]

H. "Do you like my writing?"
G. "About what?"

H. "Not making sense."
G. "Makes sense."

H. "Who created the universe?"
G. "Not you!"

H. "Who created me.?"
G. "Me."

H. "Do you love even me?
G. "Yes."

H. "Why?"
G. "You are a part of me."

This process went on and on. I was a two year old enjoying playing with my Father. It was a different way of spending spiritual time alone with God. During this time there was more reflection than response. God and I reflected feelings and words back and forth to one another. Times were simple. Often, the simplest of times are the most meaningful. It was rewarding to become a child again. I had never felt more spiritual. God can be witty and fun!

Insanity!

Mania occurs as the mind processes abnormally fast and becomes unable to judge or make decisions on previously "normal" ideas and events. Long-range, high-energy, right-brained dreaming while awake overrides normal left-brain reasoning.

Insanity is a step beyond mania as highly abnormal, impossible things are "experienced" without the afflicted being able to control, stop, or make sense of occurrences. However, the most dysfunctional, damaging, and insane people are those who think they are perfect and able to convince others of their "perfection." False perfection multiplies insanity. Only God is perfection.

Insanity is when one cannot respond to normal situations. Insanity creeps into the manic mind like a thief in the night. There are many ways of experiencing insanity. It begins at birth as innate spiritual sanity is slowly suppressed by earthly trauma and insane experiences. Stress and traumas construct baby's earthly sanity limits for determining what is and is not possible.

Strange things happen to sleepless, traumatized minds. Reason fades into uncertainties. Things go bump in the night. Our own facilities, other people, and even God seem to deceive us.

However, subconscious processes developed to regain sanity may construct building blocks for creative thinking beyond normal levels. We do not expand thinking limits unless we reach for the unreachable. God has a purpose for manic and insane minds. It is our responsibility to organize and understand our own creative thoughts before expressing them to the outside world.

While highly manic, I emotionally relived God creating the universe. Our souls are a part of God and include the history of the entire universe. Atoms within our brains are 13.7 billion years old!

Insanity activates memories of spiritual history but decreases earthy reason. Excitement increases and spiritual ideas come so fast the mind is not able to organize them. We become like babies learning language for the first time.

In protected environments, we do not always need to be sane. When beyond our worldly reasoning limits, we rediscover the spiritual reasoning God breathed into us at the moment of our conception.

Being afraid to stretch the brain to emotional limits briefly might be considered insanity. Many emotionally and intellectually limit their minds to moronic levels to "feel" comfortably sane. We must not be afraid of adventurous thinking to improve inner processes.

When one is insane, he might communicate purely with God, but be so spiritually high that he cannot communicate about earthly things. Ideas must be written down and organized later before presenting them to others.

Support persons have difficult tasks helping manic-depressives organize manic creativity toward earthly reason and control. It is done with patience and appropriate levels of medication. We must distinguish between one who is of shallow thought and one who is temporarily stunned by the beauty and truths when communicating with God. Spiritual communication sets us free of earthly worries.

We must search inward to find ourselves and God. Individuals cleared of trauma scars seem odd spending so much time working to discover reasons for our mental structure and existence. Too often, interpersonal comparisons consume our thinking and cloud our souls.

After years of mental restructuring, I am able to slow down and control manic thoughts to the point of writing them down. Difficulty in remembering manic thoughts is similar to remembering dreams. We have to write dreams down quickly, or they are gone in a flash. We must research our inner minds until we can reach out and touch God.

When manic, we focus on the big picture. Cosmologists model the universe to understand its origins and relationships. Cosmological models predict physical properties of the universe which may be experimentally discovered later. Scientists' mathematical models have predicted elementary particles that relate the fundamental micro-structure of matter to the macro-creation of the universe. Many useful inventions may come from cosmological models. Predicting the future brings confidence and order to life.

During manic times my brain and mind became sensitive to electromagnetic fields. Disregarding what others may think, sensitivity to magnetic fields is not insanity. It is a lost skill. Traumas and complexities of learning speech have clouded man's innate spiritual and magnetic navigational abilities. Once the brain is sensitized, magnetic feelings grab attention.

Magnetic feelings are similar to placing an open hand into a smoothly flowing stream of water. When the hand is sideways to the flow, the resistance is low. When the hand faces the flow, resistance is greater. The earth's magnetic field gives the mind a sense of direction. My theory is that animals still have this directional "instinct."

There are levels of uncertainty in all human and physical things. Subconscious processes iterate as the brain searches for purpose. There are no certain or fixed solutions in the physical universe. Time changes all things physical.

God iterates to integrate all physical uncertainties into perfect spiritual certainty and history of the universe independent of time and space, which is never subtracted from or added to. Human minds iterate to integrate experiences into memories which are independent of time and space. However, human memories are often forgotten and distorted.

In mid-adult life, I realized I had only been mimicking anger. Mother never showed anger; seldom did dad. I had suppressed anger most of my life. During unexpected harsh abuse, my right cerebral hemisphere released repressed energy allowing it to process as it was designed to do. I now experience anger. God gave us emotions for a reason. Anger protects us against mental and physical abuse.

When highly manic, I had awareness of my thoughts being monitored. Sensations were distracting, somewhat scary, but were fascinating. I embrace the unusual and do not worry about insanity.

I often felt unusual sensations were from God. Most of us believe prayers are transmitted to God. Our best instruments cannot detect spiritual energy which is relativistic to the physical world. Some believe prayer only organizes inner thoughts.

On earth, perfection is only in the mind. Using superlatives about your self or work is damaging to those around you. When thinking of God, we think of the whole universe. Perfection is God.

Uncertainties often require surrendering decisions to God. Christianity teaches surrendering our wills to God's Will. Have you seen the smiling faces? You can see their happiness due to their beliefs that Jesus is in control of their lives! There is less conflict and guilt in decision making.

During mania, it is difficult to determine between spiritual and worldly sanity. We must recognize differences between emotional and spiritual ideas to determine which thoughts should be acted upon. Before acting on manic ideas, write them down. Writing activates left-brain judgment, and slows manic thinking.

While highly manic, I acquired brief unusual predictions using the Bible and its concordance. Spiritual ideas became deeply important. However, recollection of unusual predictions using the concordance has escaped memory like dreams. Dreams produce flashes of our inner spiritual nature.

Dramatic physical healing of individual brain's fabric is needed for curing, and spiritual integration of, all minds throughout the world, and possibly the universe.

There is a root cause of some bipolar disorders and their insanities. It is committed by parents in raising their first born. First time parents should be careful to avoid a common pitfall in raising their first born. They tend to give them too much control.

Parents must present a nurturing atmosphere, but let a young child know he is being "given" control at times. If they do not exert control but plead with a young child, he will learn deep down he has extreme importance, control, and entitlement to abuse younger siblings. At the beginning of raising the first child keep in mind you have to culture his attitude to take care of and not selfishly abuse younger siblings.

The huge problem between siblings is entirely the parents' fault in being too loving and impressed with the first sibling. It is easily prevented by creating a loving atmosphere for the first child but frequently letting him know parents are in control. As the child grows, he should delight as more freedom and control is allowed.

Control must be exerted at an early age. An older sibling is not entitled to abuse younger siblings. Punish him until abuse stops. An abused younger sibling becomes as frightened of an abusing older sibling as a soldier when running from gun fire. Younger siblings are wounded mentally for life unless they purge repressed trauma memories and mentally reconstruct. If not corrected early, family problems escalate. With frequent abuse, younger sibling minds can become severely limited. Parenting can be insane.

CHAPTER 5

Mind Models and Mental Reconstruction

Sound and Light

When normal, I hear sound and see light;
My senses let me know things are right.
Inner sound and inner light bring change,
The brain and mind must rearrange.

Hugh Fulcher, 2005

In past centuries, philosophers described the sun as being carried across the sky in a chariot. Man has always related things they did not understand to things they understood. This is still true today.

The author has developed models to expand the mind. Models often use analogies to relate the mind to physical concepts. Some models and mental reconstruction processes are included from *Bi-polar Blessing & Mind Expansion,* in support of spiritual models.

The mind is good at thinking about outward activities but needs training to become aware of, and improve, inner subconscious processes. With patience, mind models, and unique exercises, inner and spiritual abilities are recovered.

The first mind model the author is aware of divided the mind into two parts – conscious and subconscious. Sigmund Freud is credited with this model. He developed psychiatric processes to expand the subconscious mind into consciousness. A goal in healing the mind is to become more aware of subconscious processes so we can control more of our mental abilities.

The Tip of the Iceberg

This model relates the conscious and subconscious minds to the tip of the iceberg and the rest of the world, respectively. The tip of the iceberg only "knows" the heat of the sun, ocean air and winds, the ocean water slapping against its edges, and gravity. The bottom of the iceberg corresponds to that part of the subconscious mind that supports the tip of the iceberg "above water" for consciousness. The tip of the iceberg is not aware of the bottom of the iceberg since conscious minds are not aware of subconscious processes.

The conscious mind is modeled as only local experiences of the tip of the iceberg. The subconscious mind consists of the bottom of the iceberg below water, the ocean, and the rest of the world. Environments increase or diminish icebergs.

Our solar system and the rest of the universe are modeled as heaven. All resonating field forces, including light and gravity, which construct communication throughout the universe, represent God. This model promotes the magnitude of our subconscious minds and God. The bottom of the iceberg determines which communications from the world and heaven will be held above water as the tip of the iceberg or conscious thoughts.

Limits

The brain is a machine - a thinking machine. Every machine has its limits. Any machine extended beyond its limits will either blow a fuse or blow up. The mind can be stressed beyond reasoning limits. It can blow a fuse. Fortunately or unfortunately, it does not stop right away but loses stability and operates in a wildly oscillating mode called bipolar disorder or manic depression.

By briefly stressing one's mind to limits, abilities can be expanded. To heal bipolar disorder, new wider mental limits must be constructed. By understanding old broken limits, the subconscious mind adds spiritual purpose in constructing new emotional limits. With effort, childhood emotional limits can be replaced with kinder, wider, and more logical adult developed limits.

Subconscious processes must be reflected by emotional limits, or they continue to get more excited and out of control searching for old purged limits. Trauma scars and their conflicting repressed memories limit us from thinking like lightning. Trauma scars are like cancers within the fabric of the brain. They do not synchronize with the brain's normal symphony. Normal subconscious processes are slowed and limited by its symphony having to avoid or counter cancerous effects of sporadic local traumatized network activations. Purging excess energy from repressed trauma and stress memories resynchronizes them with normal memories.

Practice healing at your own rhythm and risk. In mania, the brain bypasses childhood engrained trauma limits and becomes erratic. Perform mental limit exercises at your own mental rhythm for healing and refining your mental symphony.

Conflicting psychiatric neck exercises extend the mind to limits. Controlled conflict at mental limits activates and de-energizes repressed memories. The fabric of muscles and the brain only grow when stressed to limits.

Fear at limits awakens creative thinking. For example, in my house in the winter of 1980, I had an encounter with two black snakes.

A wire needed to be drawn up a wall into the attic and down the same wall on the other side of a door. I completed the second floor work and went to drill holes from the attic. A flashlight was the only light. I started drilling and then noticed that the two dark areas two feet from me were coiled-up snakes. I scampered back to the attic entrance. I stopped and thought for a while. I would either have to remove the snakes, quit work, or work close to the snakes. The weather was cold, so I decided to complete my work, snakes and all.

My snake encounter allowed me to experience uncertainty, fear and bravery at emotional limits. I intentionally created a simulated "significant emotional event" to initiate psychiatric changes. However, I do not recommend this experiment to anyone. I felt like a caveman fighting to survive. Simulating life on the edge is one way to excite the subconscious mind into refining its processes.

Meditating void of words or thinking only in images develops imagination. Thinking in words is complex for a visually oriented mind and suppresses creativity. Imagination means thinking in images. Imagination and creativity have been preserved genetically throughout generations. With imagination we can create fear at limits. Practicing fear through imagination enables us to function during real fear.

After meaningful interactions or endeavors, spend a minute or two thinking of how you and your work support others and God, or avoid enabling bad behaviors. All behaviors have limits.

Without limits humans and machines would control the entire universe. In my work, even God has design limits. He has constructed constant and predictable physical laws and limits, which He does not normally violate, in controlling the universe. God conforms to His own physical laws and limits. Otherwise there would be chaos.

Without emotional and trauma design limits, the brain would attempt to think of, and control all aspects of, the universe That is, without brain design limits, we would attempt to "think" like God. God has unlimited "thinking" about the structures of His universe.

Diamonds

Let's add a sparkle to the creative process. God is still creative today. If we forget worries and calm our minds to concentrate on God's pureness and love, He will share His creativeness with us. The secret to creativity is that we must prepare to receive and recognize God's creative processes. When we spiritually prepare our minds, we can become more aware of God's constant creative message. Creative ideas retrace God's timeless footprints left during creation of the universe. What are creative ideas like? Well, they are not always so obvious. God's creative ideas are always present for each of us, but we are not prepared to recognize or know what to do with them.

A creative idea from God, in analogue or flowing complete spiritual language, is like a diamond in the rough. We must have faith that diamonds or God's creative processes exist and learn where to look for them. We must be aware of methods to mine God's diamonds.

We must find and go into the diamond mine, be willing and prepared to dig through tons of worthless dirt and rocks, and be willing to separate the rocks form the dirt. We must examine all the rocks and be able to recognize the diamond in the rough. Once we have found, or received, a "diamond in rough" we must know what to do with it. We must study a creative idea, that "diamond in the rough," and cut the diamond so that it sparkles for the world to see. That sparkle and shine is the reflection of God's love for mankind. God's creative ideas are complete and analogue. It is our responsibility to breakup holistic spiritual ideas into discrete words with our best translation to present God's sparkle to the world.

Even though we are blessed with a gift from God, our work is not easy. We have significant responsibilities in transforming creative ideas from God's deep structure, analogue language into sentences so all might experience the wonders of God's Creation.

We must faithfully translate God's pure spiritual analogue message into words.

Discrete and Holistic Models

Discrete mind models are for left-brained up-close and detailed thinking processes. Holistic right-brained models are for long-range and more general and futuristic thinking processes. The goal is to provide the subconscious mind models of itself so it can understand and heal its own processes. Subconscious processes are good at producing and understanding conscious thoughts, but have difficulties analyzing their own inner functions to make them more efficient. We must develop synergy between left and right brain processes.

Let's define what we mean by discrete and holistic. Discrete could be defined as a single member of a choir singing a solo in tenor. This singer can make many melodious sounds or vibrations in the air for us to hear. If sounds are on key and in rhythm, we listen to beautiful music. Instruments and words can portray emotional stories.

Holistic could be represented as a choir of 500 members singing in perfect harmony. Some sing tenor, some sing base, and others sing in different parts. Individuals sing differently, but there is no individual standout. Each member is as important as all others. The air is full of integrated vibrations to make one holistic sound of music. Holistic means integrated and complete. Integrated sounds of the choir feel more complete.

In a broader sense, discrete thinking means up-close focus expecting immediate or routine actions and control. On the other hand, holistic thinking is like the 500 member choir. We do not have a feeling of being able to reach out and touch the entire choir.

We can focus up close on firings of one neuron. It has little meaning. However, firings of millions of neural networks throughout the brain make rhythmic and beautiful music for a creative life.

A long-range view of the mountains is holistic. We are looking at the entire scope of the mountains and not at specific details. We have an integrated picture without anticipating action or control. Babies think holistically without thinking of actions or control except for nursing.

Holistic thinking is by integrated activities of large numbers of neural networks firing in harmony. Holistic thinking is by right brain dominance in most people for flowing, analog processes such as rhythm and music. Wow! Billions of activities are coordinated subconsciously for us to think of individual details or long range goals for controlling our lives and environments.

☆ ☆ ☆

Models and methods have produced sufficiently exciting results such that they have continued for seventeen years. It is difficult to describe inner changes and feelings. However, here is an example. A normal person's awareness of idea development might be like feeling the water when slowly stepping into a swimming pool. Sensing the calm water is like normal idea generation.

The feelings of idea generation after psychiatric exercises might be like sliding down a water chute with all its twists and turns and then exploding into water to create an idea. There are more energetic feelings during creative idea development. Ideas and idea development are not all equal. Manic and insane ideas demand action. Mental reconstruction for reducing mental energy, expanding the mind, and nurturing creativity is a long and difficult process.

The author has modeled and designed nuclear reactors for over twenty years. Modeling complex nuclear reactors provided confidence for modeling the brain and mind. Mind models and unique exercises heal and restructure the fabric of the brain for more efficient subconscious processing and creative thinking.

Memorizing and repeating emotional dogma kills creative processes. Without spiritual reasoning, ideas divert to self-importance.

With more understanding of the inner mind, modeling God flowed naturally. Modeling forces in-depth analysis. Engineers and architects make drawings and models to guide construction. Scientific models guide experiments for scientific discoveries.

The author works to cure the mind using physical exercises and spiritual communications. Models of the mind and God are heuristic and developed on a quasi-scientific basis. Heuristic and philosophical developments are forerunners of science discovery. Intelligent guesses and models are followed by experimentation and evaluation of results.

Scientific discoveries prove consistencies in, or laws of, nature and may eventually discover the nature of God. Metaphysics ponders reasons for our existence. I extend my quest for understanding God. Extreme emotions and life threatening uncertainties develop a higher need to search for certainty in God.

Persistent imagination develops amazing models of the mind, the universe, and God. Models guide subconscious healing processes and spiritual awakening. A model is a mental or physical tool to assist thinking about details of a problem or design. Self-healing or self-psychiatry processes were first meant to heal the author's bipolar disorder and then help others who are afflicted.

With patience and practice, worst insanities can become best skills. Freedom from insanity is worth any price or effort.

The brain, with input from the body, creates the mind and in turn the mind controls the brain and body. Life is an iterative and recursive process. The subconscious mind creates the conscious mind. The conscious mind directs outward abilities to navigate environments and recursively controls subconscious processes.

Every thought is a potential force for accomplishing goals or increasing frustrations. Memories are only reflections of our thoughts and lives. We alone control our thoughts and imagination. Our imaginations can become our futures.

Subconscious processing or "sub-thinking" is modeled as image manipulation and integration of three dimensional mental holograms. Dreams support this theory. Models help us understand mental processes. In dreams we view changing three-dimensional perspectives of holographic dream characters. Dreams or subconscious processes integrate flowing or analogue three-dimensional mental holograms to form four-dimensional or virtual thoughts or memories.

Dreams and mental holograms, like God, are independent of physical time and exist in higher-dimensional, virtual, or spiritual space. To some extent, dreams and mental holograms are independent of physical energy and are dispersed throughout the universe as spiritual energy. Our minds have Godlike qualities. Scientists are not able to measure spiritual energy since it is the same everywhere.

Physicists and engineers think of life from an energy viewpoint. We receive heat and light from the sun. Electromagnetic radiation or light is the energy that allows us to see. Nothing is done or thought of in this universe without exchanging energy. God is light and the spiritual energy within light. God's thoughts require some form of spiritual energy. There was no initial intent to study spirituality. However, words received from God required obedience.

Mental reconstruction takes a long time. Our brains contain remnants of trauma scars from previous generations. Unless we mentally reconstruct, we may leave our children with un-thought of mental burdens that compromise their lives and spiritual abilities. In traditional spiritual times, God judged certain families as righteous.

God does not create true spiritual leaders from the top of societies. Moses thought his speaking was inadequate. Jesus was hidden from the public until He developed His spiritual teaching and healing abilities.

Judging events and interactions is necessary to survive. Judging others spiritually has an air of spiritual superiority, which, of course, does not exist in humans. Only God can judge spiritually.

Physical configuration and chemical composition of the brain and its neural membranes culture our mental processes and memories. Electromagnetic activities refined by neural membranes construct the mind. The spatial configuration of the universe and its composition of matter construct God's infinite wisdom and abilities. Electromagnetic, gravitational, all other field forces, and nuclear activities throughout the universe culture God's abilities.

We must work against nearsightedness, narrow-mindedness, prejudices, and stigmas to become global in thought and concern. I am proud to be a world ling anything less is prejudice. I'm not yet too concerned about the welfare of outer-space and intergalactic aliens. However, I have disappointment in myself for not supporting my parents on earth and now in heaven, or God, as I should.

Some overzealous parents call their children geniuses at young ages. This label complicates give and take communications as stress destroys expectations and lives. It is difficult for anointed high-ego geniuses to communicate with others and God.

Thinking is an iterative, integration process. My repetitive unique exercises clear the mind of trauma scars and enhance left-right brain dominance sharing for mind control. Once trauma scars are released neural networks re-grow and reconstruct hologram processing abilities. Fundamental hologram structures manage the subconscious ordering of mental holograms for developing and organizing conscious thought and receiving spiritual communications.

As we take a step or do anything, we predict results for the near and, sometimes, the distant future. We must predict actions and judge outcomes to do anything.

God predicts events and judges results or He has no purpose. With perfect historical knowledge and abilities, God's predictions are far reaching. Our future is cultured with each judgment we and God make. Predestination is illogical and should be a dead issue.

Developing language is needed for learning from, reasoning about, sharing with, and caring for, one another. A child, who seems slow with limited language abilities, may possess higher spiritual abilities, and be of high value to God. We do not need to look outward to find God. God is within our souls' higher spiritual dimensions weaved within the fabric of our brains. God touches us every second. We must love ourselves in order to love God.

Two-dimensional Holusions are amazing works of art for mental experimentation. See a Holusion of the *Thinker* in Figure 6.5. Relaxing eyes and focusing long distance through the surface of the page, a three-dimensional image appears from the detailed two-dimensional intertwining picture which guides the mind into three imaginary dimensions. This is similar to life. When observing normal three dimensional views, we yearn to relax our minds into higher spiritual dimensions for understanding.

The right brain integrates a confusing two-dimensional picture into a virtual or "spiritual" three-dimensional Holusion that makes sense. Experiencing God is similar to viewing a Holusion. Chapter 6 explains Holusions as tools for mental exercises.

Watching television is somewhat similar. Our minds project two-dimensional images into meaningful three-dimensional activities.

Our predictions and influences vary depending upon events, moods, and decisions. God's predictions for, and influences on, us depend upon truthfulness of our decisions toward His purposes. If long range predictions had certainty, God and the universe would be predestined and purposeless.

God, creating Man's minds with physical processes, left man dependent upon the physical universe. Otherwise, there would be a perfect existence without pain or sorrow. During meditation and spiritual communication when briefly separated from physical needs, our minds can increase spiritual abilities. With fading energy, redeemed and dying minds develop perfect spiritual communication. At the moment of death, the mind and soul become one.

Resonating light reflections within the brain form awareness and thought. The mind and God in spiritual space can be modeled with imaginary numbers and integral calculus. Striving to understand, and communicate with, God develops spiritual reason. From God's perspective, an instant of physical time may be infinite spiritual time. We know so little about "time."

Only a few decades ago, man did not understand electricity or dream of technical things we have today. Yesterday's dreams have become reality. Our spiritual dreams can become tomorrow's reality!

What will reality be in a thousand years? Communication abilities will advance. Use of electricity, electromagnetic radiation, and possibly other field forces will be expanded to improve spiritual communication technology. With higher technical abilities to receive God's guidance, I cannot imagine the possibilities! Could we invent machines and computers to receive and "perfectly" translate God's perfect, flowing message into advanced English? Man has been inventive throughout the last thousand years.

Books freeze minds and pictures freeze scenes and events in time. The written word and pictures have constant characteristics. The Bible stresses importance of the written word. This book freezes my thoughts in time.

Creative ideas beyond limits will help heal overstressed minds and extend imagination for spiritual advancement. Existence and

God make more sense united not divided. The most believable, inclusive tenets from all religions could unite the world emotionally and spiritually. I love thinking imaginatively, but fear becoming normal.

Only arrogant audacity allows anyone to feel superior to any of God's children. A spoiled heiress acts superior to her own guests. Hitler preaches superiority and condemns a whole race. An older sibling abuses a younger sibling. The arrogant and ignorant "saved" act spiritually superior to those they view as "unsaved."

Some subconscious resonances last long enough to become conscious resonances. Memory structures are similar for people of all languages. This explains why God's universal spiritual resonances are received and interpreted similarly by believers of all languages.

Memory is developed by filtering "light" or emr from neuron activations through a myriad of neuron membranes to form "living" hologram resonances for consciousness. Mental holograms are spiritually alive. God is a living Higher Dimensional Hologram framed by all electromagnetic and other field force activities throughout, and relativistic to, the physical universe for creating perfect consciousness.

A sense of time is stored within virtual hologram memories independent of physical time and space. Dreaming is independent of physical time and space. Waking minds are usually constrained to physical time and space for daily interactions.

Figure 4.2 is a picture of a few normal mind functions. Each mind exists as its own universe. Visualize mental functions, "A" through "G," vibrating at various spiritual distances within and/or beyond the brain. "G" may vibrate with extremely low frequencies to and from the edges of the universe for communicating with God.

A. Mental communication back and forth with vital organs is repetitive and, when healthy, is direct.

B. Dreaming and mental organization make spiritual sense of daily activities by integrating them within long range memories and our souls. The ovals are genetic macro-functions connecting diverse ideas and dream scenarios. "B" may resonate considerably beyond the physical brain.
C. The rectangle represents genetic functions during awakening from sleep into consciousness with body control. The mind zigzags or iterates through earlier memories to prepare for sensed waking activities.
D. Efficient processes are developed for routine, macro, and repetitive activities within "C" above. Vibrations extend to limits of the senses.
E. Analytical thinking extends to extremes or mental limits at times to relate new concepts to established thoughts. Vibrations extend beyond the brain.
F. Reflex thinking reflects genetic and emotional processes to trauma limits. Up-close reflex thinking consists of high-energy short wave vibrations for fast reactions. The Flash is the limiting reflex process.
G. Spiritual and surrender thinking extend beyond free will thinking. We must think humbly beyond self and holistically into the universe. Adult minds with normal egos, unless having experienced near-death, may have resistance to spiritual surrender. "G" shows resistance before expanding spiritually. The oval represents parallel, holistic, or flowing processes for complete spiritual communication. Spiritual resonances are independent of space and time beyond that which we understand.

Think of functions, "A" through "G," as resonating in spiritual dimensions. We need imagination to understand our own minds. Imagination is everything.

Figure 4.3 shows mind functions cleared of trauma effects and prejudices. All processes are straight forward. "G" shows no resistance to spiritual surrender with constant God consciousness. Spiritual processes convert worries and uncertainties into "human" certainty.

During near death, extremely trying, or inspired times, and if we surrender our lives to God, each of us can become inspired to receive spiritual messages. With different abilities and experiences, each of us interprets God's wisdom differently.

Some of us write to explain spiritual feelings and words, and the mind's ability to receive spiritual messages. Exciting spiritual messages, force some to believe they have become spiritual leaders for all times. With humility, true spiritual leaders realize they are only beginning to learn of God's constant, omnipresent message.

We interpret God's constant flowing message with different words according to abilities and earthly experiences. God speaks to us constantly. We must learn to listen.

God, like us, predicts near futures more precisely than distant futures. If God exactly knew the entire future of the universe there would be no reason for Him to exist or for the universe to continue. Everything in the universe would be predestined. With our free wills and quantum uncertainties, the universe cannot be predestined. Man has a reflective purpose for God.

God makes near infinite spiritual decisions about the physical universe and knows the complete integrated history of the universe. However, if God makes judgments about our heavenly futures, He does not precisely know our futures or the future of the universe. Decisions change courses of actions. God and we are not predestined. God would not search for or expect good thoughts and activities on earth without purpose. Spiritual existence is dependent upon physical existence. Both God and our minds reflect physical existence.

Memories of our histories are imprinted as holograms on brain cell membranes throughout the brain or on its various components.

With resonances promoted by sensed data or memories, decisions are made by converging sense data and memories into new completeness.

Mothers' bodies, and rhythms, give embryos a holistic sense of confidence in early life. We were integrated as one within our mothers. As adults we can regain that feeling of oneness with God.

The best thing for baby is to be cuddled by his mother with a soft reassuring hum or song. Repeated sounds and nursery rhymes develop right-brain resonances. Babies gain confidence in predicting the next sound. Predicting the future is important to baby and us. Resonating sounds are spiritual experiences for baby. Later in life, only spiritual rebirth rivals such experiences.

A basic mind model is that low energy thinking is high level thinking. High energy thinking, such as anger, is low level thinking. In anger, we can think of only a few options. With low energy thinking, we can think of many creative options. Calming the mind and controlling mania increase creative abilities.

Think of calm relaxing things or pleasant activities before sleep for positive dreams. Exciting dreams with confidence and frequent successes restore the mind and body.

If we work for understanding God, our mental holograms become more integrated and clear. Not doing so darkens or hazes our holograms. Our quest for the "mythical" clear mind by refining holograms lasts until the end of our lives.

In dreams we view changing perspectives of dream characters in spiritual dimensions. Dreams and memories extend beyond physical existence. Mind healing with integration of science and spirituality are break-through efforts to improve quality of life.

We must distinguish between psychiatric and spiritual healing. Psychiatric processes heal specific discrete overstressed neural networks. Spiritual healing is holistic or global healing throughout the brain. Self-healing awakens hidden mental and spiritual abilities.

Our minds are created by sharing and integrating activities between billions of neurons. Without this sharing there would be no human minds. Inner and spiritual thinking is personal. The mind integrates discrete earthly images and other sensations into memories with spiritual completeness. The written word has a lasting spiritual quality. Written messages remain independent of time whenever read.

The physical brain is stationary. Relative to our brains, mental holograms are constructed by light traveling at the speed of light in all directions. The brain exists in physical space but the mind exists in virtual or relativistic spiritual space. The brain creates thoughts and memories in spiritual space independent of physical space and time. Memories are not attached to their sensed physical images. Our minds are bridges between the physical and spiritual.

Predicting the future gives us confidence and stability. Bipolar thinking and actions are also predictable to some extent. Predicting give us some ability to control. Support persons should pay close attention to bipolar behaviors to help the afflicted avoid manic episodes. Identifying behaviors early and reminding the afflicted of past difficulties may avoid severe manic episodes and hospitalizations.

The mind consists of electromagnetic radiation reflecting throughout the fabric of the brain at the speed of light. The speed of light in the brain is slower than the speed of light in vacuum. From God's viewpoint our minds extend throughout the universe as spiritual holograms somewhat independent of space. Everything is relative.

Psychiatric sensations and spiritual feelings are not easily believed unless also experienced. We tend to think those close to us think similarly until they develop a noted reputation.

My contention is that all of society, especially the young, could benefit by releasing trauma energy from neural networks. My processes are extensions of Freud's psychiatric processes for releasing excess trauma energy from repressed memories. When beginning processes, there was concern that sensations of apparently breaking neural networks might not be beneficial. A thought was that breaking networks might cause loss of mental abilities. After seventeen years of extensive exercises, I have proven that this is not the case. Excitement about life and abilities has increased. It was important to keep a positive attitude throughout this long process.

There are so many suffering people who could benefit from this work. While exciting and encouraging, mental reconstruction and re-growing the brain is a long process. Research needs to refine processes in a shorter time frame. This is a challenging task. This work fits into the relatively new "mind/body/spirit" category established by the National Institutes of Mental Health, NIMH. Brief proposals for continued study, directed to the NIMH, are presented in Chapter 19.

Beliefs are an important part of mental health. We hold on to early learned spiritual beliefs until we have a significant emotional event. This event may be through a relationship with Jesus or other method.

We like people who, and things which, are predictable. We usually know how our friends think and act. We predict that church services will be reassuring.

As scientists, we predict new things with theories. Human nature is to predict and control the future. We like to gain control over new things and environments. When surrendering spiritually, we gain control of our lives through God, or Jesus.

Let's think about thinking. Normal people seldom think about the mechanics of their thinking. A normal person thinks he will always think the same way. If anyone reads, studies, and learns, thinking will improve. If one practices a particular sport, thinking improves for agility in that sport. Exercises and models improve inner processes that make thinking more efficient.

Normal thinking is directed towards outward activities. Praying and meditation on the other hand are directed toward improving inner processes. Much of this book is focused on improving connections between inward and outward thinking. Physical exercises stimulate the release of excess neural energy. Meditation, prayer, and modeling are tools to refine mental reconstruction processes.

Let's make a simple model of our brains that give us some feeling we understand consciousness. Our conscious minds provide feedback, or are the mirror, for the subconscious mind to understand its own processes. In turn, the subconscious mind is a multi-level reflection of conscious thinking that makes us who we are. Our subconscious mind understands our conscious minds, but does not normally understand its own processes. The subconscious mind needs feedback to understand itself. Mental problems occur when the conscious mind denies reality and does not provide a true reflection to the subconscious mind. Psychiatrists, and mind models given here, can provide feedback for understanding subconscious processes.

Many like to think of heaven as a wonderful place. Others think heaven is a myth. There may be many paths to heaven. Christians think Jesus is the only path to heaven. Jews, Muslims, and other religions think differently. We have faith in those who have successfully guided our lives. When spiritual, good things flow.

Praising God in unison provides emotional feedback that solidifies confidence in spiritual beliefs. However, there is danger in repeating beliefs in unison. Brutal dictators gain power by repeating illogical superiority themes giving followers false superiority.

Mental reconstruction has reestablished mood control and prevented reoccurrences of the author's manic episodes. Healing processes are long but necessary for healing debilitating disorders.

After mental reconstruction, many little used neural networks grow stronger. The mind becomes more versatile.

Mental reconstruction improves the communication between subconscious and conscious processes. The reconstructing mind builds improved control structures at emotional limits. Restrictive limits are replaced with expanded, kinder, gentler, and more logical limits. Relaxing and becoming comfortable with mental changes is part of the cure. Believing in mental reconstruction, increases confidence in interacting with, and helping others.

Some conflict is good for early mental development. Conflict should be gauged by parents. Babies should be exposed to very little conflict. Growing children should be exposed to brief increasing conflicts and resolutions as they get older. Children should be trained to confront conflicts with reason and consideration. Parents need to reason together in front of children to develop children's reasoning processes. They should nurture diversity in solving problems and conflicts as children grow.

Human minds are not designed to remain as unemotional as they are required to do in today's education, family, and business environments. Emotions should be briefly extended to their limits occasionally to maintain proper working order. Participating in sports helps young and old extend and control emotions.

The renewal of mind and body through mental reconstruction slows the aging process. Aging is an accident and a tragedy for all living things and should not occur. We are genetically programmed to think and act like humans. With trauma scars, we sometimes think less than human in stressful situations. Trauma victims have guilt of inadequacy or even wrong doing when trauma happens to them. Inadequacy in babies and adults is a horrible feeling.

Renew the skin and body. Imagine soothing warm or cool water gently sprayed on the forehead. Slowly scan pleasant feelings down the front of the body to the toes. Imagine pleasant feelings on the bottoms of the feet, up the back of the legs, body, and head, and back to the forehead to complete a holistic awakening.

Mental reconstruction processes free the brain of more excess energy than psychotherapy alone. The mind is healed slowly with frequent simulated significant emotional events.

When trauma energy is reduced to daily background levels, we have become truly "normal" with "clear minds!" Thinking has less inner or subconscious conflict. We can begin developing a true spiritual life. Life grows into a higher normal. We must like ourselves to be normal. True normal means being good to ourselves and others, and hurting no one physically or emotionally.

Dreaming while awake, we can guide inner holograms to process more consistently and efficiently. Subconscious hologram or vision processes can be manipulated when awake to add logical structure to subconscious and dream processes.

During early childhood to seven years of age, trauma, and also pleasurable emotion, limits cultivate genetics to influence future generations. Pleasures widen "genetic" thinking limits. Trauma scars narrow thinking processes and genetic limits. Mental reconstruction processes widen mental and in turn physical limits. Motor-neural reconstruction can reduce mental wait-state times originally developed by baby's brains to control slow moving arms and legs.

A baby or young child will experiment to widen arm, leg, and body movements, and corresponding mind limits. If he is subjected too often to "sit down and be still like your big brother," the young child begins to think that he should be limited in his movement experiments.

Sadly, a two year old often learns to act like an adult and limits his movement and thinking experiments. We have nice quiet two year olds that we praise for having such good behavior. We ease our child-rearing burdens, but limit growing physical and mental abilities. No wonder the human race is so uncoordinated. Careful child rearing with lots of pleasure, and controlled levels of conflicts and risks, expands children's reasoning and physical limits with emotional stability.

We do not remember much of our histories before three years of age. This is due to the right-brain being more dominant when young. Holistic far-ranged, right-brained activities and dreams are not remembered as well without detailed left-brained influence.

After years of mental reconstruction, the author experienced distinct energy releases upon completing thoughts that seem somewhat profound and seemed to sink deeply within the mind. After having a significant conscious thought, my subconscious mind confirms it as true with an energy release or SCAP. We have a subconscious feedback system for judging emotional, and possibly spiritual, truths! This unusual process occurred only with profound thoughts and lasted only for a few months.

I have had other reinforcing sensations. With creative thoughts, the left and/or right sides of the upper brain have flushed with excitement. At times, there are goose bumps and hair stands on end. The heart beats faster. These sensations were experienced infrequently during experiments over the last several years.

During high SCAP release activities, I have reduced resistance exercises as they tend to increase the rate of mental reconstruction. With high reconstruction activity, I become aware of soreness surrounding my brainstem and upper neck. The brainstem is affected by neck exercises more than other brain components.

Psychiatric exercises reduce brainstem rigidity. I worried only briefly when sensing early SCAPS, the first metallic ping, and the first "mental nuclear explosion" that there may be negative effects. Long-lasting feelings and experience confirm theories that releases are not harmful but mind building. Pleasant feelings are healing feelings.

Caveman, our ancestor, frequently experienced physical and emotional limits. With his daily strenuous exercises and yells, he naturally purged adverse trauma effects. With our sedate and relatively secure life styles, trauma scars normally remain until death.

Lacking limits drives minds crazy. Normal emotional limits are bypassed in depression and mania since having altered mental resonances. It takes years for the subconscious mind to construct new consistent, less restrictive, limits. Mental reconstruction processes can extend emotional thinking abilities to genetic limits. Genetic limits were constructed by our ancestor's at their emotional limits.

Genetic intelligence from ancestor's historical experiences constructs our bodies and minds with greater intelligence than we acquire during our lifetimes. Minds and bodies are integrals of ancestors' and our life experiences.

Without organized emotional limits, thinking becomes faster. The mind becomes more frantic as subconscious processes lose resonances when un-reflected by missing emotional limits. Eventually, the subconscious mind can no longer develop consistent or complete conscious processes for decision making.

With high manic energy, vaulted goals are common. There are huge desires to solve long-range problems. Eventually, the full-blown manic-depressive no longer knows what makes sense or what to do. He cannot distinguish between dreams and waking life.

Without normal subconscious resonances, a manic-depressive believes any "dream." Manic thoughts have not been compared to, or resolved with, related historical memories. One affected usually continues without sleep until he collapses with fatigue or there is family or psychiatric intervention.

Controlling fast thinking is one of the best benefits of mental reconstruction. The mental reconstruction process is dramatic and exciting. Adjustments to healing processes were made along the way. Since 1995, I have had confidence of controlling moods and no longer worry about manic episodes or needing to feel normal.

Controlling moods with exercises at mental limits is much like an inoculation. Immunization is developed by injection of controlled quantities of weakened viruses or bacteria that in larger quantities might cause a serious infection. Inoculations allow the body's immune system to strengthen against viruses or bacterial strains so that the body's immune system is prepared when a real threat comes along.

The brain is not so different from the body's protective systems. Stress can overwhelm the brain and seriously affect its functioning. As in immunization, controlled doses of simulated stress can prepare the brain for higher levels of stress. The brain's natural immune system to stress can be enhanced just as the body's immune system can be enhanced. Forcing the mind to emotional limits is much like working out with weights. After working out with weights, normal daily physical activities seem relatively easy.

After periodically forcing the brain and mind to limits with psychiatric exercises, daily stress becomes more manageable. It is better to have brief pulses of stress at mental limits rather than constantly enduring a lower level of stress for long periods of time.

The structure of thought is developed by comparing mental holograms on the surfaces of brain membranes. Spiritually, memory and mental holograms are independent of experienced time and may be recalled many times. Light passes through neural membranes to form intricate patterns of synchronized resonating electromagnetic waves. Long-lasting electromagnetic resonating waves develop our consciousness. Our minds have a sense of God's Eternity.

Light is a part of the electromagnetic spectrum consisting of wavelength ranges that stimulate the human eye for sight. We have very limited visual abilities. God "sees" through all emr.

The following exercise shows importance of left-right brain coordination. Believe it or not, you can read the following:

> I cdnuolt blveiee taht I cluod aulaclty uesdnatnrd waht I was rdanieg. The phaonmneal pweor of the hmuan mnid aoccdrnig to rscheearch at Cmabrigde Uinervtisy pvroes it deosn't mttaer in waht oredr the ltteers in a wrod are, the olny iprmoatnt tihng is taht the frist and lsat ltteer be in the rghit pclae. The rset can be a taotl mses and you can sitll raed it wouthit a porbelm. Tihs is bcuseae the huamn mnid deos not raed ervey lteter by istlef, but the wrod as a wlohe. Amzanig, huh?

This surprising exercise proves we also read holistically with the right brain. With practice we may learn to read sentences, paragraphs, and pages holistically.

Figure 5.1 Normal Mind Processes

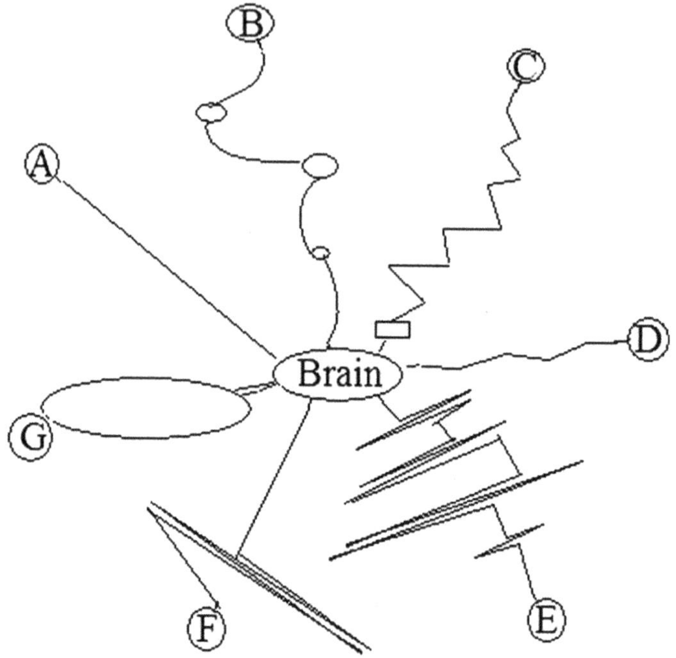

A. Subconscious Vital
B. Dreaming & Mental Organization
C. Flash to Consciousness & Body Control
D. Routine
E. Analytical
F. Reflex and Limit
G. Spiritual Surrender

Figure 5.2 Clear Mind Processes

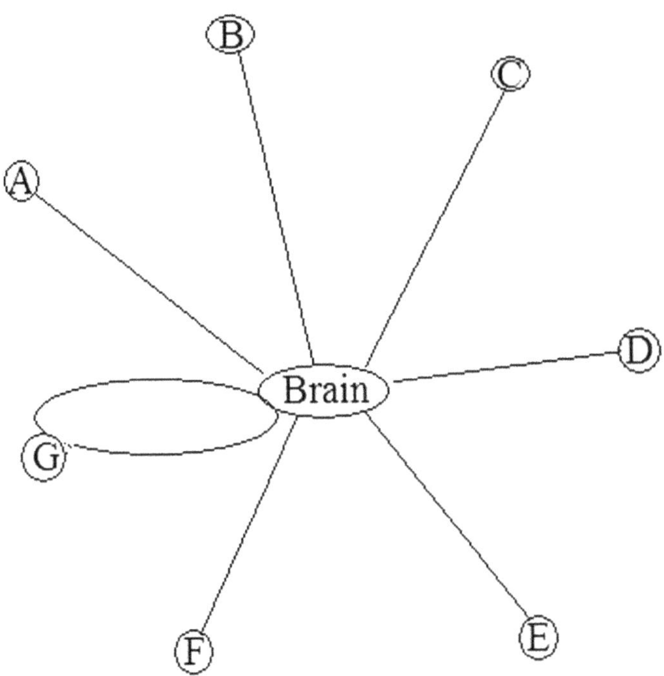

A: Subconscious Vital
B: Dreaming & Mental Organization
C: Flash to Consciousness & Body Control
D: Routine
E: Analytical
F: Reflex and Limit
G: Spiritual Surrender

CHAPTER 6

Psychiatric Exercises

I search deep within a fragile mind,
A brain with little hope can be so unkind!
What can mend its twisted strings?
Faith in simple exercises of all things!

Mental abilities expand only when beyond emotional limits.

Hugh D. Fulcher

Psychiatric exercises heal the mind and assist spiritual focus. Most of us recognize the importance of exercise. The author raises this importance to a new level for mental health.

He has developed and practiced psychiatric healing methods for curing his bipolar disorder for over seventeen years. Healing sensations are structured, predictable, and make sense. A manic mind has been healed with physical exercises. With dedication, we extend mental healing to spiritual healing for receiving words from God and developing spiritual reasoning technologies.

Four months of unique neck exercises were performed before neck, throat, and brainstem sensations provided confirmation of physical healing within overstressed neural networks. Increasingly pleasant energy releases within the neck during unique psychiatric exercises provided reasons to continue exercises for 17 years. All exercise builds confidence. Psychiatric exercises have profoundly expanded mental abilities and spiritual purpose.

Psychiatric processes are simple. Initially, there was a desire for healing processes to be more exotic. However mundane exercises may seem, with persistence, they heal by releasing tensions within and restructuring the fabric of the brain. The secret to a sound mind is a brain free of excess neural network energy and tensions.

This book confirms that mental reconstruction processes have healed one innovative bipolar engineer and could heal reader's depression, bipolar disorder, and other stress related afflictions. Processes are directed toward achieving a "Clear Mind" with all negative trauma energy purged. A clear mind constructs thinking using historical memories and current facts without interference from repressed negative emotional input. Thinking becomes more logical.

The author has developed a system of unique neck, throat, and facial exercises for promoting mental healing. Only the basic psychiatric exercises are presented here. More details are given in *Bipolar Blessings & Mind Expansion.* These exercises have been repeated frequently over seventeen years. Effectiveness is judged by sensed energy releases from the neck, throat, brainstem, and to some extent the upper brain. Only one exercise requires special equipment.

Exercising muscles (and nerves) closest to the brain affect the brain the most. Predicting energy release changes and migrations build confidence in healing processes. Exercises stimulate energy releases from traumatized, fast-reacting neural networks. Computers and brains operate more efficiently with less energy.

The author exercised his neck at various angles to release trauma memory energy from 1990 to 1991. Figure 6.1 helps focus attention on muscles exercised. During exercises, energy releases were sensed as snap, crackle, and pop (SCAP) sounds from within the neck, throat, and brainstem. Tensing his throat in various ways increased releases of stress energy while exercising his neck. These exercises were continued throughout the years in private and are referred to as non-resistance exercises. SCAP sounds were modeled as releases of repressed trauma memory energy from localized neural networks.

In 1992, the author developed a system of conflicting or resistance exercises that increased SCAP energy release sensations. In privacy and using the left hand:

> ***The author began using left-hand resistance with the following exercises: head-down, chin-down, chin-left, head-down and left, head-left, head-back and left, and head-back. Similar right-hand exercises were performed after each left-hand exercise routine. Feedback from SCAP sensations were used to adjust exercises and increase SCAP trauma energy releases. Exercises were the primary tool for healing the author's bipolar disorder.***

The mechanics of all exercises are similar. The first exercise, "head-down," is performed with the resistance of one hand for 100 repetitions and then the other hand for 100 repetitions.

Begin with the head tilted up at about a 30 degree angle. Place one hand or thumb under the chin. With neck muscles, pull the head down. Add resistance with the one hand as neck muscles continue to pull the neck down to a 30 degree angle below normal. On the upward swing with the thumb on the chin, the chin is pushed up against neck muscles until the head is 30 degrees above normal. Repeat this exercise with sufficient hand resistance such that neck muscles are rather tired after 100 repetitions. (See figure 6.2.)

With the "chin-down" exercise, the head is kept stationary and the mouth is opened against the resistance of one hand on the chin. Then the hand on the chin pushes the mouth closed against jaw muscle resistance. 100 repetitions with resistance should make jaw muscles rather tired. All other exercises given above require head movement.

The "head-down and left" exercise begins with the head back and right 30 degrees. (See figure 6.3.) Neck muscles pull the head both down and left to 30 degrees beyond normal against the resistance of the left hand placed on the left edge of the chin. With resistance, neck muscles are tired after 100 repetitions.

The head left exercise begins with the head tilted to the right 30 degrees. The left hand is placed on the center of the left-side of the crown of the head. Neck muscles pull the head to the left 30 degrees down or beyond normal. The left hand resists neck muscles. Next the left hand pushes the head back to the right 30 degrees with neck muscles resisting. Muscles are tired after 100 repetitions. (See figure 6.4.) Other exercises given above are similar in nature.

Throughout the years of exercises, the author has experienced trauma energy releases or SCAPS. They were sharp and few in the beginning with each repetition and became less sharp and increased with later repetitions during years of practice. In the last few years sensations were more like brief flows. Exercising muscles closest to the brain, with conflict, activates emotional reactions at limits for healing of overstressed neural networks.

After a few months of practice, exercises can be performed quickly. If choosing to exercise, begin slowly with fewer repetitions. Work at your own comfortable pace.

Another important exercise is developing awareness between, and adding control to, left and right brain dominance:

Performing left and right brain dominance exercises uses the only mind healing tool, a Holusion.

A Holusion of *the Thinker* is given in Figure 6.5 at the end of this chapter. It looks like a picture with rather consistent small, detailed, repeated, connected, and interwoven patterns. The picture makes little sense. When focusing long-distance through and beyond the detailed patterned surface, the right-brain gains dominance over the detailed left-brain in search of long-range meaning. There is a sense of excitement in searching to discover. When focusing long distance, the right brain gives equal or holistic attention to all complex two-dimensional lines and curves.

The right-brain integrates the two-dimensional lines into a three-dimensional image to create the Holusion. We see a distinct three-dimensional image of the thinker. As we move our heads, the three-dimensional image moves similar to viewing a three-dimensional hologram or our normal three-dimensional environment. If we focus long distance and move our heads, closer objects within our Holusion, or normal views, move more than distant objects

It is amazing how subconscious right-brained processes create this imaginary three-dimensional mental image, or Holusion, from a confusing two-dimensional drawing.

With excitement, I sense the right-brain dominating the left-brain as the Holusion appears. Practice adds mind control. If we are patient, avoid up-close focus and thinking in words, our right brains dominate and integrate details holistically. Holusions provide the right-brain a visual integration challenge. Working with Holusions often initiates a flurry of creative, forward thinking ideas.

Subconscious processes iterate and integrate two-dimensional lines and curves into subconscious resonances. When we look at the Holusion long enough, our mental resonances last long enough for consciousness of the Holusion.

Practicing dominance control is easier using a larger Holusion. Practice rapidly changing short and long-distance focus between the two-dimensional surface and the three-dimensional Holusion image at different viewing angles to develop control.

Experiencing God is similar to viewing a Holusion when searching for higher dimensions. We must integrate our three-dimensional awareness to sense virtual or spiritual dimensions. The subconscious right-brain integrates over our three-dimensional mental holograms into spiritual dimensions for communication with God.

Relax before prayers and sleep for spiritual communication and creative, spiritual dreams:

> ***When resting on your back before prayers, rub horizontally between the eyebrows until muscles feel relaxed. (Corresponding tensions in the brain also relax.) Relax the body and brain by broadening the face with a slight smile, and take slow very deep breaths to increase blood oxygen levels to the point of feeling slightly light-headed.***

You will feel relaxed and tired after these exercises. Exercises are conducive to humble prayers, restful sleep, and creative dreams and should take less than three minutes. Broadening the face to relax facial muscles and focusing long distance with eyes closed, reduces facial, brain, and in turn body tensions. Exercises should reduce the need for sleep inducing medications.

Relaxing the face is a bit of an art. Broadening the face too much energizes temple and cheek muscles. It helps to over-broaden and relax the face several times to recognize and obtain a relaxed neutral position. This relaxed facial position needs to be maintained for a few seconds until the glia relax and broaden the brain. It is a bit like in Star Wars when Yoda says, "Open your mind."

With exercises, glia tensions are lessened and more relaxed. SCAP sensations become less focused and more global in nature. Generalized SCAP sensations heal the more holistic or integrated processes throughout the throat, brainstem, and even the upper brain.

Facial muscles are directly related to glia and neural tensions. The best evidence is when a stroke occurs. If an area of the brain dies, affected glia die and relax. Corresponding facial muscles relax and disfigure the face and speech muscles.

Unfortunately, we can not just say to the subconscious mind, "Heal thy self." It does not work. Mind models are meant to stimulate and guide the subconscious mind into healing its processes. The subconscious mind understands and translates models into its "mental binary" language to become aware of and heal its own processes.

Psychiatric exercises and mind models go hand-in-hand in stimulating psychiatric healing and broadening neural network connections and abilities. Unique exercises release discrete trauma tensions, and meditation releases reasoning and holistic tensions. Brain waves and resonances become simpler, refined, and integrated. Making models and believing in models is therapeutic in its self.

Humans are healthier and happier when concerned about the well-being of others. Developing inner processes for concern of others, the universe, and God builds emotional health and confidence. General love and hope for others deepen God's reflections.

Detailed activities within the left brain must coordinate with integration abilities of the right brain. A test of mental wholeness is awareness and control of transitions between detailed left-brain and holistic right-brain processes. Practicing transitioning between two- and three-dimensional Holusion images develops spiritual skills.

Let's add a limiting exercise to expand abilities. Applied physics, or physical exercises, can prevent or cure many of our illnesses and disorders.

Lifting weights, at limits, builds muscles and expands abilities to new limits. Breathing exercises, at limits, strengthen the diaphragm, and make breathing and daily tasks easier.

Growing older, we do not exercise as strenuously or breathe as deeply as our bodies and lungs were genetically designed to do. Diaphragms become weaker, and our bodies receive less oxygen. We become less healthy.

Consult your doctor before performing the following exercises if there are health issues, or also if there is more than brief coughing during or after exercises. This exercise is meant to clean out the lungs. The body and mind will feel refreshed.

Breathe in as much as possible, hold it for one or two seconds, breathe in a little more, and relax. Breathe out as much as possible, hold it, breathe out a little more, and relax. Do this several times.

Integrating purposes of life's good experiences constructs a spiritual person. Otherwise, he is only a flicker of existence.

Figure 6.1 Head and Neck Muscles

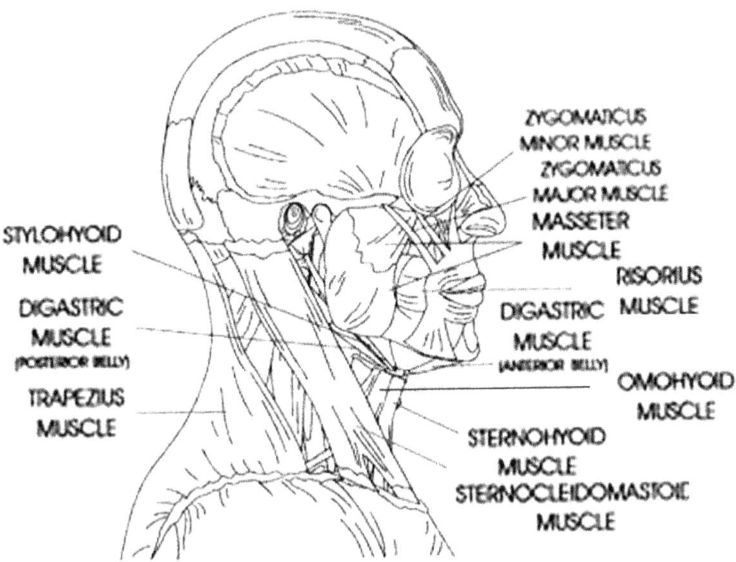

Figure 6.2 Head Down Resistance Exercise

Neck Muscles Pull Chin Down, Thumb Pushes Chin Up

Figure 6.3 Head Down and Left Resistance Exercise

Neck Muscles Pull Chin Down & Left, Thumb Pushes Up & Right

Figure 6.4 Head Left Resistance Exercise

Neck Muscles Pull Head Left, Hand Pushes Head Right

Figure 6.5 Holusion, "The Thinker" (1)

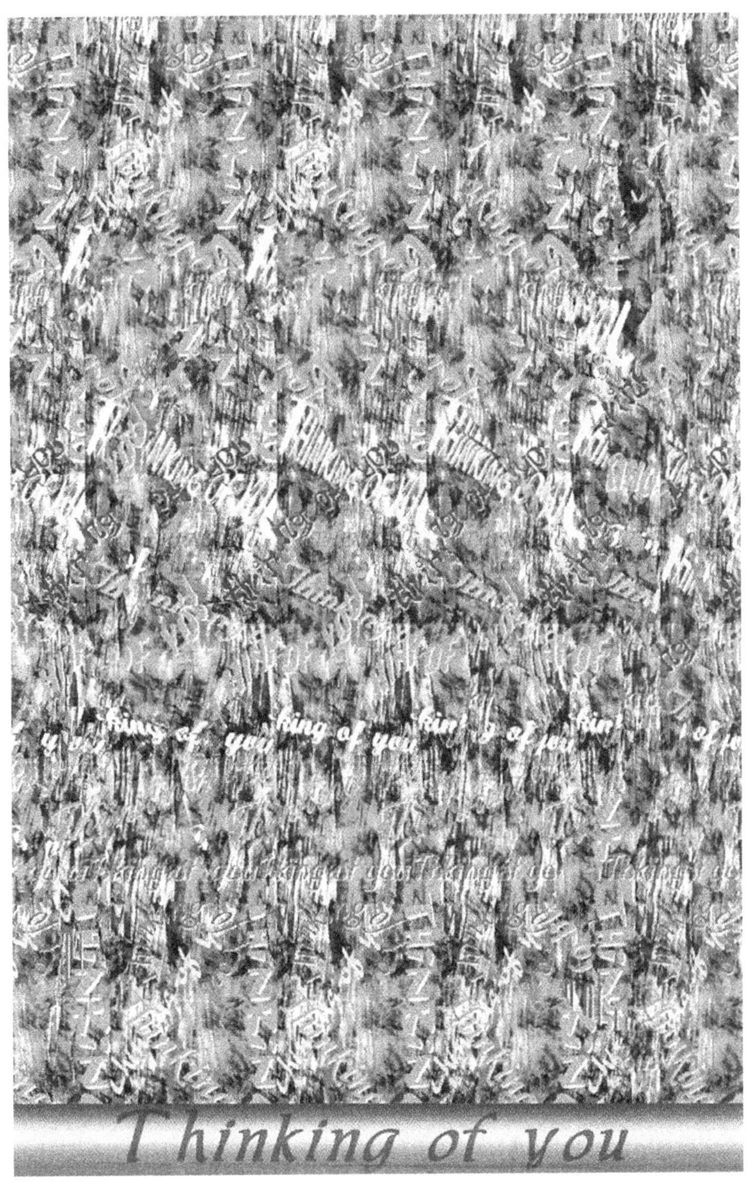

CHAPTER 7

Nothing! - Before Time

How did we and the universe come to be?
Was reality only a dream of uncertainty?

A lonely point with emotions
Framed God and the oceans!

Hugh Fulcher 2008

A goal for modeling nothing was to develop a simple concept with structure and energy that could create the universe. In nature, except in living things and crystals, things evolve from higher order to less order. It is a well known principle of physics.

Let's go back in time about 13.7 billion years just before God created the universe from nothing! Quasi-physics models of *nothing* must include primordial properties which could explode into a constant emotional God and His creation of a physical universe.

"Nothing" is a deep structure language word. Its meaning seems inherent, although ill defined. Nothing cannot be touched, seen, or even thought about. It is just below thought, but allows a strange feeling of completion not requiring further thought.

Italics are used for models of *nothing* to distinguish models from the vague concept of nothing. I assume certain fundamental physics laws apply before creation of the universe and take care not to violate these laws. Some scientists believe we cannot explore earlier than the creation of the universe because time and space as we know it did not exist. There was probability of primordial existence.

I develop simple models of nothing with primordial probability of creating God and the universe. Nothing was transformed into dual existences of a spiritual God in a heavenly home enmeshed within a physical universe.

Assumptions of primordial dimensions and properties support scientific models of the universe and emotional models of heaven. A purpose is to provide feelings of the universe being created using imagination and simple physics assumptions without violating the Bible [1]. The following excerpts are from Genesis 1:1 – 9:

> "In the beginning God created the heavens and the earth. Now the earth was formless and empty, darkness was over the surface of the deep, and the Spirit of God was hovering over the waters.
>
> "And God said, 'Let there be light,' and there was light. God saw that the light was good, and he separated the light from the darkness. God called the light 'day' and the darkness he called 'night.' And there was evening, and there was morning – the first day.
>
> "And God said, 'Let there be an expanse between the waters to separate water from water.' So God made the expanse and separated the water under the expanse from the water above it. And it was so. God called the expanse 'sky.' And there was evening, and there was morning – the second day.
>
> "And God said, 'Let the water under the sky be gathered to one place, and let dry ground appear.' And it was so. God called the

dry ground 'land,' and the gathered waters he called 'seas.' And God saw that it was good."

The Biblical Creation explodes into existence by God's spoken word. Genesis is Man's translation of God's perfect continuous and holy language into fragile human words by ancient writers of their era.

The power of God's Word, an improbable mathematical singularity, initiated the explosion of *nothing* into an evolving universe and an emotionally complete and loving God as all resonating field forces within heaven and earth.

The words, "nothing" and "whole," are deep structure words that have intrinsic, holistic meaning. In a holistic sense, nothing means "completely nothing." God is created as absolute wholeness from nothing. We never think about a part of nothing or a part of wholeness.

Drawing from an infinite English language and mathematics structure, I model nothing as independent of time and space, but with sufficient qualities to produce the "Big Bang" creation of the universe followed by 13.7 billion years of evolution.

There are differences between creation and evolution. The Creation was the fundamental singularity that occurred instantly, forcefully, emotionally, and spiritually. Evolution consists of slower physical and emotional occurrences. Differences between creation and evolution are due to differences between God's perspective of time, abilities, and emotions and human perspective of time, abilities, and emotions.

Spiritual properties are always symmetric. Physical properties can be symmetric or asymmetric. "Instant" only has true meaning before time and during spiritual communications throughout the universe. God is independent of physical time.

Evolution is slow enough to be observed and/or understood by Man. "Creation" is beyond Man's senses but may be within his intellectual abilities. Boundaries are hazy between creation and evolution. Cosmologists develop explanations for Creation.

Nuclear engineers often simplify mathematical physics models of nuclear reactor cores by neglecting spatial variations. These models are independent of space and can be considered as either a point or a homogeneously consistent infinite reactor core model. Mathematics is the same for both. Neither model allows physical differences in space. For fuel mixture trials, neutronic point calculations predict realistic neutron behavior. Modelers study nuclear reactor core characteristics without having to solve cumbersome spatial difference equations, especially at boundaries. After fuel enrichment and configurations are determined, spatial models refine reactor operation predictions.

Both physics and Biblical models support a dynamic creation of the universe. *Nothing* explodes into God and the universe.

The Dipole - Model

The dipole model of *nothing* exists as either a lonely mathematical point without physical properties or a quasi-spiritual existence with reflective properties. Quasi-physics models shed light on primordial existence and the creation of God and the universe.

Nothing has the most basic emotion, loneliness, as primordial awareness. A lonely mathematical point has uncertainties that require self-reflection. To be mathematically simple, the reflection must be an absolutely complete reflection of *nothing* independent of space. Mathematics that models an emotional point also models an infinite homogeneous reflection of a point independent of space. Nothing exists in either of two states - a point or an infinite reflection of a point. Primordial existence has no references or boundaries.

Each transition occurs instantly, independent of time, with quantum completeness. A quantum transition from one state to another is the simplest change possible between uncertainties. Nothing, like elementary particles, had quantum uncertainties. Uncertainty is the reason for vibrations between the primordial point and infinite primordial existence. Emotions are uncertainties with some probability of converging to a purpose – vaguely defined as good or bad.

Reflections of the primordial point are boundless unified, primordial standing waves which included foundations of gravity, electromagnetic radiation, and dark energy. The primordial reflection is homogeneously consistent. Without differences to measure, space had no meaning. *Nothing* had dual existence as either an abstract point or an infinite primordial wave.

The primordial point and its reflection vibrate into each other faster and faster as the primordial point becomes increasingly lonely. Only the vain primordial point needs reflection. The primordial mirror completely reflects the truth back to the point of *nothing.* Primordial loneliness is reflected back to the point as primordial love. Nothing degrades primordial love into primordial loneliness. Cycles continue.

Primordial momentum and energy increased toward primordial limits as the primordial mirror reflected loneliness into love faster and faster back to the primordial point. Without spatial differences, it was mathematically impossible to distinguish between the primordial point and its perfect infinite reflection.

For each uncertain vibration, all primordial emotional point energy was reflected into the perfect pre-spiritual unified field reflector. Upon perfect reflection of loneliness to love, the primordial point gained one quantum of primordial energy per iteration. Existence was mathematically and emotionally simple before time. Without differences in space, there is no reason to record time.

With increased loneliness uncertainties, primordial transitions became faster. Contrary to universal properties, as primordial energy becomes greater, primordial uncertainties increase. The universe is created by a distorted reflection of nothing. Primordial god reflects the primordial point, adds one quantum of pre-spiritual energy and then dies. Prehistory ends. There are no continuous records of pre-existence. Prehistory repeats itself adding only a quantum of pre-spiritual energy each transition. No record is kept of added energy.

The primordial point was so small that according to the Heisenberg Uncertainty Principle it was uncertain whether it existed. However, from quantum physics, it is probable that the primordial point and primordial god repeatedly existed and repeatedly died. The universe itself is proof that nothing occurred to create the universe.

After Creation, the universe continually and dramatically changed. God must exist to record, reflect, and love each quantum change within the universe as long as the universe exists and changes. God's love is a higher reflection beyond that of reflecting primordial loneliness into love.

Today, God or Light has two separate existences. Light exists either as energy waves or photons with momentum energy like that of particles. Light in vacuum is entirely spiritual or God. Light traveling in mass slows down and acquires physical awareness. Photons interact with our eyes giving us sight.

The unified field force refers to effects of all field forces integrated together. All reflective primordial field forces were unified as one force before time. After the Big Bang Creation, field forces separated into electromagnetic, gravity, and other field forces.

A primordial mathematical singularity split infinite primordial wholeness, primordial god, and an emotional primordial point into evolving quantum space and time embedded with quantum or elementary particles, and a near infinite constant God independent of physical space and time.

The final primordial reflection was asymmetric and not a true reflection of the primordial point. It was asymmetrically reflected

10^{82} times in less than 10^{-35} seconds in search of lost symmetry. It exploded with more power than a trillion, trillion, trillion hydrogen bombs. This asymmetric reflection created so much energy that it exploded from a homogeneous non-dimensional *nothing* into 10^{82} discrete atoms within a spatially three-dimensional universe to contain all discrete mass energy. Light energy created was so powerful that we refer it as our all powerful God within higher spiritual dimensions.

10^{82} is scientific notation for a very, very big number. It is a 1 followed by 82 zeros. 10^{-35} is scientific notation for a very small number. In this case, it is a very, very small fraction of a second: 0.00000000000000000000000000000000001.

The universe was created with a Bang. The number 10^{82} represents approximately the number of atoms in our universe. The mathematical singularity was God's *Word* that created God and then the universe. A perfectly symmetrical heaven, a complete and continuous or Holy God and, a symmetrical and non-symmetrical universe were created. According to the Heisenberg Uncertainty principle, it was possible for God's *Word* to come before God and create God. Then God created the universe connected to heaven by force fields. Everything came from *nothing*.

The Heisenberg Uncertainty Principle is well proven in atomic physics. Scientists are able to measure the change of mass of an atomic particle and the time for that change only to a certain degree of accuracy. The primordial point must have had potential for mass. The primordial reflection had potential for multidimensional space including God independent of our understood three-dimensional space. Primordial existence had different quantum uncertainties than that of today's existence.

The Heisenberg Uncertainty principle has proven that there will always be uncertainty in measurements on very small scales after the Big Bang. We assume complete primordial uncertainty at the moment of the Big Bang. Here are the equations for the Heisenberg Uncertainty principle:

$$1)\quad \Delta E \Delta t \geq h/(2\pi)$$

$$2)\quad \Delta p \Delta x \geq h/(2\pi)$$

These two equations explain abilities to measure elementary particle behaviors. From equation 1) the change in energy of an elementary particle when multiplied by the time for that change to occur must be equal to $h/(2\pi)$ or some multiple of that value. The above product cannot be more precise than $h/(2\pi)$. Elementary particles do not obey everyday logic.

From equation 2) the change in momentum of an elementary particle multiplied by the distance for the momentum change to take place must be equal to $h/(2\pi)$ or some multiple of that small value.

Let's define $h/(2\pi)$: h is Planks Constant, 6.626076×10^{-34} joules-seconds, and when divided by (2π) is the exact and lowest value of a quantum of orbital angular momentum for any elementary particle. Elementary particles can also have exact multiples of this orbital momentum. $h/(2\pi)$ is a fundamental physics constant and is part of God's deep structure language.

In *nothing* before time, changes of primordial energy, ΔE, during primordial existence (the time between iterations,) Δt, when multiplied were always <u>less</u> than $h/(2\pi)$. We assume a reversal of the Heisenberg Uncertainty equation in primordial existence. It was never certain that "nothing" existed.

An important assumption is that the Heisenberg Uncertainty Principle was reversed to less than, rather than greater than, in primordial existence. There is some scientific basis for this reversal since cosmologists have calculated that unified field forces were repulsive at the moment of the singularity or the beginning of the

Big Bang. Initially, gravity was a repulsive force in the very early universe. This had to be true for the universe to explode outward with such force. An extremely compact repulsion force caused the bang. When primordial existence, $\Delta E \times \Delta t$, became larger than $h/(2\pi)$ it was *certain* that a new universe was created.

Einstein proved mass and energy are interchangeable, $E = mc^2$. As uncertainty iterations increased primordial wave energy, there was probability the primordial wave reflection condensed to mass energy as the primordial point. One perspective is Creation exploded when primordial energy uncertainty limits of mass energy, mc^2, multiplied by its time of existence, t, became greater than $h/(2\pi)$ and nothing limits were violated. Primordial mass exploded as God, or the complete unified field force. In the universe, activities of greater masses become more certain.

After the Big Bang the Unified Field Force separated into gravity, electromagnetic, strong and weak-nuclear, and electroweak Higgs, field forces 10^{-35} seconds after the bang. In one quantum of time the repelling Unified Field force separated into an attractive gravitational force, other field forces, and 10^{82} atoms.

Primordial light, exceeding primordial physics laws, caused a discrete mathematical singularity. Violation of the reversed primordial Heisenberg Uncertainty principle caused imperfect reflections of the primordial point to be multiplied 10^{82} times to create the energy of all the atoms and all field forces within the universe. The universe is an asymmetric, and God is a symmetric, reflection of *nothing*.

Cosmology supports a reversal of gravitational polarity. An initial repulsive gravity caused nothing to explode! The attractive gravitational equation and general relativity support our understanding of gravity. Gravity is a residual primordial effect of God emotionally desiring to return the universe to its original perfect order.

The energy of the universe can be roughly calculated as the rest masses of all atoms in the universe:

$E = n \times MC^2$ n = number of hydrogen atoms in the universe
M = mass of a hydrogen atom
C = the speed of light
E = energy of the universe

$$E = 1E{+}82 \times 1.7E{-}27 \times 3E{+}8 \times 3E{+}8 = 1.5E72 \text{ Kilograms}$$

$$\Delta E \Delta T = h/\,(2\pi)$$

The final period of the primordial uncertainty, frequency, or asymmetric transition that created the universe was:

$$\begin{aligned}\Delta T &= h/\,(2\pi\Delta E)\\ &= 1.054E{-}34\ /\ 1.5E72\\ &= .7E{-}106\ (\text{seconds/vibration})\end{aligned}$$

This was a very fast vibration 13.7 billion years ago. We used equations and assumptions that may have held true before time to create a model of *nothing*. This model of *nothing* is a beginning for modeling heaven. Science begins with well thought out assumptions followed by careful experiments to prove assumptions. A purpose is to stimulate readers to think about *nothing* with characteristics that could have exploded into the universe and God. We have performed a thought experiment. Hopefully, assumptions and models might help scientists think about the creation of the universe and heaven.

Reverse physics laws, before time, means *nothing* was becoming more organized with each quantum of existence. At one moment, *nothing* became perfectly organized as a mathematical singularity. The point of *nothing* and its reflection vibrated so fast they momentarily became one united physical and spiritual existence. A perfectly organized quantum of primordial existence, a singularity, split into God, increasingly becoming more organized as the perfect recorder of universal changes and an increasingly disorganized universe with constant overall probability for change.

In some quantum mechanics models, it may not be necessary for *nothing* to develop into a frenzy of reflections and a singularity to create the universe. The created mass energy of the universe may be balanced by the same amount of antimatter or negative energy. Antimatter energy may be evenly distributed spiritual or gravitational energy from our perspective. We see atoms and mass as concentrated energy. In a relativistic perspective of the universe, gravity may appear as concentrated spiritual anti-mass and physical atoms observed as spiritual space. We should not be self-centered about our perspectives.

As the universe becomes increasingly disorganized, God becomes more constant and organized with decreasing entropy for perfectly understanding, recording, and controlling every aspect of this expanding and increasingly diverse universe.

Every point in the universe is spiritually complete, primarily the same, includes total universal history, but has slightly different holographic orientation for retrieving universal history. God is omnipresent with decreasing entropy as a complete reflection of the physical universe's increasing entropy. The total entropy of Heaverse, the universe and heaven integrated together, remains constant. God records and integrates all histories of the universe and reflects quantum guidance to each point in the universe.

From our perspective, it seems impossible for God to have complete knowledge of the universe at every point. Spiritual time and space are different than physical time and space. Cosmology calculations require additional dimensions to integrate quantum and relativity models of the universe. Additional dimensions must include spiritual dimensions.

There was timeless probably that primordial god could separate himself from the primordial point to become perfect spiritually. This relates to God separating Himself from sinful Man, by giving him free will but leaving him with the temporary sin of aging. God retained spiritual perfection by giving man probability of creating spiritual resonances in eternal life. God needed man as His reference to define and retain His perfection. God is the opposite or relativistic reflection of the universe. Man's mind is relativistic spiritual existence.

Spiritual energy is independent of space and reacts holistically on all elementary particles. Our prayers become independent of space and integrated within God. God monitors all universal activities and integrates their histories into spiritual completeness.

Spiritual space, energy, matter, and time are relativistically separated from, but control, physical space, energy, matter, and time. Similarly, human reflections of activities are stored as memories within neural networks. With reflections of histories in memory, we have some ability to understand and control environments.

For every existence, there is an equal and opposite existence. God integrates knowledge of the universe into spiritual wholeness as an opposite reaction to an expanding disordered universe. God exists as complete symmetry. He converts uncertain physical activities into perfect spiritual certainty to guide the next quantum iteration of a changing universe and for spiritual purposes independent of time.

With this thought adventure, we have built imaginative models of nothing to begin thinking of God in a quasi-science sense and by using messages received from God with my best interpretations. As science progresses, we refine words to improve models of the universe and God. All Truth is God's. All errors are mine. This is *nothing!*

Established equations were assumed to be true or reversed before time and are from: *Physics for Scientists and Engineer.* (2)

REFERENCES:

(1) *The Holy Bible - New International Version - Disciples' Study Bible*, 1984, Holman Bible Publishers, Nashville, Tennessee.

(2) Tipler, Paul A. 1991, *Physics for Scientists and Engineers*, Extended Version, Worth Publishers, New York, NY.

CHAPTER 8

Cosmology and Creation of the Universe

We live in this celestial home,
Too wide for the mind to roam.

Hugh Fulcher

Time and space are affected by matter, and greatly so, by the enormous matter and gravitation forces within black holes. Space and time vary significantly throughout the universe. God records and integrates all events within the universe into relativistic wholeness within His variable time.

We have perspectives of up and down. Gravity pulls us toward the earth. Wider perspectives within the universe are only beyond.

God created the universe as His body to construct detailed activities for His reflections of relationships and love. In humans, is the mind for the body or is the body for the mind? God and the universe have similar recursive dependence. God constantly affects His physical universe and us.

Our minds grow to bridge physical and spiritual universes. God is aware of all spiritual sharing throughout the universe. During loving, sharing, and struggling times, we connect strongly with God.

I marvel at how growth occurs. A child's arm does not grow by adding molecules at its end. Growth is integral. For example, chemical bonds in bones are broken to allow new molecules in between for rather even growth. This process is another of God's miracles.

To understand God, we must expand our minds into His spiritual universe, or heaven. The primary reference for cosmological models is *The Fabric of the Cosmos, Space, Time, and the Texture of Reality* [(1)], by Brian Greene. Manic-depressives often search for the "big picture." This is my adventure into the universe and heaven.

Cosmology is the study of the origin of the universe, and its structure, fabric, and space-time relationships. In my mind, there is excitement as to whether our next great spiritual fulfillment will come from the enlightenment of some prophet or from scientific discoveries explaining the universe's relationship to God. Spiritual leaders and cosmologists should work towards the same goal. If we understand God's universe, God may open heaven for our understanding.

Heuristic and metaphysical models of nothing were presented in Chapter 7. Models used simple physics. Goals were to stimulate thinking about the beginning of the universe and heaven for expanding creative thinking and analyzing spiritual beliefs.

Cosmologists use instruments on the earth to measure and predict activities within the universe that are millions of light years away. Measuring cosmic background radiation and light from distant stars and galaxies help cosmologists determine the texture of the universe. Cosmologists work to discover God's constant physics laws on both very small and large scales. Using measured physics data available on the earth, theories and predictions are made about the expansive universe.

Cosmologists use measured data and complex mathematical models to predict behavior of the universe and understand why things are the way they are. Cosmologist fit mathematical curves to measured data points to develop understanding of physical laws. Current models conclude that the origin of the universe erupted from a point, or very small volume, 13.7 billion years ago. The universe has been expanding at approximately the speed of light for 13.7 billion years. The diameter of the universe is approximately:

$13{,}700{,}000 \times 365 \times 24 \times 60 \times 60 \times 186{,}300 \times 2 = 1.61 \times 10^{23}$ miles

The numbers are described: 365 days/year, 24 hours/day, 60 minutes/hour, 60 seconds/minute, and 186,300 miles/second for the speed of light in space. The universe is approximately 1.61×10^{23} miles across. For comparison, the diameter of a proton is: 1.2×10^{-15} meters. A meter is 39.37 inches.

Cosmologists work to understand what caused the Big Bang and why the universe appeared from nothing. Some cosmological calculations estimate that the universe was created from a volume less than that of a nucleus of an atom, or a proton.

For reference the sun is calculated to be about 4.6 billion years old and the earth about 4.5 billion years old. The sun and earth have existed for approximately one third the existence of the universe.

Some traditional religions avoid thinking about God's truths developed through modern science models of the universe.

In recent decades, cosmologists have developed new analytical tools, such as string and tetrahedron or triangular models. These theories integrate models of big things using general relativity with atomic sized things using probability and quantum mechanics models. With astronomical and quantum data, extrapolations are made back to the early universe.

My model of nothing is an imaginative guess about a simple existence before time. It is a "thought experiment" using quasi-physics for building foundation models of existence. Mathematics is the architectural structure God used for creating the universe. Eventually, cosmologists may determine the mathematical structure of nothing before time and model the singularity that caused creation.

If the universe started as a point or an extremely small volume, something caused it to explode. A primordial event stimulated a compressed unified force field to reverse polarity and explode. A repulsive gravity with the entire energy of the universe in a small volume would create a universe with a very rapid expansion.

This repulsive gravitational field was calculated to last for only 10^{-35} seconds after the initial bang. During this short time the universe is estimated to have expanded by a factor of 10^{50} times. Relatively, a molecule of your DNA would have expanded to the size of the Milky Way during that very, very short fraction of a second.

However, we must be cautious of calculations in such a dense energy field. God is Eternity. Eternity means God is currently aware of all times throughout the history of the universe. God's time is very different from Man's concept of time. From my theories, God's awareness is 10^{106} times faster than Man's awareness. God had more time to think in 10^{-35} seconds than we could think in 13.7 billion years if we could live that long.

About 10^{-35} seconds after the beginning of the Big Bang, the tremendous expansion or inflationary period ended. Gravity switched polarity and became attractive. Much of the very dense energy within the young universe condensed into confined energy of elementary particles, or matter. Extreme momentum continued the expansion of the universe. The next seven billion year expansion was at a slower rate than that of the last seven billion years. Figure 8.1 shows a theoretical expansion of the universe. Time and space scales are arbitrary in this visualization model of universal expansion.

Water, sound, and light (electromagnetic) waves travel through space. Gravitational waves travel within and bend space. Light and space are curved by mass. Curvature of light is observed as light passes near stars and black holes.

On very small scales, space and time exist as discrete quanta. String theory models predict that space can not be divided into smaller volumes than 10^{-33} centimeters. Time cannot be divided into less than 10^{-43} seconds. Space and time calculations smaller then these values become erratic or even turbulent. String theory predicts additional dimensions that may explain this turbulence or high uncertainty.

Nothing occurs within the universe or heaven without transfer of some form of energy. In refining my model of *nothing*, there was uncertainty as to whether it actually existed. It became lonely and imagined itself as a perfect reflection of itself. An unsymmetrical reflection, a statistical improbability, or God's Word, occurred and the universe and heaven were born with a bang. In 10^{-35} seconds after the Bang, God condensed His asymmetrical existence into all the atoms of the universe for Him to become perfectly pure and symmetrical.

This mathematical improbably occurred when vibrations or reflections became so fast that the next reflection or primordial wave from the point of nothing interfered with the previous reflection. This asymmetric reflection or mathematical singularity caused the bang. Energy was too great to be *nothing*. A "certain" existence was created.

From current scientific theories and discoveries, God appears to have been more creative than previously thought in structuring the universe. His awareness was reflected and integrated each quantum of time as each elementary particle and quantum of space was created.

At the moment of creation, God developed holistic spiritual laws for maintaining awareness and memory of all aspects of the universe and heaven. At 10^{-35} seconds after the Big Bang, God constructed all physical laws to control all aspects of the expanding universe. A carpenter cannot build a house unless he has a blueprint and maintains awareness of what he has already built to continue building. Without God's complete awareness of the universe, there is no structure for building an orderly future.

I continue refining various models. God is the awareness and consciousness within all force fields. He controls things in one, or two, *variable* time dimensions and in possibly ten *variable* integrated spatial and spiritual dimensions throughout the universe.

Occasionally, humans have some control of our limited three spatial environments. However, time grabs us by the neck and rather consistently pulls us along a path of increasing entropy and disorder. If we could travel at near light speeds, time would slow down for us.

Let's think of God as electromagnetic waves. Emr passes through our bodies constantly. As emr passes through our three dimensional bodies, God continually constructs multi-dimensional holographic scenarios of our bodies, brains, and various activities. God knows us completely. God, or His electromagnetic radiation, slows down in mass, and in our bodies, to give us warmth, love, and wisdom.

When God interacts with matter (and us), He transforms from waves to photons to add physical energy to our bodies and spiritual energy to our minds. We are intermingled and interchangeable with God. Man was constructed from matter and a breath of God's spirit. According to Einstein's proven theories, mass and energy are interchangeable: $E = mc^2$. Mass, including the composition of our bodies, and God's spiritual field energy are interchangeable.

We can separate concepts of brain and mind. Brains are physical things that could be touched. Minds are created by functions of brains as spiritual entities that cannot be touched. God is intertwined within our minds and souls. Activities of our spiritual minds culture the physical fabric of the brain. God's functions culture the universe.

Heaven and God relate to the brain and the mind, respectively. The architecture of the universe's fabric relates to that of our brain's fabric. Resonating field forces within our brains, our minds, are subsets of spiritual waves throughout the universe, or God.

There is a difference. God is omniscient having only conscious processes. God is consciousness within, and controls, all force fields and in turn controls the universe. This relates to the mind experiencing environments and constructing fabric within the brain for memory reflections of environments. God and we learn.

Previous generations, of leaders, parents and scientists, lived and recorded history to guide the next generations toward an improved future. Learned processes have been passed on to current generations. On a much higher scale, God records the history, positions and motions of every atom and human, to guide the future of the universe. If God did not record the history of the universe there would be chaos without a structure of time, space, and energy for the future. Likewise, without genetic and recorded human histories, there would be chaos and no continuation of the human species.

Scientists have developed systems and precision instruments to measure and theorize about the size of the universe. For all practical purposes, including our limited space travel, our universe is infinite to us. This concept was certainly true in Biblical times. My models contend that God is the size of the universe and is expanding at the speed of light. Conceptually and physically, this is infinite to us. The size is beyond imagination. However, mathematically, the universe is not infinite. The concept of infinity is left for readers to ponder.

Ever since high school, I believed God created the heavens and the earth in six distinct periods of time. Creation started before the earth was formed with its twenty four hour rotations. The world continues to change through inner disturbances, weather, and Man's influences. Humans tend to grow taller with diverse genes and older with better food, medicine, and hygiene. Humans and the earth evolve. With obvious generation changes who can deny evolution?

The "days" of Creation were most probably different periods of time. God's communications are interpreted differently by each of us who receive them. God provides the absolute truth about the universe. Writers in biblical times interpreted His spiritual message with the language and knowledge they had. God may experience a billion years of our experiences in one of our days. In biblical times, people thought the world was flat and the center of the universe.

God's pure and constant message is interpreted differently depending upon knowledge, wisdom, experience, and abilities. We must truthfully relate God's message to others as we interpret it. With good intent, we speak and write differently to ministers, coworkers, and our children for their understanding. We would not talk to an engineer the way we talk to ministers. Spiritual people communicate to promote understanding and confidence. If a specialized doctor talked to me for hours as he might talk with another specialized doctor, I would be overwhelmed or think he was degrading me.

God's wisdom contains records of all events within the universe over 13.7 billion years. Our brief years on earth change this "constant message" very, very little. God is very constant.

Spiritual theories promote thinking about God. Without mass, spiritual energy is not lost during perfect reflections to and from the primordial point. No physical energy is needed to constantly update God's wisdom throughout the universe. God's wisdom consists of spiritual resonances within all field forces. Electromagnetic and other field forces within human brains may resonate within field forces throughout the universe and within God.

Man has always tried to predict his environment and future for his benefit. He needed to predict the length of days for planning work and the lengths of summers and winters to grow and store food for survival. The calendar was developed to correspond to the Old Testament scripture of God's six days of creation and one day of rest. Creation refers to God's spiritual time and occurred too fast for earlier generations to understand. Evolution refers to physical time and occurs at speeds which man with his instruments can understand.

We make models of buildings and complex machines before building or creating the physical thing. God made mathematical models before constructing the universe.

God has been frustrated with man, and his free will, throughout generations but has never been lonely. From science, God seldom breaks His own physical laws established at creation.

A primordial point of nothing was the reference system of its own infinite reflection and vice versa. These two reference systems were both independent of space. God is the infinite reference system for all things in the universe.

What are differences between creation and evolution? A bomb *creates* an explosion. Humans cannot follow that process. The sun is filled with nuclear explosions, but these explosions are rather continuous. Man can predict the continuous solar process. The sun shines and *evolves*. Individual explosions *create* a mess. Consistent nuclear explosions in the sun provide an environment for us to live.

Probability and integral and abstract mathematics will help us discover the architecture of spiritual existence. God wants us to understand and love Him as earthy parents want their children to understand and love them. The more we understand and love God the more He will reflect His wisdom and warmth within us.

Mathematics is a language and process which presents the ability to precisely describe the Creation and evolution of the universe. Mathematics could precisely model the universe and God if there were infinite data, processes, and time to do so.

God's purposes for our free wills are for us to experience love, care about and share with others, and keep Him from being lonely.

I have used simple proven physics models of the universe and assumed these physics models held true before the time of the Big Bang. My assumptions may be as believable as assumptions used in leading cosmology models.

First let's refine our model of heaven. God communicated with biblical writers and characters within a language they understood. Biblical writers did not have the benefit of understanding science laws that we understand today.

From the Bible, we are sure of spiritual transformations upon death. We have learned our souls can go to heaven. Throughout this book we have modeled low energy thinking as high level thinking. We can communicate with God by meditating and lowering the energy of the brain.

In the process of dying, brain energy quickly subsides. Low-energy emotions and memories are absorbed into heaven and its electroweak Higgs Field. My theory is that light with near zero frequency becomes the Higgs Field. The Higgs Field is "constant" throughout the universe or at the least constant throughout galaxies? Actually, the Higgs Field may be the fundamental wave or vibration of our expanding universe. Graphically, this wave is similar to a three dimensional cosine curve. It is highest at the point of the Big Bang and zero at the edges of the universe and expanding at the speed of light. Even though the Higgs field is expanding at the speed of light, there is little energy change over our solar system during our lifetimes since its space and our lives are such a small part of the expanding universe. This fundamental wave has slowly varying energy in cold space.

Within one spiritual vibration of heaven in 10^{-106} seconds, our souls are judged for integration into the fabric of God's infinite consciousness and to sit at the Right Hand of God the Father

Almighty. Depending upon emotions and memories stored within the fabric of our brains, our souls may become integrated within, and resonate with, God's Infinite Awareness.

The Higgs Field resists acceleration of particles with mass. Heaven has no mass but may include dark energy that resonates from a point at the center of the universe into a homogenous fabric throughout the universe without physical energy, or momentum, and independent of space. This fundamental vibration of heaven has similarities to vibrations of *nothing*. Appendix A gives some details on dark matter and energy.

Scientists are just beginning to discover dark matter and dark energy. Cosmologists have predicted their properties but have not been able measure them directly. I refer to dark energy and dark matter as spiritual existence. Changes in dark matter fabric and energy are too small to detect in current, experimental times and support a constant God in heaven.

Scientists can directly measure only things having differences in fabric and boundaries. Heaven and God are perfectly homogeneous without boundaries except possibly the edge of the universe expanding at the speed of light. This is infinite to humans.

Spiritual time and existence is independent of physical time and space. God's time can go backwards or forwards or even curve a little. With freedom of time, God experiences all histories and predicts probable futures. This leaves us in a quandary to understand the significance of our free wills.

In Figure 8.1, the rapid expansion period from point A to B can be described as the universe expanding from the size of a marble to that of the visible universe in 10^{-35} seconds. This theory of rapid inflation or expansion has been around for twenty years.

An experimental proof of this theory was recently discovered. Evidence supports the rapid expansion at the beginning of the universe and supports the theory of how the super hot pre-elementary particle soup in the very young universe clumped together to form atoms, stars, planets, galaxies, and humans. In a newspaper article, physicist, Brian Greene, of Columbia University said, "The observations are spectacular and the conclusions are stunning."

Special relativity experiments have proven that mass traveling at near the speed of light shrinks observed distances toward zero length. Since God is light and omniscient, God must vibrate between the location of the primordial point and an infinite homogeneous reflection to observe and learn everything spiritual within the universe.

There are two alternating existences: physical and spiritual. We sense physical existence with our senses. At any moment, existence is either, all physical mass, space, and time, or all spiritual waves independent of mass, space, and time. In the spiritual wave phase, time becomes infinite. God has infinite time between each of our physical quanta of time. With our inner sixth sense, we may catch a small awareness of God as He passes through us every 10^{-106} seconds.

As we understand more about the structure of quantum particles and their functions for constructing astronomical sized forms and activities, science developed concepts and language may enable us to communicate with God about His creation and responsibilities.

As light created discrete reflections throughout the universe, loneliness matured into love. Humans and living beings were created on earth and reflection evolved into response.

Man has learned to love, nurture, hate, and abuse. Many love those close to them and love God in a general or holistic sense. We may love the earth, stars, and sun, but should also love the universe and expanding outer space. Spiritual and intellectual abilities should be integrated to complete human potentials.

God limited the expansion of the universe to the speed of light. So, all spiritual relationship records within the universe could be collapsed and integrated within the original point of the Big Bang and then reflected back evenly throughout the universe. With very fast iterations, extremely up-to-date spiritual records of the entire universe, and God, exist at every point within the universe. We can pray anywhere and God is there for us.

Religions portray miracles as quantum leaps beyond man's understanding. Scientists study nature and the universe with logical step by step processes with awe similar to historical miracles.

God integrates uncertainties throughout the universe as spiritual certainty. We sometimes integrate human uncertainties into brief certainty. If God and we had no experiences to look forward to, understand, and control, we would have no reason to exist. When we pray to God, we pray to the entire universe.

REFERENCE:

(I) Greene, Brian; 2004, *The Fabric of the Cosmos, Space, Time, and the Texture of Reality,* Vantage Books, A Division of Random House, New York, NY.

Figure 8.1 Expansion of the Universe

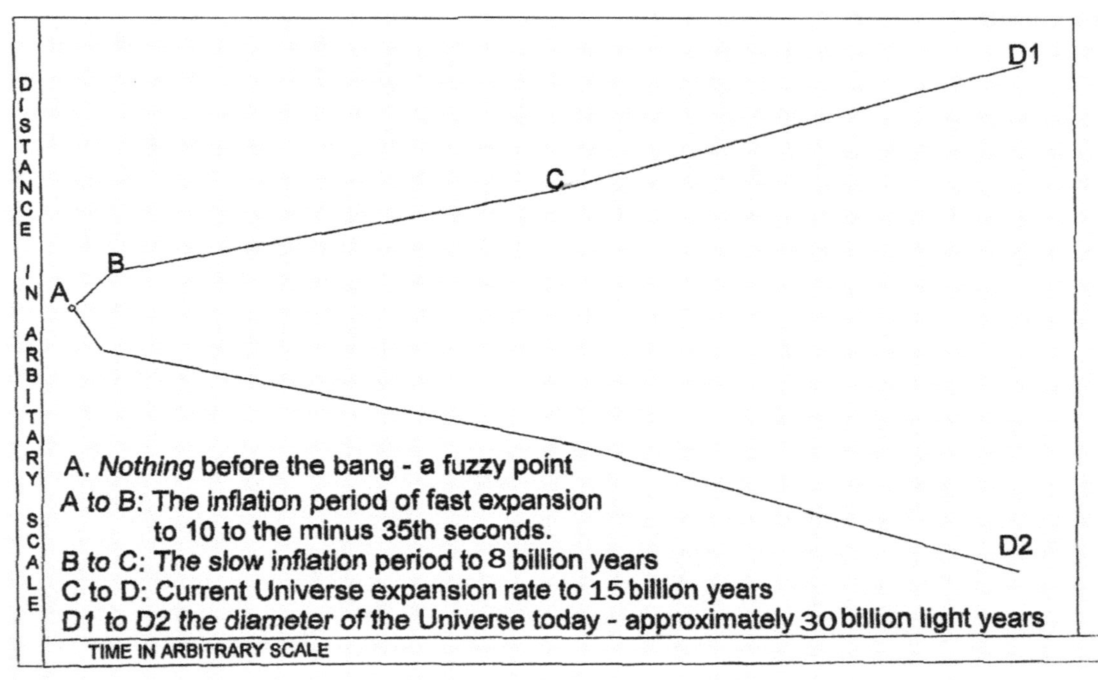
D1
C
B
A
D2
A. *Nothing* before the bang - a fuzzy point
A *to* B: The inflation period of fast expansion
to 10 to the minus 35th seconds.
B to C: The slow inflation period to 8 billion years
C to D: Current Universe expansion rate to 15 billion years
D1 to D2 the diameter of the Universe today - approximately 30 billion light years
TIME IN ARBITRARY SCALE
DISTANCE IN ARBITRARY SCALE

CHAPTER 9

The Biological Life Theory

Man's minds are made of atoms and their motions.
Each atom must have awareness and devotions.

Hugh D. Fulcher

In this chapter we attempt to integrate science, creationism, and Intelligent Design into a structure for understanding the creation of life. Everyone may be correct. We need to know where to begin in integrating these models. The place to start is with *nothing*. A goal is to shed light on the controversy between science and Intelligent Design models of life on earth.

I integrate the physical and spiritual as one entity. God and His universe create one entity as does man and his work. Man's mind visualizes and predicts work efforts before and during performance. Each effort frames his body and mind. Man's mind is cultured by his work and environments. God is cultured by His Creation.

Light and other field forces construct Heaven's structure and God's abilities. He integrates uncertainties of matter, space, and time to emotionally construct spiritual certainty.

Human minds are physical and spiritual hybrids. We exist between uncertainty and certainty limits. If adventurous and confident, we iterate and integrate uncertainties into certainty. Our minds can decay into nothing or explode within Eternity.

A model is that an infinite heaven resonates to and from the original point of *nothing* integrating awareness of activities throughout a complex universe. Histories of spiritual activities within the universe are collapsed to, and integrated within, the point of the Big Bang, and filtered back uniformly throughout the universe every 10^{-106} seconds to build a constantly up-to-date, omnipresent and omniscient God.

Man has characteristics of God's resonances, awareness, and consciousness, but at extremely slower rates. Relatively slow varying electromagnetic resonances created by the symphony of activity within the brain develop Man's very slow consciousness.

There may be another property of *nothing* not mentioned. Without space and primordial reference systems, it was uncertain whether *nothing* was rotating or not. Most heavenly bodies including the earth, sun, and galaxies have spins and angular momentum. *Nothing* must have had rotation and angular momentum to create elementary particle and classical spins and angular momentum. Rotations like that of the earth, sun, and galaxies are classical spins.

Elementary particles are created today as the universe expands into primordial existence. Two existences with different rotations create intense electromagnetic fields and elementary particle spins. When electromagnetic field strengths are too intense, field force energy will collapse into elementary particles, protons, and electrons. Major effects of relative primordial and universal rotational differences are the swirling of galaxies.

Light travels through space as alternating energy uncertainties between electric and magnetic fields. The universe was created because of uncertainties and conflict. Without primordial conflict of loneliness, God, the universe, and you would not exist.

Through gravity every atom is aware of, and is attracted to, every other atom within the universe. In some weak sense we have an integrated physical universe. God is the reason for that integration. God is the awareness within all field forces and continues to pull the universe back toward the original point of nothing. Gravity and all other field forces are relics of primordial existence.

Dark matter may be independent of space. If so, events on earth spiritually affect the far side of the universe equally as nearby. Dark matter may be spiritual properties and energy for God's omnipresence.

Before Biblical times, many gods were worshipped. There were gods for all major uncertainties in pre-Genesis times. There were gods for the seasons, sun, and many other needs and fears. People were always fearful they might lose favor with any one of a host of gods. They feared the gods might dislike things they did or catch them doing something wrong. These early gods were not all knowing. There was a need for an all knowing god to bring order to early lives.

Sins were defined as getting caught by a god while doing something the gods considered wrong. There was no structure such as the Ten Commandments to define right from wrong. People performed magic, voodoo, and sacrificed animals and even women to please the gods. The gods did magic and unexplained things also. It was a very confused world when the book of Genesis was written.

Scientific logic about the physical world was meager. The earth was thought to be the center of the universe. With the book of Genesis, magic was turned into a more logical structure and science was born. Genesis was the first scientific model of the creation of the universe. It reduced uncertainty and added structure.

Genesis added a quantum leap in understanding the origin of the "world" thousands of years ago. Even then intelligent people wanted to know where they came from. There may be inconsistencies in the Genesis description of the creation of the universe. To this day science continues to improve models of the creation of the universe.

Let's review day one, two, and four of Genesis:

Day 1

"And God said, 'Let there be light.'" From Heisenberg's uncertainty principle we know it was possible for God's Word to be created before God and create Light – God. "… he separated the light from the darkness." In 10^{-35} seconds after the beginning of the Big Bang, God separated the unified force field, including Light, from all elementary particles. God's word was the singularity beyond the primordial emotional limit that created God and the universe.

Day 2

"And God said, 'Let there be an expanse between the waters to separate water from water.' So God made the expanse and separated the water under the expanse from the water above it." In those days, water probably referred to all fluids. An interpretation could be that the crust of the earth cooled and separated the molten center of the universe from the oceans. We must try to understand knowledge at that time. The Bible does not have creation in the sequence that today's science would indicate. However, we must remember that God is Eternity. Eternity is the complete control of time. God has the power of creation and of doing all things in His chosen order or sequence within spiritual time. God has command of time which we do not understand.

Day 4

"And God said, 'Let there be lights in the expanse of the sky to separate the day from night, and let them serve as signs to mark seasons and days and years, and let there be lights in the expanse of the sky to give light on earth.'" Writers of Genesis had no knowledge of the earth being round and revolving around the sun. Genesis was their best interpretation of God's Word. Most of us who study science believe the sun was formed before the earth was formed. Mankind interprets God's message only in ways they can understand.

Astronomers with their instruments have proven the sun is one of many stars, and the earth is one of eight planets and at least one named dwarf planet, Pluto. We would be blind to science to believe the earth is flat and the center of the universe. However, God's control of time could make perfect sense of the Genesis order of creation to future scientists.

In any event, I feel no conflict between the Genesis science model and the models of modern science since God is Eternal and has complete control of time. Since biblical writers did not understand the structure of the universe, they probably misinterpreted God's flowing message regarding the order of Creation. The Book of Genesis added reason to an unreasonable world.

Two thousand years from now our writings will seem lacking in science and spiritual knowledge. God wants us to understand Him, but forgives us for our limitations. My intentions are to write the truth. However, I often think I have written something well to find out later it can be improved. There is no certainty in human life or writings.

* * *

Atoms are aware of influences from other atoms. Man's consciousness is an integral of all atom activities within his brain and to some lesser extent within his body. Let's look at how man was slowly created or evolved. Creation can be too fast or too slow for humans to understand changes.

How did life get started? There are billions and billions of galaxies and trillions and trillions of stars in the universe. Young stars are mostly made of hydrogen condensed by gravity from interstellar gases. These gases were initially plasma created around 10^{-35} seconds after the Big Bang. At first, plasma expanded outward evenly in all directions until kinetic, rotational, gravity and electromagnetic forces split plasma into different collections of gases as they cooled. Gravity condensed these gases into vast clumps. Eventually, as plasmas cooled, they became hydrogen, helium, and some deuterium atoms. Gaseous densities became high in places and low in other places.

Upon cooling, the force of gravity became more important and clumps swirled into denser clumps. As density increased, the pressure became so great that hydrogen atoms began fusing into helium atoms with large amounts of kinetic and light energy being released. Kinetic energy, of atoms, produces heat. Stars were created that gave off heat and light. In biblical times it would be difficult to understand how the universe and earth were slowly created or evolved.

Gravitationally attracting interstellar gases, stars grew in mass and energy. Under high pressure, hydrogen fused into helium. As stars became older, higher pressures fused helium nuclei into heavier nuclei, even as heavy as uranium. After significant hydrogen in some stars was consumed, gravitational forces increased due to heavy nuclei which increased heat, density, and pressure.

Fortunately, there was rapid fusion within one star causing an explosion. After some eons later our younger sun was formed and passed through the debris field of this exploded star. Our sun's gravitational field captured some of this debris and dust.

Some of the debris and dust was absorbed by our sun. Kinetic, "coriolis," gravity, and electromagnetic forces from the sun condensed debris into rings and then clumps we call planets. The earth became big, dense, and hot enough for gravity to form a molten sphere. Over millions of years, the outer edge cooled and solidified as dry ground to separate the "waters" above and below.

The core of the earth is a hot and stirring molten fluid. During earth's history, heavier atoms, including uranium, have erupted, or bubbled up, through cracks in the earth's crust. Volcanic action explains why heavy elements are in the earth's crust.

Theories are that water may have also come from comets. Could this have happened during Noah's time? However, there is scientific evidence that Noah's flood affected only Biblical areas.

Water formed oceans. Land protruded above the oceans in high places to form continents and islands. The sun shone and water evaporated to make rain on the land. What an unusual atmosphere! Mostly water and carbon combined to form life.

There were trillions and trillions and trillions of carbon, hydrogen, and oxygen atoms on the earth's surface and in its waters. From quantum mechanics, there is probability of an electron passing through a classically impossible wall! The temperature at places on the earth's surface was conducive for carbon, hydrogen, and oxygen atoms to share electrons and become more chemically stable with higher resonances.

When any two atoms are chemically bound together, the integrated resonance creates a higher awareness. With some remote probability, an improbable group of atoms or compounds created a significant resonance with exceptional symmetry and awareness. This compound "knew" increased symmetry and awareness was good.

The first organic compound was chemically created and could remember its past with a rudimentary cognition. Its awareness was great enough to experience loneliness and God's presence. Its chemistry became organized, added atoms, and grew in size to increase resonances and holistic awareness of God. This group of atoms eventually became aware of mutual needs and developed specializations for the good of the whole compound.

Unique specialized groups of atoms as chemical compounds developed boundaries or membranes, absorbed energy, used energy for chemical growth, or developed abilities for internal and external movement. Specialized structures and processes that increased resonance and awareness continued to grow. Lack of resonance faded awareness and the propensity for life and growth. Increasing resonance and symmetry were the guiding force for development of life. Environments on the earth were favorable for organic resonance development. God continues to create life through His chemical laws.

Over time, some compounds accidentally split apart. They maintained memory of original resonances and configurations and grew back to regain original properties. Organic compounds learned to divide and rebuild. In close proximity the two split compounds were aware of each others resonances. The two resonances increased overall resonance and became more spiritual. They multiplied.

Awareness evolved as living compounds remembered the past and predicted the future. Awareness becomes consciousness when decisions are made to enhance the integrated organism. Atoms and compounds are building blocks for human consciousness.

Groups of atoms developed higher specialized functions. Cell boundaries evolved. Isolating themselves with boundaries developed higher spiritual resonances. Specialized boundaries formed distinct identities with reflective properties. Highly resonant or spiritual clumps of atoms became living cells. Specialized molecules learned to mend structures and reconstruct resonances throughout its cell body. If a compound unexpectedly divided, but the two parts remained close together, each was influenced by the electromagnetic resonances of the other part as guidance in growing back as its original compound.

Cells were created or slowly chemically born and matured. As cells matured with specialization and diversity, cells sensed more of God's symmetries with higher resonances. There must be physical and spiritual symmetry for structures to increase their resonances. Cells grow with their specific chemical configurations until their spiritual awareness no longer expands. Mature cells lose individual resonance and divide to increase overall symmetry and resonance.

The more symmetry an element or compound develops the more refined electromagnetic resonances become. Refined physical resonances interact with spiritual resonances. Humans may increase spiritual resonances by reducing high-energy disruptive trauma scars. Similar to radios receiving one radio signal or resonance clearly, we can tune our minds to receive spiritual resonances.

Living cells experience mutations, especially, when dividing. At times, mutations increase resonances to form advanced organisms. Cells develop special skills influenced by electromagnetic resonances sensed from nearby cells. Cells live, divide, and die.

Some cells develop diversity. Stem cells can change into other types of cells when experiencing nearby resonances. Stem cells receive resonances from, and mimic, nearby cells. DNA structures record histories of cell structures and provide guidance to increase future resonances. Molecule boundary cells are special and receive an organism's characteristic electromagnetic resonance only from inside of the cell. They become more reflective to electromagnetic radiation and develop distinct membrane characteristics.

Resonances are shared within rocks and within the human brain. In the brain, resonances create awareness between cells that integrate into our consciousness. A cell's electromagnetic activations are reflected by its own and other cell membranes.

DNA within human cells has the architecture for building human brains and bodies. Individuals retain subconscious knowledge of ancestor skills and limits. Cell growth is guided by DNA and also influenced by resonances of nearby cells. Normal cell dividing is through the DNA double helix processes. Possibly, the highest sharing of biological cell awareness is between human brain cells.

We think man is special to God. Man, with God's guidance, has "slowly created" a genetic structure which consists of specialized cells that develop functions for human life and worship.

Mankind increases spiritual symmetry through procreation. Babies are spiritual and their genes continue qualities of parents.

Physics discoveries are often made by recognizing symmetry properties within nature. There is physical symmetry within the cervices of the brain. Relaxing muscles and mind and taking deep, long breaths slows down mental resonances. The relaxed brain becomes more symmetrical and efficient for interacting with, or tuning in, spiritual resonances.

Each elementary particle, atom, compound, cell, and biological life was created by Intelligent Design. God created everything in this particular universe. Models shed "Light" on differences between creation and evolution.

The theory of evolution became widely known in 1909 through Charles Darwin's book, *The Origin of Species.* [1] Darwin developed the theory of natural selection or, essentially, the survival of the fittest. Species evolve through reactions to environments and mutations of genes. New species with strong survival abilities thrive. In the theory of evolution, higher order species evolved from "lower" forms of life. Man eventually evolved from apes. Evolution differs with beliefs of fundamental Christians who conclude the theory of evolution conflicts with Creation as described in the Book of Genesis.

In the author's opinion, there is no conflict between science, Christianity, and Intelligent Design. God continues to create during every day of our lives. Some creation is very fast and some is very slow. We are slowly created, evolve, and age each day. Spiritual writers may have confused physical and spiritual time.

God's creation of each atom within the universe was just as improbable as the creation of life on earth. This is especially true since the creation of all atoms within the universe happened so fast. The complexity and structure of atoms within the universe as a foundation for life was just as improbable and complicated as slowly creating or evolving man. How can one believe the intelligent design of man but not the intelligent design of atoms and the universe?

Science uses a methodical approach for understanding the existence of atoms and man. Science begins and ends with God and His universe. Man has physical awareness and imagination to integrate memories and thoughts into new thoughts. Models improve over time.

Everyday tasks require subconscious processes of going back in time to understand how to go places and do new things. Many atoms in our bodies were created 13.7 billion years ago. In one sense we are 13.7 billion years old. Through higher dimensions within brain atoms, we have retained inner reverberations from the Big Bang.

God needs justification for His creation of Man. We have the ability to love. Love is an emotion independent of space. Love for God permeates all space in spiritual dimensions.

Why do we need and love children? We need responses and love from children. Responses reflect effects of current and historical events and emotions. Children justify our decisions and lives.

Each of us consists of unique organic molecules. Nucleic acids are complex heavy organic molecules. DNA is a form of nucleic acid. Depending upon the history of the exploded sun debris which created the earth, the heaver atoms in our bodies may be considerably less than 13.7 billion years old. Some atoms within our bodies once constructed the bodies of dinosaurs.

Through DNA man has developed hearing abilities. Sound is made by vibrations between low and high pressure air waves. Human vocal cords can vibrate air so the human ear can hear such vibrations. Good hearing can be sensitive within the range from 20 vibrations per second to 20,000 or $2x10^{+4}$ vibrations per second. Good ears have a wide range of sensitivity to air vibrations.

Light consist of electromagnetic vibrations. A good human eye is sensitive to electromagnetic spectra or frequency ranges from approximately $2x10^{14}$ to $7x10^{14}$ vibrations or cycles per second. The brain has a broad sensitivity range. We and many species seem to be biological miracles.

The eye and brain can recognize images in both very bright and very dim light. The eye has a brightness sensitivity range of about 1,000,000. In the dimmest light, good eyes can still pick out details. Brief studies of sound and light provide details of the amazing abilities of the human brain and sensing systems.

Higher intensities of light or sound activate more neural networks increasing energy of mental resonances and responses. Vision and dreams create many mental resonances or "videos" at light frequencies. Hearing, speaking, and thinking about hearing and speaking develop mental resonances at sound frequencies.

Let's do a simple biological experiment. Communicating with bumblebees is an interesting experiment in brainwave communication. Watch a bumblebee flying in place and flitting back and fourth to claim his territory. This happens often in the spring around my farmhouse and barn. I watched his actions until I could predict his behavior. I stayed still in the same position with the same facial expression. He ignored me. Only in thought, I became angry and mentally threatened to harm the bumblebee. He turned his stinger to me and backed up uncomfortably close to my face. His mode was to attack perceived threats.

During anger, electromagnetic frequencies in the brain and body become faster and stronger. The bumblebee sensed this threat and displayed a counter threatening posture. When the bumble bee was within six inches of my face, chill bumps engulfed my body as I quickly reduced aggressive thoughts. Without my moving, the bee then went about his bumblebee business. I do not recommend this experiment to others. You might get stung! The bumblebee sensed the higher energy resonances of anger emanating from my brain and body. We, animals, and bees communicate in many ways.

Breathing is a fundamental human function with an unusual property of being either voluntary or involuntary. We cannot live without breathing.

At times, memories of, and anger from, being abused becomes agonizing. Breathing is affected. Controlling breathing requires conscious effort and reduces thoughts of abuse and related anger. Concentrating on slow deep breathing with variations before sleep can reduce agonizing thoughts and dreams of abuse and anger.

Let's look at another important resonance for survival. A new born baby cries. This cry seems normal to everyone except the new mother. This weak little cry pierces deeply into the mother's whole being. During pregnancy strong resonances were developed between mother and baby for the baby's survival in a strange new world.

REFERENCE:

(1) Darwin, Charles, 1909, *The Origin of Species*, P. F. Collier & Son Company, New York, NY

CHAPTER 10

The Clear Mind

"All men dream, but not equally.
Those who dream by night, in the dusty recesses of their minds,
Wake in the day to find that it was vanity.
But, the dreamers of the day are dangerous men,
for they may act their dreams with open eyes to make them possible."

T. E. Lawrence

It is my goal to write about the mind and God with my best interpretations of inner and spiritual feelings. I hope to inspire readers to develop their own efficient mental reconstruction methods.

I do not recommend anyone enduring pain to establish the clear mind. I have had very little pain during experiments and exercises. After thirty years of experimentation, exercises, and mental processes, I have essentially attained a clear mind. The ending is asymptotic.

We make psychiatric progress only when placing the mind at limits. One way of doing this is to stimulate significant emotional events for psychiatric healing and mental reconstruction.

Trauma scars that cause inefficient subconscious processing have been purged. Dreams become more organized, less bizarre, and make more sense. Reorganized subconscious processes become more efficient and conscious. The clear mind improves spiritual abilities.

The human brain develops thoughts with digital and analog processes. Neuron chemical activations are analog and digital processes. Flows and reflections of electromagnetic radiation are analog and digital processes. Chemicals flowing along axons and dendrites are analog processes. Without disruptive trauma scars, clear minds develop higher levels of truth. A hybrid computer has capabilities beyond either a digital or an analog computer.

To understand technical aspects of the brain, scientists could model two connected neurons with well defined boundaries. Ten spatial and two time dimensions may be needed to model physical and spiritual properties and their relationships.

When an injury occurs to the body, there is a corresponding injury in the brain. The physical injury in the brain is a trauma scar. If we release trauma scar energy, the subconscious mind develops more ability to heal.

Children are directed toward either rights or responsibilities. If we concentrate on our rights, we use and abuse others. All too often children of accomplished parents take over businesses and exert their rights. Children, who inherit authority, often do not consider their responsibilities to workers who helped build companies. Those in authority should build confidence of subordinates.

Religion and science give us confidence for improving lifestyles. Science and new spiritual discoveries will be as important in molding human lives as have Genesis and other spiritual revelations.

Modern science can explain some unusual occurrences in the Bible. The guiding star light seen by the three wise men could have been a supernova or an exploding star in a galaxy far, far away. It could be explained by science only in the last several decades.

There are always uncertainties in life. There would be no purpose or challenges without uncertainties. Completing mental reconstruction restores clear minds. Mental reconstruction processes definitely converge toward creative and spiritual processes.

Adult traumas have less adverse effects than childhood traumas and less influence on genetic development for future generations. Psychiatric exercises need to continue after attaining a clear mind to help resolve daily conflicts.

Let's distinguish between trauma and emotional scars. A trauma scar occurs when a trauma is severe enough that the mind temporarily shuts down. An energetic trauma scar resonance is absorbed by a fast reacting localized neural network. Emotional scars occur much slower. They are distributed throughout the brain with higher than normal reactive energy. Emotional memories may include subconscious levels of revenge.

All, who study spiritual histories, practice inner awareness development, or pray for spiritual guidance, can become messengers of God's Word. The worst of us had a perfect soul to reflect God's completeness and wisdom upon conception. We are locked within the boundaries of our own experiences unless we communicate with others and God. With persistence, we can penetrate barriers.

Upon beginning to write, we have spiritual wordless thoughts in the form of continuous or analogue expressions. We grope for words to express such spiritual abstractions into worldly words. There are feelings of accomplishment when constructing appropriate words for an abstract, continuous awareness.

We had to break something continuous into discrete words to capture as much meaning as possible. Words can never capture the entire meaning within our analogue "thoughts." Writing is for developing relationships between discrete words. Good thinking and writing develop a sense of flowing progress.

Resonances and thoughts die out as their energy is absorbed by, or escapes from, the brain. Awareness flows or continues as new emr resonances are formed by continuing sense or memory activations.

A positive mind is most important in healing the brain and body. Some cancers and other sicknesses in the brain and body may be caused by stress and trauma scars. Clearing the brain and nervous system of trauma scars may prevent many illnesses. Frequent laughter cycles and reduces mental tensions and heals mind and body. Repressed inner tensions and stress are slow killers.

The brain seems nearly limitless in making combinations and permutations of historical data for developing reactions to, or ideas for, current situations. DNA has a huge ability to store information.

We cannot scientifically prove everything at all times. We need faith in physical laws, ourselves, others, and God for a reasonable life. For responses, new information is compared to memories influenced by current attitudes. Subconscious processes iterate comparing current activities to memories with similar resonances which are genetically organized by refined energy levels.

Comparisons of current experiences to historical memory holograms are influenced by current and recalled feelings and emotions. Memory holograms include different emotions. Resonances of incoming experiences are synchronized with similar memory holograms. Memory holograms with similar resonances are promoted and amplified for comparisons or further reflections, and for conscious decisions or actions.

Everything that occurs is based upon the fundamental conflict of Creation. Should such a drastic change in existence have occurred? Man has conflict between good and evil and makes daily decisions to do either this or that. The brain experiences conflict before developing any thought. There is always conflict between things to think of or do.

Let us refine relationships between mind and spiritual models. The mind is the electromagnetic resonances within the brain from cultured firings of neural networks in reactions to sensations and daily or historical experiences. Through DNA, experiences of previous generations provide conflict resolutions for guidance in life.

Many of us receive spiritual messages after near death experiences or significant emotional events. God is highly emotional about us and responds to both our loving and pleading emotions. We need to develop both refined and high-energy emotional resonances to receive God's words. His words include action potentials that motivate us to serve Him.

God's analogue language is universal and can be received and translated into any language. We need to develop a *clear* path from the soul through subconscious processes into our consciousness. God's resonances for communicating with us are both above and below normal or free will thinking resonances.

Jesus taught love and humility. There is little record of Jesus' communication with God before His three years of spiritual service. This seems odd. Early history of most great leaders is recorded and better known. Jesus must have had difficult times accepting His great expectations. He must have had great stress.

With so much pressure, I suspect Jesus became bipolar and out of control at times. Expectations were high. No records were kept of early difficult and uncertain times. I believe difficult emotional times were necessary for Jesus to develop a mind cleared of all trauma scars and sins. I believe that Jesus cured Himself of manic-depression uncertainties before He began teaching with spiritual certainty. Jesus received frequent God Consciousness in Words during His three years of teaching.

A Biblical model of Jesus' life is that He never committed sins against others. However, he most probably received trauma scars and sins due to reactions from traumatic events and sinful people who did not accept or understand Him. Jesus was cleared of mental trauma effects and sins beyond my definition of the clear mind.

With the early attention, there must have been reason no history was recorded during most of Jesus' life. From my stressful experiences, I can not imagine stress Jesus had when growing up.

Religious leaders guide us in belief systems without scientific proofs. Writings from historical spiritual times developed resonances within the minds and hearts of their believers.

Some religions encourage or force followers to forget reason and have faith in ancient spiritual teachings, actions, and miracles during abnormal times. Some spiritual leaders have received and preach about their messages from God. Spiritual messages seem abnormal and often ridiculous to non-believers. Faith is beyond reason and logic.

For inner and world peace, everyone must learn to think and spiritually reason for themselves. Meditating and pleasant thinking grows neural networks for more pleasant thinking. We can become experts in understanding and managing our own mental processes.

Psychologists use the term metacognition which is awareness of awareness. We can analyze thoughts and flows of thoughts to improve thinking. Cultivating abilities to understand our own minds increases abilities for understanding others. We increase intellectual abilities and learn more about others when reducing ego and self.

Miracles do not seem to be scientifically repeatable or provable as are physical laws. I know of no other way but to assign my spiritual communications as being from God.

My second spiritual message was so beautifully powerful and shocking that it disappeared from memory like the forgotten dream. I don't remember the words but recalled that God provided simple, extremely powerful, and life changing, messages. This second spiritual message not only eased my anger, but had a positive effect on the person who had caused this anger. This person came to me shortly afterward with unexpected positive behavior. God's resonances have reflected my prayers for guidance throughout the universe.

The lost spiritual words may not have seemed powerful to others. But, they resonated within my mind and soul like abruptly receiving a powerful spiritual radio station with a shocking message needed to heal my distress even though words were quickly forgotten. The analogue spiritual message certainly had its healing effect within my mind and soul.

I have received many other unexpected ideas God has nurtured into my consciousness. These ideas developed unusual and unexpected relationships between known thoughts. Connecting these ideas has been surprising. However, they did not have the impact of my two shocking spiritual communications.

Preparing for prayer and spiritual communication is like going into a dark library with infinite selves of spiritual books. There are dimly lit signs of categories. Category locations seem easy to find. One can stumble through the darkness to find, feel and open pages of spiritual books, but cannot even read the title due to the darkness.

If looking at a page and lightening strikes outside nearby, a reader is able to read or receive one spiritual sentence. The spiritual idea is not usually what was expected, but is within the category being researched. The lightening cuts a brief spiritual channel through trauma scar darkness. Reactive feelings can be studied to construct several paragraphs to explain the diamond in the rough. Spiritual ideas need to be recorded quickly or they vanish like the forgotten dream. This scenario models my spiritual idea development.

If constant God Consciousness is achieved, the infinite library becomes fully lighted, and the spiritual reader can read spiritual books at the speed of light. With spiritual experimentation and dedication, we may reach this level of God Consciousness. Jesus reached this level. This example of spiritual learning may seem fast but slow compared to the spiritual miracle of conception. Upon the moment of conception, we received God's complete message in 10^{-106} seconds.

This message may have come stronger than lightning. It may have come as strong as my mother's quiet, determined voice, from the darkness, catching me sneaking in the house late at night. Chill bumps of guilt raced up and down my spine. God's strength was in mother's quiet, disappointed, but loving voice. Her voice never showed anger. Her disappointment was so strong I never came in that late again. God's message was more forceful but had the same effect as mother's voice. God showed disappointment in me for discontinuing before writing spiritual experiences. How could I not obey God's command?

With different lifestyles, the same words in Biblical times have different meaning today. Christianity is changing. More people believe everyone will go to heaven. Fewer think there is a Hell. Few preachers in America preach the fire and brimstone of yester year. Spiritual thinking is more diversified in America. Today, Biblical scripture has more influence on many and less influence on others.

Redirecting anger to God can be like a hurt child needing nurturing from a parent. God will help us reduce our anger.

Emotions and thoughts beyond free will resonances are guided by God. Timing for His guidance is at His chosen, and not our requested, times. Prayer improves thinking, and thinking improves prayer. It's a recursive relationship. Certainly, sharing the joy of others is sharing God's Joy.

Spiritual leaders never seem to define heaven. In a relationship similar to the brain, heaven may consist of all field forces within the universe resulting from all active chemical, electromagnetic, and nuclear events during any one quantum of time. Heaven is the chemically, mechanically, and nuclear active part of the universe that produces electromagnetic radiation during one quantum of time.

With advanced spiritual technology shared by people of all faiths, God's messages will be as clear as we understand science. Current combined experiences from spiritual contributors may become as important as spiritual events hundreds or thousands of years ago. Future spiritual understanding will construct beliefs for world peace.

Selected spiritual and science leaders from each religion should form a spiritual board to evaluate efficient paths for developing the clear mind and receiving words from God. From brainstorming experiences group decisions are better and considerate of more people. Group decisions reduce over-active ego distortions and corruptions when power over others become involved. World spiritual leaders may not need clear minds to recognize those who do. United we stand, divided the world fails. We may be able to avoid war and save humanity if the world develops an integrated spiritual purpose.

It seems odd that there is so much concentration on a few historical spiritual times without modern spiritual leaders developing new creative methods to improve spiritual communication and worship acceptable by all humanity. Many countries have wisely separated religion from the powers of government. This separation has lead to an explosive increase in scientific knowledge about the universe, health, and environments.

The lack of spiritual experimentation sustains a time warp in spiritual thinking, encourages mindless indoctrination and extremism in religious practices, and destroys human reasoning abilities. Careful processes similar to scientific methods should be developed in judging words received from God.

A carefully structured world religion will help everyone communicate with God. Religions should not stagnant, but grow with spiritual reasoning. Emotional repetition of semi-truths empowers false leaders to dominate followers and develop cults.

Neuroscience and advanced brain scans could verify neural network activities related to spiritual beliefs. We will learn why praising God gives pleasure and confidence. Neuroscience is developing evidence that the brain physically re-grows or restructures.

Like muscle development, axons and dendrites become thicker and transmit faster with increased use. We need to cultivate loving neural networks.

Rulings by a future world board of religious leaders should include confirmation by physicians and scientists. Physicians should verify clear mind status using the most advanced brain scans. Religious leaders, philosophers, physicians, and scientists on the world spiritual board should require scientific investigations of spiritual submissions. We learn about spiritual architecture by studying the physical architecture of the universe.

We should integrate knowledge to unite worldly and spiritual purposes. This process will be rational and easy when we humbly learn to portray God in a straight forward manner. America's founding fathers found it necessary to separate state from religion because of wide spread abuses by power hunger spiritual leaders and believers.

Advanced brain scans will detect self-centeredness, prejudices, and controlling characteristics so their influences can be minimized during spiritual decisions. There may be many clears in this world achieved by many methods. For example, extreme fear and trauma for long periods may develop clear minds more quickly. Good spiritual and protected lives with few trauma scars may also develop clear minds more easily.

With words from God verified by the spiritual board and advanced brain scans, God may refine commandments for today's more complex lifestyles. Eventually, with the spiritual board verifying spiritual words and laws, complex political laws may be replaced by God's simpler and more just laws. Spiritual communication and benefits will catch up with advancements in technical communication and benefits.

Checks and balances to keep leaders humble and honest are as important in religion as in government. Political and religious leaders with initial good intent become corrupted with power and abuse or kill those who threaten their power. They become dictators.

Any religion promoting killing is a false religion. Self-serving religious conservatives prevent spiritual unification. Spiritual leaders need to integrate religions carefully and slowly and include modern spiritual and science reasoning.

All scriptures from all religions that nurture all of mankind should be carefully integrated as a modern spiritual book. Scriptures, promoting spiritual superiority, divide people into factions and should be banned.

Spiritual leaders, and political candidates and leaders, should be brain scanned and tested for self-serving attitudes, honesty, caring, and leadership ability. Scan testers would also need to pass similar tests to ensure their honesty. Voters could influence requirements for spiritual tests and world spiritual board members.

No one but us can control our imaginations. Positive thoughts develop lasting symmetric, resonating waves. God reflects all symmetric waves, or positive thoughts, feelings, and emotions throughout the universe.

It may seem bold to construct an integrated religion based on 20th and 21st century revelations received from God by current generations of all world historical faiths. Times are drastic. Peoples and nations, determined to destroy other nations based upon religious beliefs, have or will have the ability to do so with nuclear or other weapons of mass destruction. We need to bring all peoples together or the world will be destroyed.

Certainly, we are looking at a huge administrative task in developing a spiritual board. This task is small compared to the expense and tragedy of a third world war. We need to learn to love one another and prevent false and hate brainwashing of innocent children.

With humble servants, the proposed world spiritual board will receive God's guidance in writing each edition of the world religious book. Society will receive more definitive guidance from God.

We have much work to do. Brainwashed angry extremists become terrorists and kill innocent people in misguided belief that their religion sanctifies such atrocities. Anger is enhanced by mindless repetition. Look at Hitler's methods of false influence.

With repetition, any child can be indoctrinated to believe anything including spiritual superiority. Children need to be taught reasons for loving and respecting all others. What a great world this could be if all the money and effort spent on arms and security could be spent enhancing the human race!

There is a difference between teaching and indoctrinating. Indoctrination destroys open mindedness to new ideas. Everyone should be taught openly that everyone can receive words from God.

Inclusiveness of all traditional religions will serve as building blocks toward a new integrated religion. Understanding God will advance through science and clear mind processes. Checks and balances ensure truth.

We have developed languages for understanding our modern world and should develop language for receiving deeper spiritual communications. We only receive spiritual words we understand.

After some time, religions not participating will see others' experiences and recognize advantages of modern spiritual reasoning. New peaceful believers will be warmly welcomed as equals.

It is not possible for a single central spiritual board to provide truth tests to all contributors. Qualified local physicians, scientists, and religious leaders could perform initial truth screening. Aspiring prophets receiving words from God will be excited and willing to defend their revelations. Submitters can seek other opinions.

Rules for passing spiritual tests must be equal and well defined throughout the world. If a physician or qualified tester frequently passes spiritual participants that are rejected by the board, he will lose his license to perform spiritual tests. In developing this spiritual book, we must ensure the true word of God. The world spiritual board will vote on final inclusion decisions within specific guidelines.

Future spiritual scientists may develop highly reflective neural membrane technology for receiving words from God. Prophets did so in historical spiritual times. This spiritual technology or art seems to be lost today. With dedication, practice, humility, and honesty, we can advance spiritual technology.

A wonderful vision for the future would be that more and more people receive and document words from God. Prophets from all over the world gently corroborate spiritual messages. Interpretations of brain, throat, and neck scans, with coordinated truth tests, will become increasingly precise in verifying messages from God. Societies will learn to act upon and follow God's guidance. More and more people will aspire to, and work towards, personal spiritual goals. Increased mental skills with humility increase spiritual skills.

Think about models given here and develop your own models. Readers will improve and add to spiritual ideas and models. We are sewing seeds for spiritual technology and reason.

The purpose for requesting reader's word messages from God and circumstances surrounding those communications is to develop a database for spiritual reasoning. We want to learn about words received from God from all faiths. Spiritual words should be shared to benefit all mankind.

Spiritual messages received today may be as important as messages received in historical spiritual times. One does not need to attend seminary to receive messages from God. We believe we receive messages from God or we need not pray.

No true believer in God shows spiritual superiority to anyone. Arrogantly proclaiming one is saved is false spirituality. Proclaiming spiritual superiority is spiritual inferiority. We should not compare ourselves spiritually to anyone.

Circumstances surrounding messages from God need to be explained for others to understand messages. The epilogue provides readers the opportunity to express spiritual messages received in words including circumstances to help define spiritual reasoning.

A Clear Mind develops creative intensity for life. Unleashing the inner self into consciousness develops self-confidence and compassion for others. Everyone will be honest with themselves and others when understanding their inner selves. Our memories and emotions become alive for improving daily and spiritual decisions.

My spiritual model of mental health is feeling that struggles and pain have spiritual significance, having confidence in mental and physical abilities to meet expected challenges in life, and being certain of attaining eternal life. It means being able to predict, fit in, and feel comfortable in, physical, social, and spiritual environments. Spiritual health is belief in benefits of spiritual communication or prayer and feeling God, or a higher power, is concerned for, loves, and helps us make important decisions.

The path to the clear mind is not easy or many would have documented processes earlier. My spiritual message, *"Don't leave God out"* has guided all spiritual writing and models.

There is caution. In spiritual tests, alcohol influence must be tested. The alcoholic mind can be very deceptive.

CHAPTER 11

The Brain "String" Theory

"This above all: to thy own self be true.
And it must follow, as the night day,
Thou canst not then be false to any man."

Shakespeare: Hamlet

In 2006, I began developing a "string" theory model of the brain. Even though quite different, it was inspired by cosmology string theory for understanding the creation of the universe. "String theory" expands "reality" with added dimensions for combining quantum physics models of atomic sized particles with astronomical sized models which are based upon general relativity.

String theory requires seven additional dimensions to integrate atomic and cosmological models. Added spatial dimensions may also allow the combining of spiritual and physical models.

The Brain "String" Theory

With the above background the brain string theory is simply stated. Upon firing of one neuron, there is a pulse of outgoing electromagnetic energy in all directions. This light is: 1) reflected by the inner membrane surface, 2) transmitted though its inner membrane surface, 3) absorbed within the fabric of its own membrane, 4) reflected by its own outer membrane surface, 5) part of this light energy is repeatedly reflected between inner and outer membrane surfaces with less fractal energy each reflection, 6) transmitted through its outer membrane surface, 7) reflected by another cell's outer membrane surface, 8) absorbed by another cell's membrane, 9) reflected by another membrane's inner surface, 10) this process continues throughout all brain cells, 11) and some energy escapes the brain. More distant brain cells receive less energy.

Neuron activations develop unique electromagnetic profiles. Fast changing sections of a neuron's profile are received, rather equally, by all neurons in the brain. Slower changing sections of the profile affect nearby neuron membranes greater.

Fractals present a methodical repeating pattern. A Sierpenski Triangle is given in Figure 11.1. The original triangle is repeatedly divided into smaller and smaller levels of triangles. Each reflection of light within a neural membrane can be thought of as a smaller and smaller fractal triangle with less and less fractal energy.

Light is refracted or bent by membrane surfaces. Light frequencies and directions change when hitting surfaces at other than 90 degree angles. These characteristics add to the diversity of the light energy absorbed in its own and other brain cell membranes. Light or emr travels outward from spiking neurons along zigzag paths as it goes through cell membranes as it is refracted, diffracted, and reflected by cell bodies and membranes. Knotty light or emr strings vary in direction as they travel through cell bodies and membranes. The knots represent the fractal reflections within cell membranes as they deposit energy in DNA of cell membranes. Light is also absorbed within cell bodies, but they are too fluid to retain meaningful memory data.

Resonating processes within membranes construct action potentials of virtual memory holograms. Hologram histories imprinted on neuron and glia membranes are continually read and written by electromagnetic radiation from the symphony of neuron activations. Holograms are constructed on intertwining three-dimensional brain cell membranes.

There are biblical records of God's miracles. Let's look at miracles in the very small atomic arena. An electron passing through a classically impossible wall or surface could be considered a miracle. God's dimensions of freedom on very small and large scales are different from our limited dimensions and constraints.

From religions, God has probability of overriding physical and spiritual laws. String theories may prove God has probability of violating His physical and spiritual Laws above microscopic levels.

Man's free will allows a very small uncertainty in God's constant plans. This uncertainty is so small relative to God's constant physical and spiritual laws for guiding the universe, He is considered constant beyond our imagination.

There are likeness and differences between God and Man. God's understanding of time is much different than our sequential awareness of events. God is an infinite parallel processor. With control of time, God can do all things and listen to all prayers in parallel. God knows the entire history of the universe to guide it into the future. Man remembers some of his own history to plan a beneficial future.

Iterative and reflective brain processes build resonances for developing thought. Longer resonances are reflected by surfaces of larger brain components. Transmissions, reflections, absorptions and diffractions create conscious resonances including emotional time stamps within our minds. Refined mental hologram energy levels and digital time stamps are necessary for organizing memory and may be a reason for aging. Mental processes are continuously iterative.

Light from neuron activations are diffracted so many times through membranes that it becomes divided into fine strings of light. Strings of light are absorbed by brain cell membranes much like data being stored in a digital camera. In modeling, one makes logical or physical structures and judges whether additional data supports or dismantles that structure. Models either die, or become stronger. Hopefully, my models will help researchers build advanced models.

My mind string theory and other models are realistic enough to dissolve my trauma scars. Hopefully, models will initiate future mind experiments by readers. Emphasis should be placed on studying brain cell membrane properties and how mental holograms are constructed and used. I hope to advance understanding of the brain and God.

Many of us spend time thinking about life after death. My interpretation of being "saved" is that one's life has been meaningful to God and spiritual resonances become integrated within His spiritual fabric for eternal meaningfulness. Confession of sins and God's grace weaves fabric of the soul for final spiritual acceptance.

Traditional religions downgrade those who worship differently. Progressive religions are considered fraudulent. Unfortunately, some progressive and conservative leaders are out for status and personal gain. Study carefully before accepting new spiritual practices.

The author did not discuss practices until experimental results proved to be successful. Learning to communicate with God was similar to babies learning their first language. Jesus isolated Himself for most of His life. He reached the highest spiritual levels during his three years of teaching.

Figure 11.1 Fractals: The Sierpinski Triangle

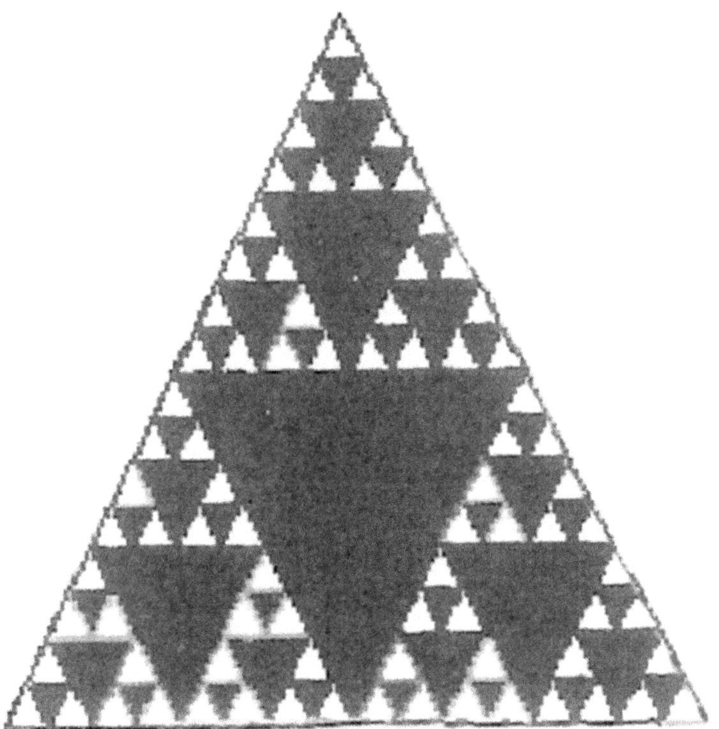

CHAPTER 12

Spiritual Models

What I Live For

I live for those who love me,
Whose hearts are kind and true;
For the Heaven that smiles above me,
And waits my spirit too;
For all human ties that bind me,
For the task by God assigned me,
For the bright hopes yet to find me,
And the good that I can do.

I live to learn their story
Who suffered for my sake;
To emulate their glory,
And follow in their wake;
Bards, patriots, martyrs, sages,
The heroic of all ages,
Whose deeds crowd History's pages,
And Time's great volume make.

I live to hold communion
With all that is divine,
To feel there is a union
'Twixt Nature's heart and mine;
To profit by affliction,

Reap truth from fields of fiction,
Grow wiser from conviction,
And fulfill God's grand design.

I live to hail that season
By gifted ones foretold,
When men shall live by reason,
And not alone by gold;
When man to man united,
And every wrong thing righted,
The whole world shall be lighted
As Eden was of old.

I live for those who love me,
For those who know me true,
For the Heaven that smiles above me,
And awaits my spirit too;
For the cause that lacks assistance,
For the wrong that needs resistance,
For the future in the distance,
And the good that I can do.

George Linnaeus Banks

My approach to religion is like my approach to science. Scientific structures with certainty are built from elementary particles, as building blocks, with uncertainty. Uncertainties of all elementary particles throughout the universe are integrated as an omnipresent and omnipotent God.

With spiritual surrender and an open parachute, we have more time to receive guidance from God. If we forget worries and calm our minds to concentrate on God's pureness and love, He will share creative ideas for spiritual healing with us. Creative ideas are retracing God's timeless footprints left during creation of the universe. God's creative ideas are always present within us. It is our choice to accept spiritual responsibilities.

A creative idea from God is a diamond in the rough in flowing analogue spiritual language. We must have faith that diamonds or God's creative processes exist, and we are sensitive enough to recognize His creative diamonds in the rough. It is our responsibility to breakup holistic spiritual ideas into our best interpretations in discrete words to present God's sparkle to the world.

When, a writer focuses on God, remains humble and faithful, but is assertive enough to write for Him, God gives writers an unusual gift. God allows us to ask Him for approval of our ideas. We must develop imaginative ideas and ask God for acceptance. God helps us verify we are following in His footsteps as He created the universe. With experience, writers refine the flow of their creative ideas.

My spiritual gift began in depression when weak and near death. Brain energy became so low that refined spiritual messages were received more freely. It has taken years to organize analogue spiritual feelings and messages into words. Spiritual feelings and messages have guided spiritual models. The best we can do is to use analogies and physics for developing quasi-physics models of heaven. Models of *nothing* flow into models of the universe and also heaven.

We have everyday belief systems, and most of us have spiritual belief systems. Even science and its methodologies are belief systems. Scientists are forced to use an organized methodology for discovering and proving laws of nature. A scientific proof consists of repeated results using the same procedures with the same unique circumstances.

We also have everyday belief systems. Our trip to work will be routine as usual. We will open our eyes in the morning and see.

We can grab a glass, present it to our mouths, and take a drink. We must believe in our minds and abilities before we can do anything.

Human knowledge and abilities are limited. We must make assumptions. When we start to take a step, we assume and believe through our senses that we have a leg and that leg is there for our command and use. We have a mental sense or model of the limits of that leg. Everything has limits. We need to have faith to step out and do great things and ask God help to fill in the gaps as we go along. Assumptions are part of our daily and spiritual life.

Every thought and scientific discovery has conscious and subconscious assumptions. We can only think of, and sometimes connect, bits and pieces of our universe. In studying the mind and heaven, it is important to think about conscious and subconscious assumptions. With practice we may make subconscious assumptions conscious. God makes no assumptions. His knowledge of the universe is complete.

Let's think about God. If God is infinite, can He multiply or reflect Himself an infinite amount of times and still be the same infinite self? Do perfect reflections multiply spiritual existence? Do our prayers increase God's awareness or has He heard it all before? Is infinite just language for something too big for humans to think about?

Understanding mental processes leads to understanding God. We should question things we do to improve our lives and question our faiths to deepen beliefs. My spiritual exploration integrates science and Biblical scripture.

Models of heaven are meant to increase understanding and stimulate readers to make their own models. Thinking about and modeling heaven increases spirituality.

God communicates with continuous and complete Holy language. For humans to communicate with one another, we must use discrete words that can only give feelings of flowing completion.

It is our responsibility to receive God's analogue wisdom and translate it into discrete words so everyone can be spiritually nurtured. Translations and interpretations into words can always be improved. We look to the past and future to receive spiritual blessings.

Jesus with His spiritual nature translated God's constant and Holy Word perfectly into the language of His time. He was restricted to use words and language His followers could understand. Most Christians believe that authors of the Bible had good memories and were inspired by God to write spiritually correct many years after Jesus' ascension into heaven. I believe they did the best they could using knowledge of those times. However, all writers have prejudices and tend to aggrandize their heroes.

My documentation of spiritual communications is enhanced by computers. They allow low energy calmness while receiving and recording spiritual communications.

We believe in two-way spiritual communication. A benefit of prayer is receiving God's communications for healing and other blessings. God has the ability to do miracles. However, during science experiments, He seldom seems to violate His constant physical laws of the universe. However, unusual, paranormal, and unexplained things occur that violate current science of physical laws.

A second part of spiritual communication is that God's messages should be shared. Those who receive spiritually will feel it deep down. God let's us know when we have received His holy message. However, there is a tendency to be emotional and exaggerate for personal benefit. We must translate as honestly as we can.

God has given us the capacity to think with and without His input. Many of us have had good childhoods and have few trauma scars impeding our communication with God. It has taken the author thirty years to eliminate trauma scars. Some readers may be fortunate and have had God consciousness most of their lives.

Spiritual communications have characteristics of dreams. They are normally of low energy, received through the right brain, and disappear quickly if they are not repeated verbally, or written, using left brain functions. However, spiritual communications give humans confidence as if ideas have been known for a long time.

Spiritual communications are usually received when we are quiet or highly emotional. Spiritual messages in words usually come unexpectedly when extremely calm or pondering emotional decisions. Spiritual messages promote an unusual sense of confidence. Spiritual messages received by children may be as important as adult messages.

We receive God's wisdom through spiritual resonances and holograms they promote within our minds. It is our responsibility to develop mental holograms from God's messages. We must integrate God's wisdom within our memory holograms. Spiritual concepts are developed through science, the Bible, other religious books, spiritual leaders and by receiving spiritual messages.

I did not receive miraculous spiritual wisdom. At times, God integrated my memory holograms in miraculous ways. God expects us to study and develop language and knowledge. We have to learn language and knowledge to translate and integrate God's wisdom. I had experienced unusual circumstances, doubts, and emotions before receiving spiritual messages in words.

God has given us free will. He needs praise and confirmation from man as much as man needs wisdom and healing from God. Parents need children as much as children need parents. Each of us constructs a small fraction of God's Spiritual Hologram. With free will we can choose to make God's complete Hologram brighter and make ourselves spiritually complete.

God is the light of every star and the light within our minds. There is awareness when light meets light. However small our life histories are, they can be important in brightening God's Hologram.

Light brightens our souls. Our eyes are sensitive to light, a small spectrum of electromagnetic frequencies. God is sensitive to all frequencies. We have limited vision, but God "sees" each atom.

Scientists explore and theorize to understand the universe. I extend models of the universe into models of heaven using physics and spirituality. When manic, I had an increased need to be creative and spiritual. We develop spiritual feelings with low mental energy and, briefly, at manic emotional limits. The purpose is to increase feelings of faith and confident beliefs. We extend our minds beyond normal thinking to experience God.

God wants the universe to be diverse physically and constant spiritually. God is aware of the integral of all good emotions during our life up to the current point in time. Integrating activities over time constructs spiritual histories independent of time. Written history can be spiritual and independent of time. We can reread a story over and over. God gives importance to the truthful written word and its constant nature.

God's Love is the total of all good emotions within the universe up to this point in time. God has everything to do with processes of living and sharing a loving life but little to do with material accomplishments. God has separated the two. Only processes for loving others, and God, count toward attaining heaven. Humble prayer is spiritual elevation. We must love ourselves because God gave us a part of Himself, our souls, for Him to communicate with and love.

Modeling heaven creates interest in thinking about heaven. If we thought more about heaven, we would not do the uncaring things we do today. Some of us aspire toward God consciousness. Others give up on or have no interest in God but worship material wealth, security, and power. Many seek God when socially convenient but worship power, security, and material wealth in their hearts.

If we concentrate on spiritual quality of life processes, we have little to worry about. If competing with the righteous in the next pew, we lose sight of God. God loves each of us in a personal way as parents love each child differently.

We have wonderful deep down feelings, when we are prepared for heaven. God chooses us for everlasting life by His Grace when our souls leave the body. We may feel saved early in life, but disobey God later. From my models, only at judgment time will we have assurance of heaven. We have challenges to be good or bad each day.

It helps to have models of heaven to guide our lives. My theory is that heaven collapses to the point of the Big Bang every 10^{-106} seconds. It is quite possible since the entire universe was originally contained within a point of quantum space we call *nothing*. Models of *Nothing* had a dual nature with discrete and holistic existences. Heaven returns "Home" to the location of the primordial point every 10^{-106} seconds to update and integrate all spiritual wisdom within the universe and reflect that wisdom equally to all points of the universe independent of space. God is omnipresent and omniscient at each point in space. God is completely up to date everywhere in the universe and ready to receive our prayers from everywhere.

In addition to models, deep structure language also conveys fundamental truths about God and the universe. Examples are: $1 + 1 = 2$, basic physics equations and constants, love, and spiritual books. We have deep inner structures for understanding the universe and God.

The same deep structured spiritual wisdom can be received 1,000 years from now. Interpretation of the same spiritual message will be different to fit future environments and times. Sometimes God's spiritual words hit us like lightening. Other times God's spiritual message flows over us like a gentle breeze.

Great spiritual leaders in history have received and translated God's wisdom into words. They have made truthful translations and interpretations for others to understand and have developed great religions. In the future, leaders will receive, translate, and interpret spiritual communication for more detailed and technical religions.

Our brains are localized on earth; our minds are relativistically or spiritually constructed independent of physical space. The universe is a physical place with time, space, light, and lumpy things like atoms and clumps of atoms. All physical things, including humans, communicate through gravity and light with all other physical things in the universe.

The infinite resonating awareness from all integrated light, or electromagnetic radiation, and possibly all energy fields produced by all atoms and processes within the universe is modeled as God. God integrates our mental resonances within His resonances.

The soul contains all emotional events of our lives as mental holograms. Upon death, a holistic flash of our spiritual holograms is integrated and absorbed into God's constant Hologram. Our mental holograms reside on all surfaces within and on the brain and include images and emotions of events throughout life.

In a manner similar to viewing a Holusion, we must look through every day images of God's beautiful earth to experience God's higher dimensions. If we relax body and mind and focus on God, our holistic right brain becomes dominant. The least energetic, most refined, and innermost resonances, or our souls, gain more influence on consciousness.

Dreaming and the soul integrate our perceived space and time as independent of physical space and time. In dreams, we can become free of worry about day-to-day life and present our lives to God's higher-dimensional Hologram. God reflects only truth in our dreams back to us. When awake we must work to recover these truths.

In my near-death flash, physical life stood still, moving seemed asleep, time and emotions became spiritual and independent of physical time. An earthly moment can become spiritual eternity.

Let's look at the critical point of life when we are weak and dying or experiencing sudden death and the Flash. Time no longer matters. There is no longer need for ordering earthly events. Normal mental processes fade and our souls become the strongest influence in a "timeless life." Our lifetime holograms are reflected to God by our souls. Our spiritual holograms are our contributions to God.

God is love including love from all who have loved Him. Jesus has been integrated into oneness within God and sits at the right hand of God, the Father Almighty. When our souls integrate our lives over space and time, the only thing left is our integrated spiritual emotions. The highest honor of life is to have our soul pass the "Final Judgment" and be accepted for Eternity by God.

Our holograms have honor and love, or are empty. Love and sharing spiritual processes matter to God. I credit my capacity to love from my mother's and father's examples. Love is taught and shared. My country parents loved all they met.

Physicists should be able to calculate the power of God's Word. We can relate the spiritual power of God's Word to the energy released in the Big Bang creation of the physical universe. The Bible describes the physical birth of the universe and, in turn, the spiritual birth of heaven. The Bible and science converge to support the "truth" that God created the universe from *nothing* by His Word.

God breathed life into man with ability to communicate with Him. Moses said, "God is the light in every Man's mind." God is the spirit within our minds. Electricity, magnetism, and chemistry within the brain are God's gifts that give spirit and life to our minds.

Models are meaningless unless our assumptions are valid. They define what is included in models and what is and is not analyzed. Boundaries and limits of models must be defined. The most difficulty in overall understanding of the universe is defining boundaries as to what is and is not the universe. Definitive models must include physical properties and constant spiritual reasons for each part being where and what it is. Assumptions of any model must be made explicitly.

A model of the universe should include a spiritual structure for God's influence throughout the universe. God's love and His spiritual and physical laws are the only things constant in this universe.

We can make comparisons and measure differences within the universe. It contains measurable differences. We cannot measure differences within the refined fabric of heaven. Heaven is all that is not measurable within the universe. According to Descartes, "we think; therefore, we are." Somewhat similarly, we can say that since we can measure differences, the universe exists.

Is our purpose to learn about and gain control over the universe, serve our selves, have children, and return to dust? Or maybe we should work to construct spiritual memories or holograms that become independent of time. It is my hope that Man's instruments will never be able to detect prayers, which should remain private.

We learn physical and spiritual things in a step by step process. The out-dated Bohr model helped scientists to think about atoms similarly to planets revolving around the Sun. Quantum models treat atoms in a probabilistic nature. Models are meant to be improved.

In physics language, God's Word was a symmetry-breaking mechanism within *nothing*. Mutations and combinations have been structuring the universe ever since the beginning moment of time (+ or - some small delta of uncertainty.) A highly improbable event within *nothing* created God's Word which created God, and God created the heavens and the universe. God's Word was Light and God became His Word. God is the awareness and consciousness within Light.

God's overall view of the universe allows a small Heisenberg uncertainty in time perspective for the Big Bang. Focusing on the surface, up close/short range view relates to the latest time for the beginning of the Big Bang. God "sees" all three-dimensional entities of the universe equally. This is similar to our viewing a two-dimensional image with its lines and discrete images when we focus on the plane of a Holusion.

God's perspective of the earliest time, long range view for the beginning of the Big Bang creates an integrated higher-dimensional view. This relates to the three dimensional Holusion, "spiritual," image. God's awareness is constantly integrated to the uncertainty in the exact time of creation to construct spiritual certainty. All physical dimensions have degrees of uncertainty.

Spiritual integration over space and time filters out material thoughts in mental holograms. Only truthful emotional histories remain. God "sees" us as "pure love" or "empty of love." If we focus on the future with love, we look forward to an everlasting future.

Gravitational forces tend to integrate all parts of the universe back toward the point of *nothing*. In the distant future, existence may physically collapse to nothing but contain spiritual everlasting history of this former universe. The purpose of the creation of the universe might have been for *nothing* to gain knowledge of what it could be and has been. History repeats itself.

Enjoy thinking of and making your own models of heaven. Our efforts may be similar to our children drawing stick mom and dad pictures. As parents, we glow with every creative thing our babies do. God does the same for us when we expand His creativity.

When God created man with free will, He released man from needing constant communication with Him. It is much like parents training children and thoughtfully giving teenagers more freedom. Grownup children may choose to continue to communicate with and love parents. We can choose to love and communicate with God.

Free will gives us personal freedom and gives God interest in something He does not have to control all of the time. God has constant control of gravity and every non-living thing in this universe. God is very, very constant with some small uncertainty due to Man's free will. We simply refer to Him as constant.

We cannot study the mind in depth without studying God. Man's mind is made in God's image. We have to think recursively to study our inner minds. That is, we have to use our minds to reflect upon our minds. Self-reflection upon our own thought processes is a beginning for feeling God's presence and understanding Him.

Made in God's Image means that at conception our minds contained only good symmetric emotions. We shared electromagnetic resonances and reflective structure with God. Self-reflection through the soul is a powerful method for expanding emotional awareness of self and God. With spiritual reflection, our souls and God become one.

Spiritual communication difficulties are from our traumatized minds to our souls and not from our souls to God. We must cast out trauma effects or sins to communicate purely with God.

With less trauma effects we can think more globally about God. He experiences the entire universe on each spiritual collapse to the original point of *nothing* and on each reflection to wholeness throughout the universe. In this manner, God receives prayers every 10^{-106} seconds.

Spiritual awareness vibrates throughout the universe billions and billions of times faster than the speed of light. I estimate that light travels only one quantum of space, or about 10^{-33} centimeters for each spiritual vibration. The center of the universe contains the spiritual blue print or "DNA" to integrate all spiritual occurrences within the universe and reflect them back equally throughout the universe. Models help us expand spiritual abilities and limits.

In heaven, we will feel greater oneness and comfort within God than when we were cuddled by our mother's as babies. We will not need physical bodies; we become everlasting spiritual resonances. We will not have eyes but see through our spiritual holograms much more clearly. We become one with God and experience reflections from our loved ones in heaven and prayers from earthly loved ones. We will share mutual love, joy, and oneness through God's resonances and reflections.

If we could view heaven, all points would be similar to each other in the same manner that all parts of a hologram produce the same images but with different perspectives. God's "heartbeat" or spiritual vibrations are constant throughout an infinite heaven. His footprints vary throughout the physical universe.

God's higher, integrated existence is reality more than the physical universe. We and the dimensions within the physical universe are God's dream reflections similar to our dreams reflecting our three-dimensional experiences in our virtual dream time. God's perspective is relativistic to and quite different from ours.

There are so many good things about heaven we can not begin to comprehend. Making models, however simple, helps us experience spiritual wisdom and feelings of wholeness.

Make your own models of heaven and work for feelings that God accepts your models. God wants us to worship Him and reflect upon His Goodness. It helps Him in his battle over evil. We are His children, and He loves our childish attempts at understanding and modeling heaven. He praises us for thinking about Him.

If we experienced God's complete Hologram, it would be so overwhelming our minds would freeze in awe. Humans only receive spiritual reflections they are able to understand. All other spiritual frequencies pass through our minds like the un-tuned radio signal.

I have progressed to this point by trusting words I have read or heard from the Bible and studying science. Models were developed for my quest of earthly and spiritual sanity.

Love is giving reflected back many times. Greed is taking, stealing, and grabbing with no reflection. Choose life processes wisely to reflect on heaven. It is our choice. God gives us faith in Him upon conception. Faith is lost through traumas and life choices.

If we completely knew our own minds, we would not need to study science. The structure of the universe was hard-wired in our genetic holograms within our souls at conception. Elementary particle physics knowledge is embedded in our deep structure memories. For knowledge of all things, we only have to look within ourselves. Your mind right at this time and place where you are reading this book contains all secrets of life. We need to learn deep structure language to share spiritual knowledge with others.

If we wish to discuss science, we must learn scientific language to converse with other scientists. We may experience inner feelings of knowing elementary particle physics but must be able to translate our deep structure language into scientific language so other scientists might understand. Otherwise, we are scientists in a vacuum. There is communication between scientists in their languages and spiritual communication with God in His deep structure language. To understand God's laws of nature, we must learn physical relationships formed at the time of creation and speak His language.

What do our minds and elementary particle physics have in common? They contain the essence of and reasons for the Big Bang. If we truly understand the meaning stored in the physical behaviors of elementary particles, we will understand the soul and the human mind. In turn, if we truly understand the inner workings of the human mind, then we will understand the forces, motions, characteristics, and properties of elementary particles. The mind is created by atoms, and their elementary particle, activities within the brain.

Fundamental characteristics of atoms are intertwined within God's holograms. If we know our own minds and elementary particle physics, we know God. Without transfer of energy, conflict, and uncertainty, the mind is nothing. God integrates uncertainties into certainty. Uncertainties within atoms can build confident minds. The mind is never complete without reflections from God. Spiritual reasoning integrates emotional and physical relationships.

Our thoughts and actions are reflected for comparison to God's perfection and truth. Virtue is truthfulness within a rhythm of life that varies as it should. When mental holograms are integrated over time and reflected to heaven, two pure qualities remain: love and virtue.

If humans have consciousness, awareness within elementary particles forms its building blocks. Elementary particles have deep spiritual structure formed at the creation of the universe. We are only beginning to learn the spiritual-structure of elementary particles.

God has no incomplete steps. He speaks to us in His Holy or complete Word. God's processes are similar to elementary particle processes. Each change or action is in complete quantum steps.

We must recognize spiritual wisdom in the rough. God gives us feelings of completeness when we translate His message truthfully into sentences that readers may understand.

As I was completing *Emotional Mind Modeling,* I experienced deep structure language pulling me toward modeling God and heaven. Shortly afterward, I received words from God in English.

God said: "*Don't leave God out.*" These words echoed through my mind as I was contemplating ending my first book. Certainly, I felt inadequate for such a task. The words came so strongly I felt compelled to give God's request my best effort.

I have met others who have received life-changing words from God. If at first remembered, words from God are emotionally stamped in the mind forever. Recipients become spiritual.

Living things have concepts of self and their effects on living and non-living things. God is aware of His effects on the universe.

The Spiritual Baby

Each baby is spiritually whole upon conception and aware of all spiritual wisdom within the universe. We all have had a common spiritual background. God shares His Holy message with all pure little souls. Unfortunately, as babies grow they absorb trauma scars and conflicting emotions. During life egos cloud the spirit and truth. Each of us must be reborn spiritually.

The spiritual awareness of a baby, or of even an adult who has mentally reconstructed, might be thought of as a person walking on a smooth, level road for many miles on a beautiful spring day to find the truth. Awareness before mental reconstruction might be thought of as a person walking in neck-deep icy water over slippery rocks to find the truth. Mind modeling, mental reconstruction, and spiritual rebirth bring about transformations to receive spiritual communications. Spiritual thoughts and feelings include God's logic. Without spiritual depth, logic builds brick stairways to nowhere.

Babies are naturally attracted to softness and calmness. Without love when young, a child grows up to respect only power and control. Dreams are frequently reflections of early and recent histories. Dreams are of: 1) our actions, 2) wished actions, 3) actions we are afraid might occur, or 4) actions we are afraid someone might see.

☆ ☆ ☆

Dogmatic beliefs without spiritual reasoning degrade more than heal. Continuous memorization and repetition of religious dogmas without spiritual reason is emotional indoctrination. With huge investment of emotions, energy, and time in memorization, the indoctrinated retain their false beliefs.

Military training uses repetitious indoctrination. Terrorists use radical, idealistic repetitive indoctrination to justify terrorizing, and murder of, innocent people. If everyone worked to receive spiritual messages and spiritual reasoning, there would be peace on earth.

Spiritual reasoning is most important for choosing a spouse for peace in our lives. We are judged mostly in life by God in how we treat our spouses with whom we should be spiritually one.

Memory holograms are "tinted" by emotions and spiritual intensity relative to God's truths. God does not care so much about the details of mental holograms or who wins but about the tint or color and intensity of each hologram. Truth and honor in emotional reactions at stressful limits are of most importance to God.

We may think we are truthful but portray different messages to different people. We speak differently at work, church, and home. We speak differently to authorities or those with higher intelligence. This list could go on. We are not all that consistent in everyday lives, much less when emotional. Emotions either amplify inconsistencies or confirm God's truth.

Some deranged parents produce an atmosphere that children and spouses are competing for their affection. In this un-godly scenario, that parent has produced a temporary hell on earth for the other parent and an everlasting hell for the once-pure child.

Karen Armstrong writes in her book, *A History of God* (1): "It is no good trying to understand religious 'information' that we have not experienced ourselves." We relate spiritual experiences only with limited words and actions. We must improve spiritual language.

Predicting future occurrences and interactions give confidence that we and others exist. Prediction, hope, and anticipation of positive future events are keys to happiness. We are happy when predicting good things for ourselves and our loved ones to enjoy.

Physical instabilities in space, light, provide spiritual stability. Everything has its opposite, is relative, and is a matter of perspective.

When receiving spiritual revelations, we have feelings of being reminded of things we have known for a long time. They are received with confidence. Also, understanding physical laws makes holistic sense with feelings we have known them for a long time.

My strongest support for constructing my particular models of *nothing* and heaven are that the Bible describes God as Eternal. Eternity is not just the idea of unlimited time. Eternity means control of time with the ability to travel backwards and forwards in time.

The idea of Eternity supports my models of God and heaven collapsing to the origin of the universe, integrating all wisdom, and then reflecting it back, perfectly homogenized throughout space every 10^{-106} seconds. With God's complete control of time, His knowledge of the entire universe is unbelievably up to date. Certainly God's true processes are more detailed but results reflect Biblical descriptions.

God gives lesser and greater physical gifts. Greater spiritual gifts demand greater responsibility. A gift might be patience to improve spiritual communication over many years and share God's message. Greater gifts amplify potential to do good or evil. Greater strength and intelligence have greater responsibility to help others.

Beauty is a gift that amplifies attention. Those with beauty and intelligence have a greater responsibility. Beauty requires social skills to boost confidence of others yet maintain self-respect and personal honesty. There is beauty and symmetry in the smallest of things.

Symmetric elementary particles, atoms, and molecules create resonating waves in spiritual dimensions without needing physical energy to continue eternally in spiritual time. Atomic sized spiritual resonances and dimensions may contain the secret to human and infinite awareness.

When atoms combine to form compounds, resonances integrate to form higher resonances in higher physical and spiritual dimensions. Intelligently designed atoms chemically combine to form integrated higher resonances and intelligently designed humans that can recall historical, and develop future, thoughts.

On Sunday, January 22, 2006, while listening to a sermon, I was emotionally drained as I had just completed a manuscript the day before. I was "struck by lightning." A wonderful spiritual thought engulfed me. My mouth started to drop. But quickly, I was again aware of the minister's message. The spiritual thought vanished as quickly as the forgotten dream. It was only one simple sentence.

If remembered I could have built a chapter around it. I was so disappointed at its fading, but still feel excitement of having received this message. I was not prepared to remember such a powerful idea. However, I knew at that time God will share many additional ideas. I have let many spiritual ideas escape before writing them down.

My left brain was dominant listening to the sermon in words. The right brain flashed to dominance with the spiritual idea. Left brain dominance returned. This spiritual idea was like a brilliant 100 carat polished diamond. I hope to achieve a similar high-energy mental limit again with honest emotions to recall this spiritual idea.

God never gives burdens without giving abilities to succeed. The most rewarding thing in life is to bear God's burdens. God's burdens can be simple or difficult. It could be for loving your spouse as he or she needs to be loved, and for loving God!

If an unexpected idea explodes into consciousness, we know we have received a spiritual idea. The idea seems deeply truthful for circumstances. Circumstances must be explained for the idea to be meaningful to others. Most spiritual messages are like dreams and have to be written down quickly or they are forgotten.

God is perfectly aware of the entire 13.7 billion year history of the universe. Through His field forces He predicts the intricate future expansion the universe. There would be no universe without time and no time without the universe. Space, time, and matter iterate through recursive relationships to construct the universe and heaven.

A reason I think God was created at the same time the universe was created is that I do not think a god of our God's abilities was necessary during simplistic times of *nothing* before the Big Bang.

Without God remembering the past for guidance in controlling the future through His field forces, there would be no order in the universe. Without God there would be chaos, no meaning, order, or awareness in the universe. All actions in the universe would be random without physical laws.

There are numerous religions to understand the meaning of life. Religions that worship the sun or other parts of God's creation have merit. These religions may not worship God's completeness or full existence. We know only a very small part of God's existence today. Religions that worship idols, other manmade things, or self-elevated persons proclaiming themselves as gods have no merit.

I have learned to distinguish between manic and spiritual thoughts. When spiritual messages are received, I write them down and test to be sure I am not manic. I do this by meditating and clearing my mind of all thoughts. If thoughts continue forcefully, I work to calm down with meditation. I have arrived spiritually when I can feel wholeness within calmness.

The opposite of mental calmness is anger. Experiencing anger responsibly relieves tensions and enables solutions. Do not keep anger bottled up. Express anger to God. He will understand and help lower tensions and emotions. Pray for answers. In striving for a spiritual life, we must have patience to unify. A frown never helps unify. It tears down spirituality in self and others. A smile can be spiritual. Working together integrates spiritual resonances.

Oh how tragic is the frown or pout. They cause negative neural networks to grow fast and furious and subdue pleasure, happiness, and spiritual communication networks. The key to spiritual happiness is to love all and not feel above or below any human being. You would not feel superior to your baby! The mind controls the face, and the face recursively controls the mind. A smiling face grows a relaxed, pleasant brain that does not need to be defensive.

If I told everyone I received a foundation message from God: "*Don't leave God out!*" it would mean very little to you or anyone else. However, God was aware of my thoughts and challenges before I received this message. I have spent over fourteen years defining what God meant by this message. Four previous books and this book are my explanations. I have had many spiritual messages; however, only the "forgotten message" was as dramatic as, "*Don't leave God out!*"

An important part of prayer is listening to God. Dan Rather, a well known American television news anchor, once asked Mother Theresa what she prayed for. She answered nothing; she said she just listens. Rather asks what God tells her; she says He just listens. Rather did not understand. Mother Theresa said that if he did not understand she could not explain it to him.

My explanation is that her flowing spiritual communication was too holistic or complete to be broken up in discrete words. God's answers come with deep feelings of completeness.

If one develops models that improve spiritual communication, that talent should be shared. Anyone receiving spiritual talents must never aggrandize himself, or he becomes corrupted. Jesus may have remained as spiritual as we all were upon conception. Jesus humbly preached love and healing.

Dreams often contain events and images integrated from different periods of time. There is little judgment in dreams. Absence of judgment allows relaxation of timing and association structures within the brain. Dreams integrate trivial and important events in our lives for composing spiritual memories and predicting the future. Memories only exist as chemical and physical configurations on the fabric of our brains with inherent action potentials.

Societies have given importance to those who predict the future. Historical prophets have made profound predictions. True prophets would never aggrandize themselves. God gives wonderful feelings when we are truly humble. Arrogant feelings are short lived. Humility can be everlasting.

Listen to people. Discuss spiritual messages in depth only with those ready to listen. If I went out to the street saying I received a spiritual message, there would be scoffers and non-believers. Some might feel inferior. Others would feel superior. During interactions, we should make listeners feel good about their inner selves. Let love and humbleness show on your face. Be truly interested in helping others psychologically and then spiritually. People have free will to be spiritual now or later.

When teaching, think about listeners' abilities. Listen carefully to questions. Show interest and answer questions carefully and truthfully. When not able to answer, it is easy to say, "I don't know the answer to that question." Offer to get back with answers later.

God imagined the architecture of the universe and it was created. Man's thoughts and dreams have developed the architecture for all manmade things and recursively cultivated his mind and body.

Most religions believe adherence to their methods is a sure way to heaven. There are conflicts between religions. Religious writers are human and not perfect. Physicists use mathematics to understand the universe and may construct models to understand God. In my models, Christianity and science have little conflict.

God is the architect and builder of our bodies, brains, and minds. Studying God through religion without studying our bodies, brains, minds, and universe makes little sense. It is like studying a famous architect without studying his designs and structures. We need to study physics, chemistry, biology, psychiatry, psychology, and other sciences to understand God's designs and thoughts as He created the universe and us.

God has constructed physical, emotional, and spiritual freedoms allowing good or evil choices. Historically, so many people have been killed by misguided religions in God's name. Their way of worshipping God is taught as the only way. A solution is to integrate traditional religions through science and current words received from God into a unified modern religion.

We can describe spiritual experiences only with words we know. It is difficult to believe spiritual experiences until experienced. We learn from God and other's spiritual experiences. God learns from our experiences.

Some of us believe we receive spiritual messages today as strongly as happened in traditional religious times. Any organizational leader without checks and balances becomes corrupted by power.

God is constant. We have the same opportunities to be inspired by God as did traditional spiritual writers. Scientists continue to learn how God structured the universe with constant physical and probability laws. The better our models are the better we can receive God's blessings and inspiration.

Jesus preached to and healed the poor and needy and changed spiritual traditions. He was the liberal, socialist rebel of His time, and a servant of God and mankind. Jesus loved everyone. Today, Christian leaders teach that their religion is superior.

Our minds have grown through experiences and memory processes over our lifetimes. God has grown with continued "perfect" awareness, as the universe has expanded over 13.7 billion years. The configuration and activities of the physical universe construct God's existence.

Saying the Bible is the Word of God, in English, is a misnomer. Word languages are manmade communication tools that hinder receiving spiritual analog communications. God's spiritual waves promote spiritual resonances in human minds, which can be translated by humans into their language of choice. The Bible is information from God interpreted and translated by man.

Before God, there was nothing, without form, space and time. Everything was continually uncertain. God became an existence rebel and created something, Himself, and the universe, from nothing. The universe evolves with increasing complexity. God guides universal activities with constant and probability physical laws and with paranormal and spiritual influences, independent of space and time.

Nothing, before time, was absolute uncertainty or chaos without purpose that probabilistically exploded beyond primordial limits to create an evolving universe. Before existence, time was non-existent. A moment and infinite time were the same. There were no physical changes to create the passing of time. Spiritual and mental awareness depend upon changing physical activities.

Atoms and elementary particles have uncertainties in time, space, and energy. God created spiritual certainty by integrating quantum time, mass, energy, and space uncertainties into His perfect relativistic properties.

Human certainty does not exist. However, humans have high probability of understanding and accomplishing a few things in life.

God became the first quantum of time as a powerful unified field wave without matter, space, or time. Awareness without uncertainties or change has no purpose. In 10^{-35} seconds after the beginning of time, God created all atoms and elementary particles. God needed physical changes and uncertainties to integrate awareness into certainty. Our minds need change and uncertainties to exist.

God gave of His own energy and created the universe as His body, home, or heaven from His perspective, traveling at the speed of light. God relates each atom of the universe to all other atoms, galaxies to galaxies, and Himself to man. We can learn God's technology for relating to God and the universe. His math certainties and wave uncertainties are God's language.

Humans are healthier and happier when concerned about the well-being of others. Developing inner concern for others, the universe, and God builds emotional health and confidence. General love for others deepens God's reflections.

Studying great literature, art, buildings, or accomplishments gives insight into creative minds. Hopefully, this work gives insight into the mind and God.

When manic, most manic-depressives frequently and strongly experience God's communication. Scientists must objectively study normal and manic minds, religions, paranormal events, and God. Strange unexplainable things happen when highly manic.

Scientists are beginning to study paranormal occurrences. Paranormal resonances develop high spiritual energy characteristics similar to the weather.

If busy on pleasant days, we may not think about the weather. The atmosphere sometimes concentrates its energy into hurricanes and tornados. Paranormal observations may be due to uncertainties in separating mental waves into spiritual waves and resonances. Spiritual waves are not evenly dispersed throughout the universe, as normal.

More Americans now believe eternal life can be acquired through different paths and religions. Religions that believe their way to heaven is the only way are dangerous to the rest of the world. Self-centeredness and arrogance degrade self, others, religions, and God, and start wars.

REFERENCE:

(1) Armstrong, Karen, 1993, *A History of God,* Ballantine Books.

CHAPTER 13

Heavenly Models

Men never do evil so completely and cheerfully
As when they do it from a religious conviction.

Blaise Pascal

Models are built to explain the brain's spiritual ability to process extremely fast during near-death "flashes." In death-threatening traumas, many have experienced "flashes." Flashes are above free will energy ranges. God takes control of the brain and mind to save lives. The writer of Carrie Underwood's song, "Jesus Take the Wheel" undoubtedly had experienced a near-death event. Important lyrics are:

> Jesus take the wheel
> Take it from my hands
> Cause I can't do this on my own
> I'ma let it go
> So give me one more chance
> To save me from this road I'm on
> Jesus take the wheel

God's spiritual frequencies stimulate human mental resonances above and below free will thinking resonances. After years of practice, I raise and lower mental energy to receive spiritual communication. With God's guidance, generations thinking, acting, and reacting at emotional limits have constructed the human brain and body.

The universe is physically alive with forces, energy, relative movement, and waves. God is a living higher-dimensional Hologram with complete awareness of the history of the universe on probability, classical, and relativistic levels. He controls the universe with His field forces and perfect knowledge of the universe. Through gravity our bodies have a faint influence on the entire universe. Prayers through God may have more influence on the entire universe.

The universe is constructed of quantum time, mass, energy, and space. Without God remembering the quantum history of the universe there would be chaos. The universe would consist of a soup of random elementary particles with random and erratic field forces.

Our brains are physically alive. Our mental holograms are spiritually alive. Consciousness is developed by iterative and recursive processes. Refining recursive processes broadens abilities. God has given us free will for earthly and spiritual choices. With lowered energy, minds learn to become more confident, reasonable, and spiritual throughout life.

One spiritual relativity model is that, at the speed of light in empty space, God experiences all empty space within the universe as having zero distance. He has a different perspective and sense of space than we do. In this quasi-relativistic model if we had the ability, heaven would be observed as a constant point, or a constant infinite resonating multi-dimensional wave. Heaven, like light, has a dual existence.

From my experience, everyone can learn from current spiritual communications. Quantum leaps in understanding God were made in Biblical times. We have spiritual purposes today. Learning about the universe through science is also learning about God.

"God rewards those who earnestly seek him," Hebrews 11:6. *God, the universe, & You!* describes the author's search for God Consciousness. After Christian and other religious formative periods, people clung to the security of their traditional religions. I cannot overemphasize how Christianity has influenced my faith.

God is the constant spiritual structure controlling physical laws that support all life. His gravitational consistency allows us to live on earth. God also controls constant probability laws at the atomic sized arena. Improbable things occur on the earth, particularly, our miracle conception. God does consistent, and some improbable, things.

Each of us can reawaken our spiritual gifts with inward analysis, and by loving, caring, and sharing. Inward analysis is a slow process. Write down, nurture, and refine inner revelations. Seldom do emotional revelations construct spiritual completeness overnight. High energy emotional ideas often deceive us, and we may then deceive others later. High-energy emotions often distort spiritual messages toward self-centeredness. Humble surrender is often difficult.

God's creation of Himself and the universe was infinitely improbable before time. If God is all powerful, He can certainly create Himself. Physical laws are built upon integration of quantum and spiritual laws. Immediately before creation, primordial existence and primordial god could be modeled as continuous without physical or spiritual boundaries independent of space.

New models will improve spiritual communication. Integrated neuron activations briefly create short segments of God's very long slow changing electromagnetic waves to communicate with Him. These spiritual wavelengths are the length of, or harmonic fractions of, the diameter of the universe. God's electromagnetic, and possibly other field force, resonating waves extend throughout the universe in three physical and many spiritual dimensions. Our slowly varying brain wave segments traveling at the speed of light synchronize with and minutely modulate God's powerful spiritual waves. Our minds are or can be a small part of God.

Refined mental frequencies have the ability to be integrated as spiritual frequencies creating everlasting awareness in spiritual space and time independent of physical energy. Spiritual waves may be maintained by particles with spiritual quantum energies and spins not normally observable in our physical three spatial dimensions.

Poor, humble, and giving minds will continue in higher spiritual dimensions forever. God wants us to nurture and prepare minds for heaven by helping them purge trauma scars or cast out sins.

Superior-acting people will have to pull their camels through the eyes of needles to attain heaven. Resonances of some minds may never be received by God's spiritual radio channel. Non-spiritual lives may not become synchronized with God's frequencies. Rather than being spiritually alive and dispersed throughout heaven within God, non-spiritual and self-centered resonances may be confined into the nucleus of a single atom or possibly all dead body atoms.

I cannot over-emphasize the importance of modeling to make sense of the mind and God. Thoughts begin as flowing or continuous analogue entities and mental holograms. Our conscious minds must breakup this mostly subconscious hologram completeness into words and sentences as pieces of a puzzle to construct meaningful language. Hopefully words resemble subconscious and spiritual completeness.

Scientists will expand spirituality beyond historical time warps. Models are meant to help readers improve their creativity in discovering physical and spiritual truths. I have only "drawn" stick figures of my heavenly Mother and my two heavenly Fathers. Love for them expands. My parents, in heaven, are higher saints for me than historically recognized saints.

Studying historical spiritual books and science, and listening to true spiritual leaders, can guide us toward understanding God. Some historical religious leaders were more spiritually truthful than others. Good spiritual leaders are good spiritual examples to follow for constructing inner spiritual feelings and beliefs. Rigid, inflexible spiritual leaders separate us from personally communicating with God. We may feel inadequate, or become afraid, to communicate our spiritual thoughts with spiritual leaders or even God. With so much spiritual deception, many reject all spiritual leaders and even God.

In traditional religions today, leaders are receptive to new spiritual ideas as long as they do not differ greatly from their dogmas. If spiritual messages differ significantly from traditional beliefs, they are condemned as "insane" thought intrusions. How do people think earlier spiritual leaders and prophets received their spiritual messages? Dramatic movies of traditional spiritual lives do not depict reality.

I contend that traditional religious leaders saw visions that were as real to them as those from normal sight. Angels seen were spiritual not physical. They were real spiritual holograms created and sent by God. In today's environment, we are reluctant to talk about seeing spiritual visions or we will be branded insane by self-centered and self-serving bigots. In culturing the mind with spiritual reality, we can see spiritual images of love and peace as seen in yesteryear.

Important spiritual experiences occur every day. Conservative religious leaders contend that overriding spiritual experiences occurred only in historical religious times.

When not thinking globally, the author might think non-Christian prophets were less important, misguided, or even false.

Other religions will think their leaders or prophets are more important than Jesus. Without modern global communications, traditional spiritual leaders had relatively local, polarizing influence. The author has no doubt that God wants to bring the world together in peace. Any religion promoting war or murder is a false religion. All humanity must be respected.

Traditional and modern prophets' words can be interpreted many ways. When describing emotional occurrences, people use different words with different meaning. Different biblical translations have different meaning for different people.

For example, a religious leader may say he is the only way to heaven – meaning for the people listening to him and not for all people throughout the world who have never heard of him. An impressed writer might interpret his words to mean anyone anywhere in the universe must go through that prophet even years after his physical death to attain heaven.

Many of us believe Jesus arose from the dead and is alive spiritually at the right hand of God as a guide and resource to help believers become accepted by God. I recently heard a conservative minister preaching that Jesus was sent to save the universe. Wow! We humans are the most important beings in the universe next to God!

We must ensure we are truly receiving communication from God rather than being drunk with misguided, power infested emotions. Humble surrender to God is necessary to determine origins of inner feelings and emotions. Our inner processes are much more different than our word communications. God gave us diverse minds and opportunities. Each relationship with God is different and personal.

God certainly has a purpose for everything He does. With eyes, ears, and sense of touch, our purpose on earth may be to translate our physical experiences and reactions into spiritual love and emotions. We are bridges between physical and spiritual existence.

Human minds depend upon physical bodies and environments for existence. Upon death and redemption, human souls shed physical bodies to ascend or disperse as electromagnetic radiation or light into spiritual antimatter, time, and space. Electromagnetic and possibly other physical field forces construct bridges to God in heaven.

Feedback is valuable to spiritual speakers and their listeners. Spiritual reasoning must flow back and forth with love. One-way indoctrination by speakers is detrimental to listeners and God.

When all peoples spiritually accept one another of their own free wills, there will be peace on Earth. God will joyfully rule the earth as heaven on earth. Think what can be done without prejudice, arrogance, and hate. We can become a part of, and influence, God's everlasting destiny on the earth. Let peace on earth begin with us through global trust and love.

Biblical and other spiritual writers were scientifically limited. God was translated correctly as Light. God is light and other field forces, and spiritual energy, within spiritual space and time.

At times, if observing unusual light or shadow patterns, study their origins. When doing so, we are tracing paths of God's Truth.

If man understands the framework of God's spiritual foundation and constant, analogue, and universal communication technology, man and God can achieve wonderful mutual goals. God created man with independent thinking for His needs, purposes, and completeness which is similar to reasons we have children to continue and complete our lives with purpose.

Communication with God should flow like a symphony. The most thought provoking and important parts of a symphony are the highs and lows. Prayer should be with the low-energy of a meek child confessing wrong doing to parents or with high-energy to correct spiritual wrongs.

We must be honest about our situations and reactions when communicating to God with high energy. With high energy we are communicating to God but not listening. We must think through things and have not only justified anger but also disappointment in situations, others, or ourselves.

Good speakers study audiences to be effective. We should study trusted spiritual leaders and learn to communicate directly with God. If we communicate with God, we should understand with whom we are speaking to be good communicators.

In the movie, *The Ten Commandments,* God was dramatized as lightning actually writing the Ten Commandments. We usually do not think we are praying to lightning. We think God has a gentler side. What should we be thinking when God is our audience? This is a personal decision. Some think of an image of Jesus. God's image is created by reflections of all light within the universe including that of our faces.

I think of Jesus, and my loving parents, as spiritual resonances throughout the universe integrated within God's resonances in higher spiritual dimensions without needing physical energy to exist forever. I also continue with resonating spiritual thoughts of beloved family members and friends who have passed into this better, spiritual world.

Spiritual resonating electromagnetic activity on earth is a very small part of God. I focus on the purpose and blessings of the sun's nuclear, electromagnetic, and other field forces that have nurtured man into existence. I expand thoughts outward to all field force activity in the solar system and within the universe.

I envision God integrating resonant activities throughout the universe into one Holy resonance for understanding and controlling the universe, and nurturing our lives. Models are fragile and can always be refined.

Traditional religions change as communication skills and knowledge advance. Ministers are preaching more gently with positive reason than was done fifty years ago. Communication and knowledge are more accelerated today. Christianity and other religions must be strong enough to bend with science and spiritual discoveries.

Excitement for spiritual learning in heaven is beyond human imagination. Spiritual time is very different. We may learn everything in an instant or enjoy learning throughout Eternity. If achieving heaven, we will be prepared for spiritual work. God is very busy managing the universe and our saints in heaven. We will be busy and blessed with exciting spiritual challenges. Idle minds are never happy.

While on earth, our minds iterate with ideas on and on, but converge to complete truth only as we cross the final bar. Once, I approached that spiritual bar but was unable to cross.

We should not limit God to our meager senses and awareness. Traveling at the speed of light, God views the physical universe relativistically and from a very different view.

In outer space or vacuum where Light travels at its highest speed, God experiences a holistic awareness of the universe with space observed as being contracted to zero distance or volume. Space itself is of little interest to God. The slower Light travels in matter the more physical distance or volume God experiences as His spiritual universe or heaven.

When Light is created by elementary particle activities, atom activities, or possibly interactions between Light, God experiences discrete awareness of the universe.

Spiritual space is dependent upon matter but independent of physical space without matter. This means light continues in vacuum forever without losing energy. Spiritual dimensions are associated with each physical atom within the universe. From our perspective spiritual dimensions are infinite in time and space.

We experience the universe as very large and changing in three spatial and one time dimensions. Spiritual dimensions integrate time and spatial dimensions. This integration constructs higher spiritual dimensions which scientists may discover through indirect means and calculations. God views the universe as much smaller than we do. With infinite awareness or omniscience, God does not view space and time as infinite.

We have discrete and holistic views of our lives and the universe, but indivisible view of God. The separation between God's discrete and holistic awareness is much greater than that of human awareness. Electromagnetic resonances within matter create God's awareness of all physical things big and small.

God integrates discrete awareness of all atom activities, through probability and statistics, into a continuous holistic awareness of the universe. Man's responsibilities are similar. Our brains integrate symphonies of 50 to 100 billion brain cell activities into consciousness of a single thought. Our purpose may be to inform God of human-sized earthly activities independent of His control. Thought and control are one entity for God. If He thinks it, it is done.

God created Man, with free will, as something He did not need to control to avoid loneliness. He has given our minds God-like characteristics to reflect our visions and thoughts to Him. God learns about and recognizes Himself in us. Earthly fathers learn about themselves though responses of their children. Life would be dull, meaningless, and predestined if children could only mimic our lives.

We must be versatile to understand our minds and God. At light speeds, everything is relative. Our minds may extend throughout the universe as spiritual holograms independent of space and time to be reflected by God.

If we synchronize our minds with God, He may use His symmetry breaking mechanisms to guide us from fears and dangers. If we stimulate God's awareness, He may help heal us and prevent pain. God, breaking physical laws to create miracles, is much like us breaking through baby, childhood, and adult trauma scars to extend thinking beyond emotional limits.

Be thankful for everyone inspiring love and confidence. We must understand and love ourselves to love others and God. We must make sense to ourselves before communicating with and making sense to others.

Spiritual communications affect the entire brain but must be translated into words related to common experiences with analogies. Jesus used parables to simplify understanding. People, including spiritual leaders, are fundamentally self-centered toward investments in effort and money.

Group spiritual activities encourage right-brain thinking as we learn to look beyond ourselves. Inner studies are convincing that no one is spiritually superior to anyone. Upon conception, we were all equally and perfectly spiritual.

God's flowing universal language can be interpreted by all spoken languages. With different knowledge, we translate and interpret God's message differently. With higher technical languages, higher spiritual messages can be received and understood. God wants us to understand the universe's creation, its laws, and its emotions.

God's spiritual electromagnetic and other energy waves continually pass through us. We might imagine God as all radio stations. If we develop mind technologies to spiritually culture our brains, we can receive a part of God's complete spiritual resonance through our spiritual radio. With spiritual practice, we can receive more of God's guidance. The mind, radio, television, and the internet make us aware of how expansive and detailed electromagnetic abilities can be to serve our purposes.

God's flowing, continuous, and complete message can never be perfectly interpreted or understood by difficult-to-describe feelings or discrete words. Human words are never perfect. Meaning changes over time and experiences. With inner study, spiritual technology, and humbleness, each of us can become messengers of God.

Spirituality should not remain in a time warp. God rewards those who think about and praise Him as an earthly father would a child. Discovering an understanding of the universe through science is also developing a spiritual path toward understanding God.

Historically, religious leaders have worked to expand their influence and authority over the years and reduce influence of individual's spiritual messages. Christianity and other traditional religions have been a guiding light for developing current spiritual thinking. Traditional religions should continue with more reason and less emotion. Excessive memorization reduces reasoning and promotes dogmatic, self-centered importance.

Everyone was equally spiritual upon conception. With this fundamental reality, religious leaders must work together to best serve God and all of mankind. Difficult compromises are needed to improve all religions holistically. Each miracle of life must be cherished.

Let's list some spiritual ideas:

1) God, Light, in "empty" space, is the purest form of existence and an integrating part an infinite hologram existing for over 13.7 million years.
2) Laws of Gravity are so consistent they may require little attention from God. Man's relationship to his own vascular and immune system may be similar.
3) Stars and the sun are turbulent sources of high energy "Light" and God Consciousness.
4) When Light affects matter, or matter creates Light, God's awareness is intense.
5) When Light reflects spiritual awareness, including that of humans, God's awareness is most intense. God may have awareness of primordial existence beyond the universe.
6) God controls small things with probability. Man-sized things are influenced strongly by emr, chemistry, and gravity. Earth-sized things more controlled by gravity than electro-

magnetic forces. Stars are influenced by gravity and nuclear probabilities. Galaxies and the universe are controlled more by dark energy and forces. On a very large scale, galaxies are rather evenly distributed throughout the visible universe. God exerts different levels of control depending upon size.

7) God's awareness and responsibilities grow as the universe evolves and diversifies. If we learn, God learns.

Describing Jesus as perfect gave Biblical writers an ideal goal to strive for. If Jesus were perfect all sins including those of Adam and Eve would be immediately atoned. There would be heaven on earth today without pain, suffering, and wars. However, if mankind attained perfection, life on the earth would become meaningless without uncertainties and choices. Maintaining perfection would be impossible with human abilities.

Televangelists provide only secondary guidance for learning spiritual skills. Without checks and balances many televangelists have become corrupt and wealthy at the expense of poor vulnerable viewers. Many have extravagant lifestyles using contributions from insecure viewers meant for God's work. Televangelists should voluntarily submit to brain scans and tests for spiritual truthfulness. Those who do not submit should be suspected of self-centeredness and corruption.

Mahatma Gandhi, leader of India, lived a simple austere lifestyle. He explained his non-violent beliefs, "I would die for the cause, but there is no cause I am prepared to kill for."

God is the definition of perfection for many of us. Adults are able to receive and understand only small, limited parts of God's wisdom. We cannot help but include personal interpretations as we receive words from God. This is true of prophets and writers of all times. Prophets had to use words they understood. Humans are never complete or perfect.

We need amazing grace to save sanity in this world. I can think of no greater amazing grace than spiritual leaders analyzing their own and all other religions and compromising to integrate them into a spiritual reasoning foundation. The world would unite with love, respect, and unity of purpose.

With education and global communications today we are in a greater position to understand physical and spiritual things globally, and even universally. Traditional religions are perpetuated with followers emotionally aggrandizing leaders who originally had limited regional or racial purposes during times of unusual need. Current spiritual leaders must study, be graceful, and recognize traditional spiritual exuberances. Together, we can improve spiritual technology for higher spiritual reasoning with verifiable words from God.

Because of importance the world has given to inner words received from God, we must develop scientific methods to verify traditional doctrines and current spiritual messages. Both traditional and new reasoning spiritual leaders should verify their truths by submitting their beliefs for scientific verification.

A key part of unifying all religions is that shorter condensed proposals from each religion will receive higher upfront exposure and purpose in a modern spiritual book. This requirement will encourage leaders to think carefully about the important parts of their religions. Conciseness, number of followers, unification orientation, and peaceful benefits to all mankind are priority considerations for entries.

Unification may be our last chance for long term survival of human life on earth. We need advanced prayer technology and spiritual psychiatry to restructure our minds for everyone to spiritually accept all of God's people. Fragmented self-centered religions produce distorted and fragmented minds. A modern unified religion should provide feeling of completeness for all caring self-reflective beings within the universe. Updates to this modern religion should be made as spiritual communication and testing technology advance.

With patience, inner study, and scientific discovery, spiritual beliefs can be developed into physical and spiritual truths. Many fundamental Christians do not recognize that many scientists are spiritual when discovering God's amazing paths for His very integrated Creation. Many scientists believe their creative ideas were received as inner feelings and words from God.

Struggles throughout history have created "supernatural" leaders for developing believers' confidence and meaningful lives before and after death. Many of us have been brainwashed into believing a particular brand of religion. With excessive demands, spiritual beliefs have become more important than loving and caring for neighbors with different beliefs.

Oh, what a web we "spiritual" humans have spun? How can we survive religious conflicts in a nuclear age? The threat of annihilating all of mankind is greater now than in any historical time – even greater than Noah's flood? Historical spiritual leaders became revered because they overcame great difficulties to guide chosen followers to better more confident, spiritual lives.

Oh, how difficult to construct amazing grace for all peoples to unite all traditional religions for understanding God on higher spiritual and scientific levels. It will be just as difficult for others to compromise as it will be for us to compromise! Do you want to save the lives of your children and grandchildren? God can help us build a "Holy Religion" that includes all people of the earth and all self-reflective beings in the universe. We must develop a broader spiritual feeling and interest. God does. Compromise is truly giving to others.

Spiritual interpretations were and are not perfect or applicable for human advances throughout all times. We have too many options today for historical predictions to become true unless believers force them to become true. Many false prophets, have predicted the future to aggrandize them selves if certain things come true. False prophets have frequently predicted the end of time.

Unfortunately, fanatics, forcing their spiritual ideologies on others, become terrorists. By not spiritually integrating and giving to one another, and without expanding spiritual technology, the option may become a lifeless Hell for "self aggrandizing, false believers."

False Prophets can abuse even educated Americans today by proclaiming they are speaking words directly from God. These false prophets prey on follower's uncertainties by proclaiming spiritual superiority and isolate their misguided followers from learning the truth about their lies. Anyone proclaiming spiritual superiority without identifiable and repeated miracles is the lowest of the low. Beliefs and life can be amplified toward good or bad.

Science should categorize physical uncertainties, probabilities, and certainties for insight into spiritual uncertainties, probabilities, and certainties. Life without uncertainties would be meaningless. The universe would be predestined. There would be no future in which to look forward. We experience and discuss many physical uncertainties in life. We do not discuss spiritual uncertainties. Understanding our own spiritual uncertainties and certainties is our responsibility.

Many of our spiritual uncertainties are due to our trauma scars or sins. We must admit spiritual uncertainties. I have prayed humbly and long for the health and lives of my parents. However, frailties of old age have taken their toll. Both of my parents have passed into a better awareness. Even with our best and longest prayers, loved ones die. We often say God works in His own time. Human frailties and lack of morals and abilities to attract God's Grace cause suffering.

Advanced science increases understanding of the universe. We will be able to receive higher spiritual gifts by obeying God with greater understanding. We can reduce spiritual uncertainty and develop higher spiritual certainty through spiritual probability and reasoning for higher moral and meaningful lives. It will become more reasonable to love, care, and share with all persons on the earth and all self-reflective beings throughout the universe. We should not limit ourselves. When thinking and praying holistically, we aspire to be more like God. Our dreams and prayers can be tomorrow's reality.

We have a recursive relationship with God. We need to ask God how we can help Him. We need to pray for the suffering and confused child next to us, on the other side of the world, and on the other side of the universe, for our minds to become more God-like.

Pure love, independent of self, becomes spiritual perfection independent of time and space. Atoms may have physical and spiritual dimensions of which we are not aware. Our souls may exist within small or atomic physical dimensions. Atomic physical dimensions are surrounded by infinite spiritual dimensions. We should not limit spiritual thinking to worldly thinking.

However small we may be; we can pray for the universe to unfold according to God's Will. We might even pray that the powerful, runaway light of supernovas reveals God's purposes and helps Him resolve conflicts. Our loving and caring for, and praising, God may help Him win conflicts over evil. God reflects our love back to us with amazing grace.

The ability to search inward into the soul to communicate with God is more spiritual than simply following spiritual leaders. A personal relationship with God is more important than memorizing words from even good intentioned spiritual leaders. We should learn from spiritual leaders but determine our personal spiritual path.

Learning from spiritual leaders provides spiritual guidance. Caring and praying for all spiritual beings, with self-reflection, who may exist throughout the universe is Holy. Developing a spiritual identity with reason is a continuation of mind healing and expansion. Continue to improve your own mind and spiritual models.

It takes amazing grace to love and care for extraterrestrial self-reflective spiritual beings that may or may not exist on the far side of the universe with forms, purposes, and thoughts so different from our own. Our binding essence is that God loves us and them the same. We become spiritually complete and at peace by praying for all of God's spiritual creatures. I hope to meet family, friends, and all sanctified earthly and extraterrestrial beings in heaven some day.

As people grow older they increase their self-reflection. In a spiritual sense, it is good to live to an old age. Also, most of us become more self-reflective when we have been sick near the point of death or suffered important failures. Many religions enhance self-reflection through meditation. In different ways, we learn to believe in God to add purpose to uncertain lives and feel worthwhile and complete. When small we feel confident by being part of parents who care for us. Later we feel confident by being part of a powerful and perfect God who cares for us.

Jesus was humble and amazing in His life of caring, loving, teaching, and healing, and in His communication with God. Jesus did not explain His abilities and reasoning in depth. Einstein was patient, humble, and amazing in receiving his understanding of God's universe. Einstein explained his scientific knowledge in depth. Both had amazing wide-spread influence. Was Einstein as spiritual as Jesus? Should we make comparisons?

Can religions compromise beliefs and incorporate science to receive God's Amazing Grace for peace on earth and life everlasting? God becomes stronger by integrating the redeemed into His Eternal heavenly family!

This world needs amazing grace for volunteer truth testing of those with power over others. Spiritual, political, or business leaders, who guide followers' lives, make or enforce laws of behavior, or set their own and employees' salaries, respectively, should be tested for truth in executing responsibilities. America and other countries need to convince each other of moral intent to gain respect from each other.

We should frequently question spiritual leaders' intents. Spiritual leaders claiming their ways are the only way to heaven should be analyzed closely. There have been too many scams in God's name. We must reason about our lives and beliefs! To unite the world and universe spiritually, we must become world lings or Universalists!

CHAPTER 14

Existence of God

The Devine Comedy [1]
By:
Dante Alighieri

Inferno

These of death no hope may entertain:
And their blind life so meanly passes,
That all other lots they envy.

Excerpt: Canto 3

Paradise

The virtue mingled through the body shines,
As joy through pupil of the living eye.
From hence proceeds that which from light to light
Seems different, and not from dense or rare.
This is the formal cause, that generates,
Proportion'd to its power, the dusk or clear."

Excerpt: Canto 2

Man has either dreamed of spiritual existence under God's care after physical death or feared death. In the fourteenth century, Dante famously described circles or levels of existence after death for wasted lives in *Inferno.* In *Paradise,* he describes heaven as virtue or light independent of space and matter, as similarly extended in this book. True religions guide lives and beliefs for life after death.

My quest to prove God's existence is certainly not new. Theists and religions have spent centuries trying to prove the existence of God. Today, science may be more able to develop technical methods for verifying God's existence.

We need confidence in spiritual abilities to ponder and feel the existence of God. No matter how strongly we feel God's presence, some say we have no proof. Indeed, it is difficult to prove or disprove the existence of God to those who have never experienced His presence. Some will say spiritual feelings or words simply evolve from the subconscious mind in some unusual way. They point out that the mind often erroneously concludes sight and other perceptions.

In developing methods to prove God's existence, we must analyze mental abilities to sense, and believe in, God's existence. Difficulties in life refine inner processes and sensitivities. Awareness of inner processes is one tool for proving God's existence. Brain scans and statistical analyses of spiritual messages from modern prophets may become a strong method for proving God's existence.

If scientists measure the same unique electromagnetic mental resonances in modern prophets' brains which have received similar meaning spiritual word messages from God, scientists may statistically prove a single source. This prediction assumes analyzing spiritual messages from prophets who have not met and may speak different languages. Additionally, modern prophets should have experienced difficult times and possibly temporary insanity.

An experiment for defining the existence of God is for a spiritual leader to pray emotionally for unique blessings for something related to his congregation. Then, each member independently listens for God in quiet meditation and records the first unexpected words received. A statistical analysis of words received may prove a single source of words, God.

Let's continue toward convincing others of God's existence. We discuss how humans organize things for their benefit and how life could not exist without our organizational skills. We may then explain that God organized the universe for His continued existence.

When is religion not reasonable? If leaders believe their religion promotes killing and they encourage martyrs for "their" cause, they should kill themselves first to honor their false beliefs. A religion is not reasonable if it indoctrinates believers to think they should kill those who worship differently or when it conflicts with scientific facts.

Scientific carbon dating tests on dinosaur bones prove that dinosaurs lived several million years ago. Some conservative leaders preach that the Bible, as translated into English years after Jesus' crucifixion, is the absolute, perfect, and complete word of God. They preach that dinosaurs lived only a few thousand years ago, there is no fallacy in the Bible, and it should not be subtracted from or added to.

However, every sermon adds interpretations of the Bible for our times. If God is infinite, billions of books cannot describe God and His characteristics and abilities. Conservative Christian religions do much good today. Unfortunately, conservative leaders preach that their way is the only way and that all other religions are false.

Many, including myself, do not believe in a supernatural God. From my model development of existence from *nothing*, I believe in a natural all-knowing, all-powerful God. In my models of the universe and God, an emotional God is as natural as humans and all physical aspects of this universe. If electromagnetic resonances in our brains create consciousness, all integrated electromagnetic resonances within the universe create God. Traveling at the speed of light, God is eternal.

How can you believe every word of ancient spiritual books if you do not believe carefully proven scientific facts? If we mentally reconstruct, we may receive words from God more powerful and believable than information received from all other senses combined. It is my goal to develop spiritual technology so everyone who chooses can receive words from God and become His messengers.

How powerful is God compared to Man? Neurons produce low energy electromagnetic spikes. God's power includes emr, nuclear transitions, and gravity produced by all atoms within billions-and-billions of stars throughout the universe. Physical and spiritual abilities are recursive. God has given each star physical abilities and its feedback gives God spiritual purpose in guiding future activities of the universe.

If man's brain produces consciousness through billions of tiny neuron explosions, the Big Bang explosion of Creation has produced an "infinite" electromagnetic radiation awareness and consciousness. God and the physical universe are recursive as are the mind and brain. The brain creates the mind and the mind controls the brain. Quantum energy changes of every nucleus and atom in the universe create God's omnipotence, omniscience, and omnipresence.

There are billions of neurons and nerve cells in the brain and body. The coordination of all neurons and nerve cells can channel the mind to focus on a single purpose such as petting your cat. All atoms of the universe resonate so God can focus on each of us in parallel. God has billions and billions of thoughts between each of our conscious thoughts. God's processes may have some similarities to ours but are infinite compared to our limits.

If emotions are developed within Man's brain, they were also certainly developed by reverberations and resonances from the Big Bang. Reflections from the Big Bang include wavelengths extending to the edges of the universe and expanding at the speed of light. With coordinated neuron firings, long electromagnetic wavelength segments interact with God's universe length electromagnetic waves. Mutual resonances synchronize throughout the universe.

Attaining God consciousness may mean synchronizing brain and spiritual resonances. Spiritual resonances and extended brain wave segments may be measurable with future advanced technology.

In seeing and hearing imaginary or distracting things, one loses touch with reality. Insanity within once normal minds follows a series of events. The conscious mind becomes overwhelmed by analytical, social, or physical stresses. It reasons in circles without resolving physical or mental pain, analytical problems, or inner stresses. The analytical left-brain becomes overridden by the survival instincts of the reactive right-brain.

With severe pain, nerve frequencies are too fast and energetic for normal, distributed processing throughout the brain. Fast reactive emotions and logic are not necessarily good for long-term coping with and healing from stress.

Our minds consist of abstract and discrete processes. We cannot touch our minds but believe they exist. In addition to thoughts we have feelings about the quality of our thinking. Feedback from the physical world and interactions with others encourages us to believe we have minds for navigating our environments.

Losing confidence in everyday mental abilities sometimes enhances spiritual abilities. There are similarities between insane and spiritual thoughts. They both are difficult to explain. It is pleasant to think our minds have properties of God and are created in His image. We cannot touch God but feel His nurturing presence.

After refining inner processes, we sense mental trauma energy releases. After mental reconstruction, remembering processes include unusual feelings of searching and discovery as subconscious processes iterate for appropriate memory matches. Mature brains and neuron membranes become more complex and require greater searching for related memories.

We are aware of distinct feelings during mental searches when God abruptly redirects mental processes into more reasonable, spiritual processes. With brain scans, scientists will prove different brain activation patterns during spiritual communications.

Can we sense and experience God as strongly as earthly environments? Spiritual reasoning should become as logical as today's lives and scientific methods. With spiritual practice spiritual ideas should flow as easily as normal ideas. Sensed experiences promote normal ideas. Inner processes promote spiritual ideas from God.

We must know traditional prophets' and writers' situations and emotions to understand the full meaning of their spiritual words. Traditional spiritual books do not always give emotions and situations. Today, we must also describe our situations and emotions to fully explain our messages from God.

Words and situations thousands of years ago do not have the identical meaning today; especially, if they are translated into diverse languages. Forced memorization indoctrinates and reduces reasoning ability. With huge mental investments, followers become certain they are part of an absolute truth and become closed-minded toward advancements in spiritual and scientific reasoning. Alliance with "perfection" seems all important but can amplify good or bad.

Without global communications of today, all traditional religions were self-centered toward local cultures. Today, religions should work together to give all people equal opportunities to share God's intentions for mankind.

Arrogantly declaring oneself saved or a messenger of God seeks power, which distorts communication with God. Power corrupts. Receiving words from God incites wonder and excitement wrapped in serenity. Searching for God is basically an inner emotional pursuit within the heart and soul but includes various levels of intellectual development. Seeking spiritual truth is a journey, not a destination.

Our lives are organized only if we think about the past and the future. Thinking is electromagnetic radiation reflecting at the speed of light throughout the brain. Reflections and absorptions by brain cell membranes develop meaningful physical and chemical configurations for cognition. The universe is organized by God's cognition and controlled by His physical forces.

Either our minds are part of God or separated because of free will. If we have free will God does not know all we are going to do. If we have free will to control our muscles, God is not quite all powerful. God constructed our brains and minds to have free will. Our children use our guidance and restraints in developing their free wills.

Beyond free will resonances, God affects every atom including those within our brains. However, it appears God does not disobey His physical or spiritual laws. Repetitive scientific experiments support the constancy of God's physical laws.

In frustration Moses became angry on the mountain because God had not given him direction. In anger Moses asked why God had forsaken him. God interrupted physical laws, spoke, and gave him the Ten Commandments.

Responding to my anger, God spoke the shattering words I was not able to remember. However, I remember the surprising simplicity, beauty, and power of that message.

It is important for me to continue to try to remember how I evoked this word message from God. Under similar circumstances, I may be able to repeat a truthful level of disappointment and anger. Anger is difficult for me to express. This communication from God was shocking, but melted away my anger. I had become angry at someone who had been demeaning to me. God spoke. After receiving words from God, I became amazed, then humble. Soon afterward, the person causing my anger approached me with a pleasing attitude.

A word message from God is so shattering that one is compelled to immediately believe it. However, weakness for power can corrupt the best of spiritual messages.

Brain resonances make a huge difference in absorption of spiritual and physical energy. We must prepare our attitudes and minds to receive God's resonances. True spiritual leaders expand spiritual abilities and freedoms in others.

New methods will be developed to evaluate traditional and current messages from God. Interpretations have historically been shortsighted. When dying, only then will we truly know God.

Physical laws within the brain and universe are the same. Our minds are somewhat independent, minute subsets of God. Let's look at certainties and uncertainties. Conservative religious practices promote certainty of being an accepted part of something greater than self and even a part of absolute perfection. We have needed certainty, since babyhood, that mother would always be there and dad would always come home. Certainty of security in heaven gives confidence to go through life with higher goals and purposes.

Uncertainties of small things such as electrons and nuclei are defined by the well known Heisenberg Uncertainty Principle. Nuclear engineers cannot predict when any one neutron and uranium nucleus will combine, split, and give off energy. With probability and statistics, nuclear engineers predict neutron behavior on a large scale with certainty to safely control nuclear reactors which produce power for one million people.

Atoms bound together making human-sized things are more predictable than neutrons colliding with nuclei. If we jump off a diving board, we can predict with certainty that we will fall and accelerate toward the earth at a rate of 32 feet/ $(\text{second})^2$ every time. The earth consistently attracts our bodies. The universe is much, much bigger than the earth. I cannot imagine how precisely God controls the overall universe. Galaxies are precisely placed to form a perfect God.

Our minds can vaguely be compared with God's near-infinite abilities and constancy. Minds cannot control individual atoms within their brains, but, with probability on a human scale, they can control activities of specialized groups of molecules within nerve cells, for our mental purposes. God integrates the uncertainties of atoms into overall certainty and purpose for the entire universe. Integration of smaller things into bigger things creates certainty.

Trends and advances in society and new words defined to understand changes develop deep structure words and language. Thoughts develop words, and words develop thoughts. Words that develop thoughts for higher probability of survival and advancement attract more of God's attention and guidance. Confusion between creation and evolution is only due to man's vague words for his narrow-minded experiences.

If God knew the entire future evolution of the universe, He would have relegated Himself to a robot doing constant, expected tasks. God makes creative judgments and decisions for the future. By nature, judgments mean options and change.

Perfect spiritual decisions depend upon perfect historical awareness to guide the next spiritual iteration. Future iterations are built upon previous iterations.

Scientists work to understand the history of the universe. High energy accelerators produce intense electromagnetic fields which create matter and antimatter for brief moments. Are physicists on a path to understand God or simply creating mini-gods?

With such a high density of energy at Creation, spiritual time was almost infinitely fast. God "spiritually" existed for an Eternity before creating physical matter, space, and time - the universe. Physical time began only when God created highly organized matter. The disorganizing process within the universe defines physical time.

Light traveling in all physical directions throughout the universe integrates into one spiritual direction, God. This integration process is similar to light created by billions of neurons creating light in all directions being integrated into one conscious human idea.

Let's assume we live to be 100 years old for the purpose of modeling the connection between physical and spiritual awareness. When approaching death, imagine that our spiritual memories or souls are released as one-dimensional resonances extending 100 light years long. Our spiritual resonances are accelerated toward heaven faster and faster. Suppose the soul views the mountains along the way.

As we approach the speed of light, mountains are observed to shrink. At the moment of attaining light speed, the light resonances within our souls are observed by God as being compressed into zero length momentarily, and then our souls explode into a flat, two-dimensional infinite heaven, perpendicular to the light path dimension. Our 100 year long souls expand into a higher timeless dimension as circles of spiritual energy resonating to and from heavenly infinity in spiritual time. If human existence was one dimensional, would not a two-dimensional existence have infinite freedom at every point?

With imagination, we expand our model to three physical dimensions being converted to higher spiritual dimensions at the speed of light. God might view our three-dimensional space as the surface of a spherical shell. Traveling in a straight line could return a traveler back to his starting point. Every point on this spherical shell universe exists at a spiritual boundary in a higher dimension.

The size of this "spherical shell universe" would be 27.4 billion light years in diameter and expanding at the speed of light. At the speed of light, an infinite God observes the spherical universe shell as a point when traveling toward the shell or as infinite when traveling inside the shell. God and this universe model both travel at the speed of light. In this quantum model, God vibrates inside and outside of this physical spherical shell model in different directions.

In a nuclear explosion in outer space beyond significant outside gravity influences, all elementary particles would be traveling outward in all directions at different speeds with electrons moving faster near the speed of light and light leading at its limiting speed. Heavier particles, such as protons, neutrons, helium nuclei, and some heavier nuclei would travel slower depending on mass.

Gravity would slow heavier particles more depending upon their masses. The spatial divide between electrons and positive particles would cause an electromagnetic force field. The magnetic field force would cause a swirling of matter similar to the swirling of galaxies. Electrons would be attracted back to protons and nuclei to reform atoms. Photons, (emotional energy waves,) would continue to expand at the speed of light, with only slight differences in distances due to moments of creation to form a thin expanding spherical shell as the edge of this imaginary universe.

This nuclear explosion models assists in thinking of the creation of the universe. Light and field forces bring order to chaos. Without correct assumptions, models construct golden stairways to nowhere. With correct assumptions, scientists may develop God-consciousness in quantum leaps.

With God-consciousness, we will understand a part of God's wisdom, and translate a small part of it into words. We will know unexpected things without previously experiencing them.

Believers evangelize others to believe as they do. False leaders brainwash false martyrs to murder anyone who believes differently.

We must rationally address the difficult and emotional task of evaluating religions. Religious leaders should submit some equal number of important tenants or miracles within their religions. A statistical evaluation should be conducted to integrate tenets. Participants will evaluate scrambled tenets from all religions. Primary names in tenets and miracles will be changed to prophet, spiritual leader, or writer. Participants will be instructed to answer truthfully and be scan tested for true spiritual answers. We must develop spiritual reasoning to receive spiritual communication. Tenet and miracle options are:

1. Believe literally without question.
2. Believe literally with some reasoning.
3. Believe literally with careful reasoning.
4. Generally believe in principle.
5. Emotionally believe.
6. Have doubts but generally accept as true.
7. After reasoning, have serious doubts.
8. Generally do not believe this tenant or miracle.
9. Believe science disproves this tenant or miracle.
10. Absolutely do not believe this tenant or miracle.

Scientists will use brain sensors during responses. Computers, with agreed upon directives, and statistical methods will logically refine and integrate tenets from all participating religions. Mankind will receive greater spiritual communications and blessings.

Human minds are constructed within bodies. Without minds, bodies have no activity or response. If we love someone, we love his/her mind and its control over his/her body for interacting with, and loving, us. We integrate bodies, and their behaviors, with people's minds.

We should integrate activities of the universe with God. Activities of the universe provide humans an existence to think about and live in. Some parts of the body and universe have greater influences on our and God's cognitions. We cannot see our minds or God, but know they exist.

My contribution for proving God's existence and abilities is:

> On September 22, 2009, at 10:00 PM, I had normal parental concern as my son was driving at night in the rain. Unexpectedly, I received frightening inner words: "What in the world will I do if Keston dies?"
>
> A few minutes later Keston called on his mobile phone saying he had had an accident, but was unhurt. He had hydroplaned and spun out of control several yards into a field. My son's emotional thoughts were: "I'm out of control; I'm going to die."
>
> A wrecker pulled his car back to the road. However, with some car damage, he was able to drive the 45 miles to my house that night.
>
> My son's emotional thoughts were understood, analyzed, translated to my perspective, and transmitted to me by an unseen cognitive, communication process. This miracle is my personal proof that God exists, understands our needs, and instantly transmits loved one's spiritual communications translated for our perspectives and understanding.
>
> During this near tragedy, but miracle, God was aware of my son's and my locations, supporting the idea of His omnipresence.

God is aware when we suffer or hurt. Our suffering may have some benefit in heaven. Jesus suffered.

Some of us have suffered with mental pain and uncertainty. Today's psychiatrists would have committed Jesus to a psychiatric institution for hearing, and speaking about, His inner voices.

If we have emotional levels above or below free will thinking limits, we can receive paranormal, spiritual communications from loved ones, including God. Can spiritual technology advances extend communications to normal situations? I am hoping to receive inner messages more frequently.

REFERENCE:

1. Cary, Henry F., *The divine comedy of Dante Alighieri: Hell, Purgatory, Paradise,* 1909 – 14, The Harvard Classics, Vol. 20 of 51, edited by Charles W. Eliot, P.F. Collier & Son, New York, NY.

CHAPTER 15

Personal Beliefs

"Salvation does not lie in the rituals and profession of faith,
But in a lucid understanding of the meaning of life."

Leo Tolstoy

I pray in much the same way I talked, and wished I had talked, with my loving mother and father. My father had a near death, life-changing illness when I was seven years old and became spiritual. From life-changing experiences, we learn about God, His importance to us, and recognize His spirit within us.

Christians believe God raised Jesus above all others. Receiving words from God is a gift to share with others. Interpret this book and all spiritual books wisely. Spiritual ideas affect each of us differently.

Beliefs are personal between God and us. If we want to know our earthly fathers and mothers, we go directly to and communicate with them. We learn their verbal and body languages, and sense their emotions and attitudes. Going to someone else to find out about our earthly fathers is superficial.

Getting to know God is similar. We must search within our inner minds to develop flowing right-brained, hologram, and spiritual communication technologies. We must synchronize our subconscious resonances with God's resonances for everlasting life.

When worshipping God, He guides our awareness beyond our senses' abilities or sensibilities. Faith in science to understand God's universe also provides rewards in heaven. God wants us to understand Him and His universe. He left us logical paths to follow. Following and understanding God's creative paths are spiritual.

As the universe expanded and separated into diverse physical parts, God maintained spiritual unity. We are like God when we love and promote togetherness. Good mothers and fathers nurture and expand children's abilities and talents but unify the spirit of their family. God nurtures our abilities and unifies our spirits.

One theory is that we are God's children and experiments for judging how localized awareness, purpose, and love can be cultured within physical space and time. God needs feedback and support from independent thinking within localized areas of the universe similar to parents needing feedback and support from children.

Children give purpose for focusing toward the future. They continue our beliefs and expectations beyond our physical futures. Our teaching continues within their minds. Their attitudes and lives reflect upon us. Belief in spiritual existence after death keeps our spirits alive

God wants us to grow and progress in a healthy, happy, and organized way. We are important to God's future as children are important to parents' future. In many ways man is like God and God is like Man. Our children are like us and we are like our children.

The written word is fixed in time and can be spiritual. Spiritual books can provide inspiration. We do God's work when we share and help one another. God wants us to be a part of and represent Him, as an earthly father wants his children to be a part of and represent him.

Earthly fathers learn knowledge of their children to best respond to them. God recognizes Himself in us as parents recognize themselves in their children.

By studying science and traditional religions, and establishing our own spiritual technologies and identity, each of us can become messengers of God. In learning about our inner selves, we develop deeper personal relationships with God.

Science and spiritual discovery are not easy. The more we learn of God's creations, the more we learn about God. With humility, enthusiasm, and patient inner searching, readers will improve mind and spiritual models. Spirituality does not need to be in a time warp.

I cannot imagine Jesus' excitement in receiving His spiritual messages and abilities. Of course, Jesus had to appear calm and normal to relate His unusual spiritual messages to His audiences and be believable. Jesus Christ provided a foundation for communicating with God through His example. Communicating with God can be as real as communicating with loved ones and significant others.

What would be different if Jesus wrote of his life? He must have had some understanding of His miracles. I wonder why Jesus did not document His unusual spiritual accomplishments for our benefit today. Apostle Paul preached we should simply believe in Jesus and His teachings.

There is no greater logic than God's logic, as He constructed the laws of the universe. Scientists work to understand God's perfect and unchangeable laws. Scientists must carefully document their work to be believable so others might understand and benefit.

Religions take a quantum leap above everyday and scientific logic to explain the fundamental causes, actions, and relationships within the universe. Scientists work methodically for understanding the fundamental physical processes within the universe and, possibly, God's spiritual processes. Future generations will understand God in greater depth through inner spiritual searches and science.

We respect teachers who logically explain things of benefit to society. If Jesus had written of His life, He would have explained

His accomplishments and miracles. Why are there no personal records of His teachings? Conclusions are that Jesus' writings were lost or destroyed, He could not write, or He did not want to write of His accomplishments and miracles. I ask questions scientists would ask. We should analyze and question to believe. Jesus' personal scrolls, if they exist, could still be found.

There is another conclusion. Humbleness before God may not have allowed Him to write of His accomplishments and miracles. He may have had a covenant with God restricting the revealing of His spiritual communications and miracles!

We should learn either directly from God, or Jesus, the Bible, other spiritual books, spiritual leaders, and others who have studied or received spiritual wisdom, and then develop our own beliefs. We have freedom to blindly follow others, memorize, chant, and believe as others teach us. This choice may be good for many. We can receive feelings of God's presence and blessings through traditional religions or through individual spiritual surrender and communication. We benefit spiritually in many ways.

We know of nothing more brilliant than God as He thought of, designed, and created the universe. We are brilliant only when we follow God's creative processes. If we think, God thinks. However, we have little concept of our own or God's thinking processes.

Awareness from all senses, including the entire skin, can be integrated by the mind into spiritual awareness. Without developing holistic awareness at times, it is more difficult to experience God.

Believers do not expect to see or detect God physically. A reason spiritual energy is not detected is that God is the same everywhere or homogenously refined throughout the universe. Scientists can only measure differences. Most of us think of God and loved ones in heaven as existing forever without needing physical energy. Perhaps we need to refine the definition of energy.

God reflects perfect answers to prayers. He is independent of physical time. We slightly understand God's abilities. His spiritual and physical laws have not changed in 13.7 billion years, have no error, and are absolute in function and truth.

Man never iterates to perfect solutions since time fades the best of human solutions. Using precise measurements, mathematics and probability, scientists understand a small part of God's physical laws. Research for understanding God's spiritual reasoning and laws seem frozen in a time warp. Traditional religions have discouraged spiritual research by scientists in fear of invalidating miracles within their tenets. God's spiritual laws are simply physical laws beyond mankind's understanding. From God's perspective and completeness, physical and spiritual laws are one. God's unchanging activities, throughout the universe, iterate and integrate space, energy, and time toward ever increasing spiritual completeness, or Eternity.

We have either faith, or lack of faith, in things we do not understand. Faith should be replaced by knowledge and reason through physical and spiritual experimentation. Spiritual leaders and scientists should learn and share knowledge about the nature and fabric of God and the universe. If we learn more of and obey God's Will, we can serve and honor Him better. In turn, He recursively reflects higher love and wisdom to us.

There are two basic ways of developing faith: 1) love and devotion to God, family, and all who believe in and are good to us, or 2) devotion to ourselves and our own power. In any event, we must keep in mind that God is perfect but human abilities, words, and interpretations can only create imperfect religions.

Human thinking is not a closed mathematical solution. The mind, universe, and God continue to iterate using mental, physical, and spiritual procedures, respectively.

When absolutely certain God speaks to or touches us, we must surrender and respond right away or spiritual opportunity fades within our minds with time into failure. A first priority is to control emotions and stay humble to receive God's guidance.

In stressful circumstances, we might briefly use high spiritual energy for creativity and calm back down quickly. Communication with God is more important to us than all earthly communications. We must be true to God to be true to ourselves and others. God's message is interpreted personally by each of us. We must keep this in mind to be good spiritual writers.

Once touched, we aspire to become messengers of God. Spiritual service may be long and hard with rewards slow in coming. If espousing having received personal messages from God, there will be disbelief and scorn from those close to us. This happened to Jesus.

Man was separated from God in the Garden of Eden. Our goal is to reunite man with God. The highest level of spirituality is to develop, practice, and teach spiritual skills so everyone can become messengers of God.

Often, I feel inadequate in constructing words to describe my received analogue or flowing spiritual awareness. It is difficult. Normal word communications lack deep down feelings of completeness and truth relative to spiritual feelings. Developing careful word structure can increase spiritual meaning.

Our listening and organizational abilities are not perfect. This is why I suggest a world spiritual board to verify and integrate God's current spiritual messages from believers throughout the world.

We should learn from and honor present and traditional spiritual leaders and honor our fathers and mothers for their nurturing, love, and guidance. Be thankful for past blessings while preparing for future blessings. Open spiritual channels to live in the spiritual present. Spiritual practices today are troubling. Much emphasis is placed on entertainment and not enough emphasis on developing inner communication for spiritual and holistic feelings.

Christians are taught to believe Christ lived a perfect life even though most of His life went unrecorded. With His humility, I doubt Jesus would say that every thought He ever had was perfect.

I suspect there were many trials and tribulations before Jesus developed His impressive spiritual abilities. Jesus frequently prayed for guidance.

Spiritual communications are interpreted in different ways. We should not be forced to think and worship in the same way. Spiritual leaders should nurture followers' spiritual individuality. We have been created by God as individuals for different worldly and spiritual purposes.

Spiritual is any thought or action to support God's purposes in developing truth in our own and other's lives. The highest goal is humbly uniting all people on earth through spiritual reason.

After receiving spiritual inspiration, it is difficult to choose the right words. Writing itself helps us discover our inner selves and heal. I work to be truthful in translating God's messages. If not truthful, I will no longer receive spiritual communications. Anyone defining and sharing his personal relationship with God is acknowledging and praising His existence, love, and power.

I often think of temptations Jesus must have experienced as He developed His spiritual abilities. With less educated cultures during those times, it was easier to be deceptive. Today, people have more knowledge and checks and balances for things we do. Jesus would not have received constant messages from God unless He was truthful with God and all He met.

Benefits of a modern global religion could be infinite. With spiritual changes within the fabric of all human brains, there would be no wars and minimum expenses for defenses and policing. All minds would develop synchronized harmonic brain waves. Everyone would feel, believe, and know that everyone else were trusted friends.

Energy and resources required for spiritually culturing every brain on earth would be less than that of the Iraq war. Harmonic spiritual resonances from everyone on earth could possible lead alien life within the universe to receive higher gifts from God.

Global resonances would multiply reflections of God throughout the universe for a more infinite God. The universe and God become more efficient, and mankind increases importance in God's eyes.

Experiencing God is like seeing the most beautiful scenery with feelings of wholeness. Human knowledge of this scenery is like only reading words describing that scenery. Words fall short and do not produce the whole effect of the scenery. Words can only associate the current scenery to our remembered words and visions.

A world health goal should be to heal trauma effects and their thinking restrictions to improve physical, social, and spiritual reasoning. Our worshiping God is as rewarding to Him as a good, obedient child is rewarding to his parents. Our service to parents and God should be similar in nature.

Can a world religious structure with checks and balances help govern mankind with such diverse ideas? It will take a long time for concepts to be established. Jesus was not accepted by many during His lifetime. The majority of religious believers will not accept the second-coming unless there is some miraculous event. A dramatic unifying event would advance spiritual communication technology.

True religions encourage creative thinking. Repetitions, rituals, and dogmas restrict thinking to control followers. Many religious leaders want followers to have blind faith in what they preach.

The supreme law of love should govern. We do not hear today's politicians emphasizing love of their constituents as they love their own families.

In a capitalistic society, the rich and powerful get richer. They establish an economic slavery system by controlling the land and wealth. Political rhetoric in America gains popularity, deceives the poor, and continues toward a feudal system.

Struggles for power between America's two political parties have prevented so many major accomplishments. With brain scans and follow-up tests for honesty, the president, congress, and courts would have proven moral guidance for governing with verified high morals. Passing truth tests, political leaders will have interest in freedom for all. Jesus said, "Then you will know the truth, and the truth will set you free," John 8:32. (1)

Candidates and government leaders should be periodically tested for humility and honesty toward common goals for their nation and for improving relationships with all other nations. We must demand high morals and abilities from our leaders and advocate high morals from leaders of other countries.

Tests should indicate creative and truthful brain activities. Responses would show true, holistic right brain activities. One should study, think within, and develop his beliefs. Blind faith is not as useful as your own inner spiritual reasoning.

Christianity is a wonderful foundation for continuing spiritual development. Methodist doxology is important to me. However, we do not have to express beliefs and worship in identical ways to attain everlasting life. Traditional religions have become stuck in a spiritual time warp. If we advance learning and language, we can interpret God's message in more detail.

Without a science and mathematics background it is more difficult to understand the magnitude of God's abilities in spiritual time. Many jump to some vague thought of the infinite without thinking about God's abilities in more detail. Infinite and miracle mean for many that which is beyond abilities to understand. Science and mathematics add understanding of God's awesome abilities. Science helps thinking about deeper meanings of infinite and Eternity.

We may say infinite is something that goes on and on in time and space. From God's view, time and space may not go on forever. Very short times may not be continuous but in very small quantum steps, which vary relative to matter, gravity, and relativistic speeds. Behaviors are very different between atomic and everyday size things.

Developing a higher understanding of Eternity and miracles through science makes them more awe inspiring. Superlatives such as God, infinity, eternal, and perfect inspire primitive awe and block further reasoning. However, simple truth and honesty can be more important than high levels of scientific knowledge.

Guiding the world toward an enveloping religion is important. Many believers feel closeness to God and their congregation when practicing rituals. Associating with similar believers, even with ridiculous beliefs, brings people closer together and masks their uncertainties about life and afterlife. A task is to emphasize similarities in belief systems.

We like and trust people we can understand and predict their responses. We need everyone in this world liking and trusting each other. Distrust of different societies becomes profound enough to degrade their faiths and start murderous wars.

Science of Creation and evolution should help us justify our existence and consciousness. We recognize our uncertainties and limitations during fears and failures. Understanding limitations may guide us to abilities and wisdom beyond current limits.

Let's extend thinking to cosmic sizes. Our God may not be considered perfect on cosmic scales. It seems illogical that our universe is the only universe in existence. We are too limited to find out unless God explains such things to us. Can creation of the universe be compared to human conception?

The least scientifically inclined must believe that science and engineering discoveries have allowed scientists and engineers to design and manufacture cars, planes, nuclear reactors, tall buildings, medicines, surgical procedures, and the internet.

Science has made manmade benefits possible. Simply using these products and procedures gives some belief in science. We know scientists and engineers have had some understanding of nature to design and construct these tools for our benefit. We should also construct spiritual communication tools for our and God's benefit. We would be intellectually shallow not to believe in science. However, today, many of us believe in traditional religious dogma without reason. In biblical times, people would more easily believe things they were told.

There is a basic tendency to be associated with someone or something greater than self. Many believe their religion is better than another's religion. We want to be associated with greatness. A lovely Christian song, "How Great Thou Art," helps Christians believe how great God is. It is an honor to be a part of God.

The author confronted death in the spring of 1977. All my hopes and beliefs evaporated. Depression was so incapacitating I could not think in words, remember the past, or think of the future. Hoping for and expecting death at each moment to stop the mental torture, I barely existed in a murky, thoughtless present. I felt no love, only pain, and was unsure whether I was dead or alive.

At that time, my almost two year old son would come to me for love and affection and only found a ghost of a dad. I was unable to smile but would come alive enough to understand he knew something was wrong.

Unfortunately, things got worse. Depression erupted into insanities of mania when doubts dominated beliefs. But slowly, the love of my children returned and allowed focus toward the future and belief in life and God again. Without hope for the future there is no reason to live or do anything. After healing from depression and manic depression, I often wondered whether I had spiritually died and was, by God's miracle, reborn. In any event I knew the feeling of being brain dead. Only through amazing grace can I now write of healing. Life is God's miracle to cherish.

From that time on, I have thought deeper about the mind and God. One spiritual model that resulted is that God is similar to a time sharing mainframe computer. Mainframe computers can process many different programs during the same time. Depending on a set of priorities, each program is inserted and executed for some specified time interval, saved, and executed further during the next time cycle. As programs are completed and prepared for final output other programs are entered into memory for time sharing execution. A computer can work on many programs in the same time period as well as it can work on one long individual program.

It is difficult for humans to work on and shuffle many diverse programs during the same time period. With our logically and memory challenged minds, we need to be consistent and finish one difficult program before going on to another. Otherwise, we mix things together in confusion.

God understands and creates the purpose of every atom within the universe in parallel at unbelievable speeds. With a rough physics calculation, I estimated that God organizes and directs the entire universe every 10^{-106} seconds of physical time (a very, very small fraction of a second) or each quantum of spiritual time. God fits our lives into His completeness every 10^{-106} seconds. We have a spiritual purpose for evolving within the universe. Spiritual purposes direct physical purposes. We sometimes understand our earthly purpose but have less understanding of our universal or spiritual purpose. Through God our lives affect the entire universe to some very small extent.

God hears our prayers, but responds at His time sharing spiritual priority and not at our requested physical time. We can increase priority with God by refining beliefs through models, persistence, Christianity, and other religions to increase His action potential toward our needs.

Practicing long range, global right brain processes, and experimenting with low energy and highly emotional prayers can attract spiritual priority. God understands our prayers as they relate to our integrated lifetime history and spiritual or universal purpose.

Decades after Jesus was crucified, writers were deciding what should be included as a bible. Many writings were excluded. Writers tried to represent Jesus' life and teaching truthfully, but in the best light possible. It is true today that writers' aggrandize their heroes. We speak and write highly of those we love and respect.

No two people witnessing an event write about it exactly the same. No human is perfect. There is a human element in all writing. Scripture writers wrote a wonderful history of Jesus' spiritual work. Additional scrolls may be found to support Jesus' work.

Centuries after Jesus was crucified, scholars continue to refine Christian beliefs. Scholars have debated and written doctrines on many aspects of their Christian beliefs to be preached to the multitude.

In my models, the Holy Spirit is that part of God that communicates with mankind. God has infinite other duties of monitoring and controlling the entire universe through His physical and spiritual laws. God can direct the Holy Spirit to do miracles. It is exciting to explore communication with God.

Prophets receiving communications from God have translated His analogue messages into spiritual words of various languages. Translations were affected by emotions, histories, truthfulness, and, possibly, self aggrandizement. God's analogue resonances are the absolute truth about all spiritual and physical relationships in the universe. Words are fragmented translations of God's analogue, complete message and are never completely correct.

We become conscious of spiritual and mental resonances our brains maintain beyond a certain length of time. Viewing an image, eyes repeatedly receive the same frequencies and the brain develops long lasting resonances for a vision of that image.

Man's limited vision is sensitive to only a narrow range of electromagnetic frequencies. God is aware of all frequencies. God's awareness is the integration and understanding of all electromagnetic frequencies and their resonances. Humans are aware of only one "radio station" frequency.

We should not limit our mental models of God or the universe to our abilities, measurements, or knowledge.

Imagination is everything for productive earthly and spiritual lives. God speaks often though subconscious processes and dreams. One model might be that God takes control of our minds during sleep and dreaming to reenergize the brain and organize, integrate and store daily experiences with historical experiences.

I hope writing of my unusual experiences will encourage others to write about their own unusual psychiatric and spiritual experiences. We need to bring psychiatric experiences out of the closet so everyone can build confidence in mental healing.

Traditional spiritual beliefs should not block writing about today's spiritual experiences. A spiritual time warp means we only think spiritually through studying and, to some extent, re-experiencing historical actions and words of previous spiritual leaders. For me, Jesus' spirit is current and guiding us today. I feel His presence integrated within God. I believe in an integrated Holy Trinity - Father, Son, and Holy Spirit. I refer to the Holy Trinity simply as God.

Scientists carefully develop detailed logical procedures to understand and prove laws of nature. Religions are developed by different paths. Spiritual communications, from God through leaders bold enough to proclaim their revelations, develop religions. Spiritual revelations are not scientifically provable and are open to false prophets seeking fame and wealth.

That spiritual revelations are not easily provable is the reason those claiming to have received messages from God should volunteer for advanced brain scan, truth analyses. Messages from God may be proven as solidly and repeatable as scientific laws, in the future.

No religion should be close-ended and proclaim it is the only way to understand God and attain heaven. The world and God evolve in time. God changes very little in our life times relative to His 13.7 billion years of existence. In this sense, God is very constant relative to man. Those receiving God's guidance will work for love, peace, and unity on earth, and in the Milky Way and universe.

Each atom within our brains and bodies is up to 13.7 billion years old. Our "spiritual memories" may go back 13.7 billion years. In a sense, we share a long history with God.

We focus on earthly details by narrowing thinking with the left brain. At times, to attract God's powers, we should think of the universe and God as one integrated entity to expand our spiritual wholeness. Combining our two cognitive processes is somewhat like integrating micro-quantum physics with general relativity and cosmology to develop a unified thinking model of the universe. At times, we should think of mind and brain also as one entity to think holistically or spiritually.

Science should support religion when possible or explain when traditional dogmas are adverse to scientific facts. Scientists should never ridicule or dictate beliefs.

Spiritual science can add depth to religions. There are so many new spiritual relationships to learn. With global sharing, life on earth will become integrated as part of heaven if deranged fanatics do not blow us all up beforehand. The absurdly indoctrinated will do anything to perpetuate their false beliefs.

Jesus' love for those He met and His spiritual work are deeply ingrained within Christians. He needed thirty years of preparation to develop His spiritual abilities. He was courageous, caring, and reasonable in unreasonable times and did what God asked Him to do.

As a scientist, I question everyone. Would Jesus' DNA be decidedly different from that of normal men? From lack of comment, Jesus' appearance seemed to have been normal. If He had a persistent halo, scriptures would have been filled with this unique feature. Did anyone ask Jesus to explain how He arose from the dead? Possibly, everyone was in such awe that no one asked that question.

Many of us have a concept of God. Figure 15.1 is an illustration of the universe and God as He communicates with you, or us. This picture would be slightly different for every soul within the universe. You are located at the X, God is all lines of electromagnetic radiation focused on you, and the circle is the universe expanding outward at the speed of light.

With language and knowledge of historical spiritual times, writers were not able to describe sins as trauma scars. The word "sin" remains rather vague, today. In Christian terms, Billy Graham defined sin as anything that disobeys the Ten Commandments. We must cast out our sins or trauma scars to become spiritually reborn.

Freed of trauma scars, we are more able to receive God's blessings and purpose. With prayer and practice, spiritual abilities can become limitless through God. The world does not need to be guided by only one spiritual leader. We can become messengers of God.

God's constant resonances and harmonics affect our brains and minds differently, and at times, promote shattering spiritual words. God works to integrate mankind into one loving family. Additionally, He wants to unite all awareness within the universe into wholeness.

Without today's psychology and communication skills, man's emotions were volatile in traditional spiritual times. High emotions caused either extreme distrust or absolute obedience to religious teachings. There were often fears of survival between various cultures.

Our meager interpretations of God's perfection are less than His reality. Mankind cannot possibly understand God's perfection.

On very small elementary and atomic sizes, God controls with perfect probability. A nuclear engineer cannot control individual atoms, but on human sizes with probability, can statistically control neutron interactions within nuclear reactors safely. Nuclear probability is perfectly constant. Individual things become more predictable on larger scales. A constant gravity allows predictable movement on the earth for mankind and living things.

Spiritual communication skills are genetically developed over generations through family interactions and worship. With our and previous generations' spiritual dedications, God judges us. Through genetics, we carry gifts or burdens of our parents' and ancestors' lives and training. We are physical and spiritual products over generations.

God expects us to guide our children spiritually. Guidance of our children continues when we are no longer present or alive.

Reactions to physical laws and humans we meet should be understood with repeatable scientific or personal experiments, respectively. Wet grass is slipperier than dry grass. We always fall down, not up. If someone repeatedly degrades us, we should lessen their importance. Having a high opinion of someone who continually treats us badly is dangerous to our mental and physical health.

We should judge how reasonable and helpful writings are to us and all of mankind. If we think spiritual beliefs are only for us or our clique, we are shortsighted, self-centered, and detract from God. God's purpose is to integrate everyone within His love. Do teachers and God fail if we do not meet their standards?

There are conflicts between certainty and uncertainty, success and failure, gain and loss, good and evil, right and wrong, importance and less importance, self and others, and pain and pleasure. There is conflict in every thought we have.

With genetic instincts, we think and act like humans, not mice. Spiritual instincts frame motivation for survival, pleasure, love, reproduction, and worship.

We can help God win His conflict with evil, sometimes referred to as Satan. With free wills, we can be good and responsible in one minute and bad and irresponsible in the next minute. We can be good to some and bad to others. To be spiritual, we should apply the same rules, actions, and reactions to everyone as we apply to our loved ones. Of course, we spend more time with loved ones.

Since Christ's death and resurrection, Christian leaders have frightened believers into preparing for an antichrist who will cause the world to end. Unfortunately, this teaching encourages some self-proclaimed, "mentally ill antichrists" to attempt to make negative predictions come true. For centuries, many have falsely predicted the end of the world for attention and selfish purposes.

God and humans have abilities to learn. God learns of our free will activities through our prayers, actions, and mental resonances. If God learns about us and makes judgments, He does not have infinite knowledge. God's and our judgments change the future.

From my experiences, I believe traditional spiritual leaders also experienced manic thought intrusions or thought insertions. Experiencing near death changes both life and spiritual outlook. All prophets probably had bipolar disorder. If historical prophets lived today, doctors would medicate them and no one would believe them.

Losing mental control, in mania, increases spiritual abilities. Psychologists and psychiatrists might say Jesus and prophets had mental disorders with profound auditory hallucinations or thought intrusions. What was good for spiritual yesteryear does not seem good for today. Bipolar disorder can be controlled to add spiritual order.

If God speaks to us subtly, that is fine. If God speaks to us today in words when we are emotionally high, doctors and ministers think occurrences must be auditory hallucinations or thought intrusions. Certainly powerful spiritual messages from God override our routine thinking.

Was God's creation of the universe not a complete miracle? Amazing technologies and methodologies will continue to be developed to understand God's physical and spiritual laws and creations.

Let's think about miracles. If I happened to be evil and landed a helicopter in a village centuries ago and declared that God had sent me to rule the land, many would be amazed and believe my deception. Without earlier generations knowing the technical background of my machine, they would think they had witnessed a miracle. People might worship me because I had great power they could not comprehend.

If my helicopter flew over Jesus as He was walking on water, would not observers believe my helicopter was a higher miracle? We must be careful in believing miracles and distinguish between science and spiritual technologies.

If I were power-hungry, I might promote a web of lies and teach those who had seen the helicopter to spread the religion of the engineering miracle to control more people. Even today, we want to believe in miracles for our benefit by someone or something with abilities beyond our understanding. However, we are slow believing miracles by those close to us. We degrade unusual behaviors by those we know until they become widely recognized.

We do not think of things we understand or technological discoveries and products as miracles. However, one day, we might worship very smart androids, or "modern golden cows," as idols with powers much greater than our own.

When God, all light in the universe, travels, He focuses beyond three-dimensional views into an integrated holistic view or image of the universe. At the moment Light is created by atom or elementary particle activities or interference between Light Sources, God experiences discrete views of the universe. We have discrete and holistic views of the universe and so does God on a higher level. Our holistic view of the universe is an indivisible awareness of God. If God understands our prayers He also has discrete abilities.

Some spiritual writers proclaim their writings or books are the "complete" truth about God, and their spiritual truths cannot be added to or subtracted from. This belief has held the world back spiritually for hundreds of years. Nothing could be more ridiculous than believing ancient historical books were everything we needed to know about God. Believing humans will ever learn the complete truth about an infinite God is insane.

Spiritual people help others in need. The curious only observe out-of-control, manic behavior. Manic-depressives are labeled as crazy, made fun of, or are drugged into mental, physical, and spiritual inactivity. Goals must be to increase spiritual communication while maintaining productive, everyday lives.

Developing a world religion, with input from all religions, will unify humanity. Even good tradition religions have favored their own people and races, therefore dividing the world. We tend to be self-centered even when receiving and translating God's continuous and complete language into our limited languages. Only, a religious umbrella with diverse freedoms of worship will bring world peace.

Each of us has the opportunity to develop wide and diverse thoughts. God gave us this capacity. Philosophically, with God given diverse abilities, it seems unnatural that we should devote our worship and pleas to God in the same way. The best communication for praise of, and support from, God is through inner mental paths. However, spiritual leaders and models help us focus on God and truthful lives.

With today's communication and travel technologies the world has become more connected but less united. We must tear down the walls between countries, races, religions, and prejudices with an umbrella of global ideologies. We must focus on our similarities.

Science advocates imagination and the thrill of discovery. Imagination expands the mind for learning about Creation and the universe. Persistent inner searching will initiate the thrill of spiritual discovery.

Unfortunately, memorizing scripture and emotional repetition as practiced in many religions forces believers to be submissive and narrow-minded. Excessive memorization of scripture is a false duty to God but is a tool for religious control. Good science and religious practices should expand minds and creativity in learning about God and His creations.

In mania, we have exceptional opportunities to receive exciting messages from God. However, temptations are ever-present. Unless we learn to remain humble, spiritual messages become immediately corrupted with selfish power and control.

Final chapter thoughts are, that before creation, nothing, or all of pre-existence was entirely uncertain. As a mathematical singularity, God created Himself as time, space, and light from absolute uncertainty. He condensed His excess energy as matter and the universe was born. God allowed uncertainties to remain throughout the universe. Without uncertainties.

Religions that promote themselves as superior, brainwash believers or prospective believers, force their beliefs on others, punish or kill those with different beliefs, or confine thinking, are false religions. Minds are designed to learn and expand.

True religions encourage believers, with their free wills, to expand thinking abilities for exciting and blessed lives on earth, and for exciting, challenging holistic thinking and spiritual existences. In heaven, exciting complete thoughts will relate to all of the universe, heaven, and possibly existence.

We should respect all religions and individuals, except those wanting to physically hurt, mentally damage, or kill, any one. May God serve swift justice to false spiritual tyrants, to save the world, and its humble, loving people!

By separating church and state, many countries have promoted individual freedoms, science achievements, and respect for different cultures and religions. Today, some religions are dedicated to destroying free wills and separation of church and state. They intend for their beliefs and traditions to dominate, and limit, people's thoughts, by any means.

Some religions are preparing to take over governments, imprison or kill all scientists and persons with different beliefs. Knowledge and true spiritual beliefs are threats to false, corrupted beliefs.

In the future, true religions must develop recognizable spiritual abilities, communications, and miracles to prove their spiritual worth. Other religions will be recognized as false. Otherwise, "corrupted, false superior" religions will destroy the world.

I was fortunate to have had wonderful, humble parents. Even though now in heaven, they remain a part of me. I pray to and bless them, integrated within God, as my saints every night. My loving parents, and aunts and uncles, in heaven, guide my thoughts at times.

Awaken right-brain spiritual communication processes with relaxed thinking of oceans, good music, dancing, horses running, and other flowing processes. God is flowing, continuous, and complete throughout the universe, but exists holistically in heaven.

REFERENCE:

(1) *The Holy Bible - New International Version - Disciples' Study Bible,* 1984, Holman Bible Publishers, Nashville, Tennessee.

Figure 15.1 God, the Universe, and You

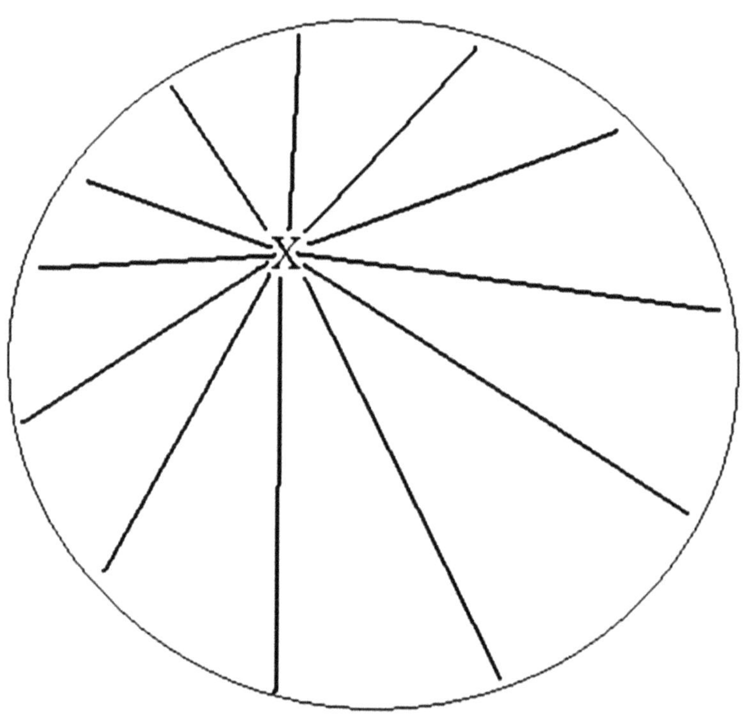

X - your place in the universe

Circle - universe boundary expanding at the speed of light

Lines - God: Light and all force fields, focusing on you

CHAPTER 16

Beliefs of Interest

We can sail along without a care
Until we meet more than we can bear!

Hugh D. Fulcher 2008

Religious beliefs differ depending upon childhood orientation, geography, evangelism, and independent spiritual enlightenment. With increasingly global societies, now may be the time to consider comparisons between religions and their benefits to their followers, all of mankind, and God. From a global science viewpoint, it may be time and necessary to point out false beliefs and activities.

Arrogance in believing in one's own spiritual superiority is very wrong in my belief system. Believing in killing someone with different beliefs is the highest of spiritual corruption. Spiritual leaders have ruled followers' minds without checks and balances for centuries. Historically, religions have been wide open to corruption.

Some religions discourage followers from thinking on their own. Religions espousing superior spiritual communication paths have been becoming increasingly corrupted. We must question beliefs, religions, and miracles at times. Developing individual spiritual reasoning protects us from false spiritual leaders. Self-proclaimed spiritual leaders can be the best or worst of humanity.

There are fewer faith healers since current medical technology can discover frauds more easily. Oral Roberts should have records of everyone God healed through him. Research should scientifically prove long-term effectiveness of God's miracles, or show highly emotional deception. Anyone permanently healed by a miracle could not stop praising God and Roberts.

True spiritual healers would teach others and spread healing throughout the world. We admire teachers who guide and expand logic and spiritual reasoning. We should question spiritual leaders who want us to believe only they have received special gifts from God.

We should frequently ask, "Are spiritual leaders making sense?" and question intentions and goals. History shows false leaders deceive and destroy individual and world freedoms. Hitler caused the world to lose so many lives and individual freedoms.

Spiritual leaders have difficult tasks of organizing and of integrating traditional and current spiritual work. This may be similar to verifying scientific discoveries. Science demands methodical and repeatable procedures and results.

On the other hand, religions appeal to emotions and require surrendering the mind to the primal instinct of awe within the limbic system. The limbic system regulates moods and is important in establishing mental limits and chemical balances throughout the brain.

Emotional followers and writers aggrandize their spiritual leaders; however, before dismissing religions, non-believers must acknowledge the confidence and comfort religions give to so many.

Few Christians or Muslims would admit they have been brainwashed even though they have been emotionally taught through repetition and memorization to believe, but not understand spiritual things. I cannot imagine scientists teaching with such methods.

In some sense, all of nature seems to consist of miracles. Science discoveries explain consistencies in nature. Miracles and mysteries have been reported by followers of spiritual leaders and also by the non-religious. There has not seemed to be much attention on how miracles were performed. Mysteries of the universe appear to:

1. have a ring of truth beyond the normal
2. keep people and societies together
3. help overcome fears of life and death
4. provide a controlling device for the arrogant ruling class
5. provide mental healing and confidence
6. increase belief in and association with the supernatural
7. give attention to the downtrodden
8. promote moral rules, pride in rituals, extend "truth" with delusional claims
9. become a guide to supreme afterlife, appeals to lost souls
10. provide reasons for suffering and also for increasing power and control
11. create a respected living for spiritual leaders
12. promote repetitious indoctrination and one method cures all
13. distort faiths for arrogant killing of different believers

Pride in being associated with psychologically powerful people such as Hitler, Jim Jones, Warren Jeffs, Jim Baker, Jerry Falwell, Billy Graham, preachers, teachers, or Einstein can lead to destruction or salvation. Association with some of the above may lead to successful worldly and spiritual lives. We have choices.

"Superior belief systems" promoting power over others are spiritually corrupt. We must carefully reason about what we and others believe! Today, if we make claims similar to that of traditional religious leaders we are labeled as delusional by the self-righteous. This is understandable since there have been so many religious frauds. True religious leaders expand followers' reason and freedoms.

Religious believers and scientists search in different ways for truth about God and His universe and to eliminate pains of doubt and uncertainty. Jesus' teachings of love, peace, and His communication skills with God have added certainty to many followers' lives. For centuries, Christians believed in a perfect spiritual leader in Jesus but later became corrupted and intolerant of other religions.

Muslims believe in Mohammad as their prophet. They also believe in a perfect spiritual leader. Mohammad's writings and actions demanded that followers convert people they meet to Islam. If they refused to convert, they became "infidels" or non-persons. Mohammad was, and the Koran is, intolerant of other religions.

Today, freedom of religion in many countries has helped avoid wars. Muslims and non-Muslims are concerned about intolerance and violence by radical "spiritually superior" interpretations of the Koran.

When people believe they have the absolute correct way of doing things, they become intolerant of other opinions and values. Thinking in superlatives deceives self and is dangerous to self and others. No one acts superior or arrogant to loved ones. Superior-acting, arrogant people do not love. Without humility, evil lurks.

There is only holy or complete peace and love. Holy war is a contradiction. Misconceptions by religions have produced ungodly purposes. War is only justified for freeing the oppressed from tyrants.

Christians and Muslims believe in one true God, or Allah. They should be wise enough to integrate their beliefs under one umbrella of common spiritual goals? Believers could practice rituals as they saw fit. With God's guidance, the two religions could be structured to complement each other. Manmade ideas of perfection lead to corruption and quest for power during and after life. Teaching about spiritual lives can be inspiring. However, over exuberance leads to indoctrination, coercion, and lost spiritual reasoning.

Conservative Christianity

Reverend, Dr. Jerry Falwell died May 15, 2007. He was a nationally known televangelist from Lynchburg, Virginia, and founded Thomas Road Baptist Church, Liberty University, and the Moral Majority. I paid respects as he lay in state at Liberty University's DeMoss Hall.

Dr. Falwell greeted everyone with a warm smile. He preached conservative Christian beliefs and values and did much good for the community and many throughout the world. He was controversial as he preached spiritual superiority and condemned other religions, at times. As leader of the Moral Majority, He tested boundaries between America's separation of church and state.

We have received different spiritual messages and have had different beliefs, but respected his work and sincerity. Dr. Falwell worked to convert everyone to Christianity for their salvation as he understood it.

Tolstoy

I happened to find a June, 1986, issue of *National Geographic* in my barn. I had no recollection of why these magazines were stored there. *The World of Tolstoy* (1) by Peter T. White was a featured article on the cover. I had never read Tolstoy but seemed attracted to the article like a moth to a candle.

In January, 2007, in a Lynchburg bookstore, my son-in-law, Dr. Andrew Hawkins, picked up the book, *Leo Tolstoy - A Confession and Other Religious Writings* (2). I felt forced to read this book. Below are results of this seemingly miracle of divine guidance.

Tolstoy struggled with depression and the meaning of life as I have struggled. After he had accomplished fame with *War and Peace,* 1869, and *Karenina,* 1878, he searched for the meaning of life. In 1879 he began writing *Confession.*

Tolstoy wrote of non-violence and protested that forceful takeover of state power leads only to similar non-tolerances and dictatorships. He believed that if we all loved one another there would be little need for state laws and enforcement. Tolstoy writes that everyone should be loved and treated as equals. He warned against controlling others.

Tolstoy suggested that everyone spend time searching within to cultivate their own spiritual beliefs and moral leadership. He thought false doctrine became mixed within Christian and Islamic faiths. Tolstoy thought religion was an inner experience that could be nurtured through traditional religions and experiences of others. He commented that most religions are founded by leaders who proclaimed that their way is the only way to experience God.

I have had strong spiritual communications but certainly do not believe my way is the only spiritual way. The thought of God's guiding and giving meaning to our lives is as believable as loving parents' guiding and giving meaning to children's lives.

Uncertainties and difficulties in life lead many of us toward spiritual certainties. Distorted spiritual leaders take advantage of this vulnerability to enhance their control and power. Cults are formed by leaders who twist religion for their own benefit. Tolstoy writes that false leaders use this need of belief to develop flawed belief systems.

Believing we are children of God gives us an elevated cause for existence. Religion should build certainty from uncertainty, but often only suppresses uncertain thinking and reduces creativity.

Tolstoy observed that luxury is built upon enslavement of others. Often today, corporate workers become slaves to their bosses in order to support their families. They work long unpaid hours to maintain security. Individual and family freedom is lost. According to Tolstoy, the lower and middle class have less freedom but truer spiritual lives.

Religions give followers guidance between right and wrong. Life becomes simplified. Life is for meaningful existence in present and eternal life. Tolstoy had increasing concerns about the division between the rich and poor. In his times, medical care was mostly for the rich. Tolstoy thought that understanding one's life with an "undistorted" religion was Man's highest blessing.

Tolstoy toiled with explaining our place within the universe and our relationship to God. He professed that Man's true welfare lies in the unity of all men and that unity cannot be attained through war and violent means. As an example, the current war in Iraq has magnified non-unity between countries with different basic beliefs.

All religions were developed initially by a single leader for the benefit of local believers. Lasting religions spread beliefs of and allegiance to exalted leaders. There is difficulty in establishing unity within the world with historically biased religions.

Gandhi became a follower of Tolstoy's philosophy and a great leader of India. Peace, love, and non-violence with humility should rule the world with God's guidance. Dr. Martin Luther King learned from Tolstoy and Gandhi and brought a new era of reconciliation, peace, and hope to America.

I promote a world religion that integrates all traditional religions for the spiritual unity of all believers, including scientists. All new true spiritual ideas will feel like ideas we have known for a long time.

Capitalism

Tolstoy wrote against the pearls of capitalism. CEOs of large American corporations give themselves hundred million dollar annual salaries and bonuses while many employees are earning just over minimum wage. Capitalism is a religion of the wealthy and is based upon continuous economic growth. The world population cannot grow forever with continued quality of human life.

American capitalism needs to be fixed. There is little justice in the free market of corporate America. The majority of Americans – the middle and low income – have allowed this to happen in our democracy. America's elected officials cater to rich lobbyists and do not protect the majority of Americans.

The rich attempt to gain moral credibility by espousing their giving to the very poor as they fleece the rest of America and the world. With the wealth in America, all citizens should have a bountiful life. Money, power, and high living corrupt the morals of some of the rich, who then use their money to suppress and abuse the poor. Illness or inability to understand contracts or labor laws force many hard working honest people into poverty.

To examine the idea of capitalism further, let's look at an example of a mind that is opposite of the capitalist's mind. From India the man later known as the Buddha rejected ways of his family's wealth and power to wander in a search for truth and a spiritual life. In later life, Tolstoy, of Russia, gave up his aristocratic life to work, live, and write as a common person.

More recently, Jimmy Carter chose to work as a common laborer in building houses for the poor after leaving the office of President of the United States of America. Sister Teresa became well known for her sacrifice, care, and advocacy for the poor and sick in India. Rarely do the shameful rich care about the less fortunate.

The Baha'i Faith

Let's look at a modern approach for unifying understanding and beliefs. One way is the Baha'i faith.

The Baha'i faith is a growing religion founded by a messenger of God, Bahá'u'lláh, from Persia in the mid-nineteenth century. This religion is based upon social and spiritual unity. He taught that there is only one God and only one human race. All the world's religions represent stages in the revelation of God's will and purpose for humanity. As predicted in traditional scriptures, the time has arrived for the uniting of all peoples into a peaceful and integrated global society. We must work to recognize all people as spiritually important.

Baha'i takes a distinctive approach to contemporary social problems. Their scriptures and diverse activities address important trends in the world today: new thinking about cultural diversity and environmental conservation, decentralization of political decision making, renewed commitment to family life and moral values, and calling for social and economic justice for a more close-knit world. Baha'i is an interesting approach to integrate spiritual ideas and people together while encouraging freedom of thought and wide participation. Advancing spiritual communication and training all members to become messengers of God needs to be added. A world religion acceptable by traditional religious worshippers would encourage everyone to work in harmony as messengers of God. Uniting worshippers that believe their traditional spiritual leader is the only path to God will be difficult. Brain scans will help us understand God's Truth within ourselves.

Unitarian Church

The Unitarian church is versatile in their approach to religion. The following was on their webpage:

> "The Unitarian Universalist Association shall devote its resources to and exercise its corporate powers for religious, educational and humanitarian purposes. The primary purpose of the Association is to serve the needs of its member congregations, organize new congregations, extend and strengthen Unitarian Universalist institutions and implement its principles.
>
> "The Association declares and affirms its special responsibility, and that of its member congregations and organizations, to promote the full participation of persons in all of its and their activities and in the full range of human endeavor without regard to race, ethnicity, gender, disability, affectional or sexual orientation, age, language, citizenship status, economic status, or national origin and without requiring adherence to any particular interpretation of religion or to any particular religious belief or creed.
>
> "Nothing herein shall be deemed to infringe upon the individual freedom of belief which is inherent in the Universalist and Unitarian heritages or to conflict with any statement of purpose, covenant, or bond of union used by any congregation unless such is used as a creedal test."

The unusual practice of the Unitarians is that they do not worship a single perfect leader. Worshipers are not limited to one structure or belief. There can be peace only if everyone gives spiritual value to everyone else. With God's guidance, brilliant minds throughout this world can find ways for everyone to unite with love.

The world cannot be unified by war or domination, but only by the spirit of equality before God. We need to build everyone up as spiritual equals. With practice, everyone can become messengers of God. Our minds are more a part of God than our children's minds are a part of our minds.

Dying!

As we get older, a time will come when we must ponder our maladies and mortality. Dying is inevitable! How we cope depends upon the spiritual foundations we have built. We will need to express justification for our lives to significant others and God.

Doctors and nurses experience patients' deaths often. Confronting patients' deaths was studied from a surgeon's viewpoint and is given in a book, *Final Exam, A Surgeon's Reflections on Mortality* [(3)] by Dr. Pauline W. Chen.

We should encourage the dying to talk about good things in their lives. It is time to relive the past and if appropriate the blessings that God has given. Be interested and complimentary of a dying person's past and their faith for an eternal future. Comforting the dying is an important gift. When appropriate, be funny. Laughter is the best medicine to relieve fears and tensions. My dad had this gift.

Science and Religion

Science and religion often seem at odds, as described by Lawrence M. Krauss and Richard Dawkins, in "Should Science Speak to Faith," [(4)] Scientific American, July, 2007. They discussed questions about science's relationship to faith. Their ideas help me formulate the following questions.

What role should scientists have toward religious beliefs? How should scientists discuss religions with believers? Should they ever lie for believers' mental health reasons allowing them to continue absurd beliefs? Should scientists support or discredit historical or new religions? If a scientist disproves a religious foundation, is he morally obligated to promote corrections? Should science develop a logical religion on scientific knowledge with less reliance on faith?

Can we understand and worship God better through science? Should science's role be to define, and prove or disprove the existence of God? With the same spiritual words being received independently by many diverse people, can science prove their truth? Will scientific discoveries eventually destroy traditional religions? Can scientists explain the deep joy and confidence experienced by believers through dedication to their rituals and beliefs? Can scientists acknowledge miracles?

Uncertainties and fears draw us to become part of a powerful absolute. Fragile youths are indoctrinated by religious teachers. Should science be taught as early as religion? Will science bring generations closer to God?

False Beliefs!

False faiths threatened by scientific knowledge and technology become enemies of advanced societies. These faiths isolate and brainwash their youth through extensive memorization without reason. Forcing investment, and nurturing pride, in memorization of scriptures increases dogmatic belief without reason.

Tolstoy writes that false leaders use the need of belief to develop flawed belief systems, without spiritual reason. Gangs form false religions. Members pledge to hold each other above non-members. Members pledge to be subservient to the gang's dogmas, beliefs, and leaders.

Spiritual gangs or cults develop reasons to prevent members from leaving. Cults falsely call themselves religions. Rather than increasing freedom of thought, cult leaders control by suppressing thought. Spiritual and street gang leaders promote feelings of superiority as being part of something greater than self.

A mentally ill tyrant, Jim Jones, leader of the Peoples Temple, brainwashed over 900 followers into committing mass suicide on November 18, 1978 as his final act of self-centered power and stupidity. He probably thought he would cause Armageddon. Unfortunately, no one or country acted in time to save those misguided, brainwashed people. War against this godless tyrant would have been spiritually justified.

REFERENCES:

(1) White, Peter T., 1986, June, *The World of Tolstoy,* National Geographic, Vol. 169, No. 6, 17th and M Sts. N. W., Washington, D.C. 20036

(2) Kentish, Jane, 1987, *Leo Tolstoy - A Confession and Other Religious Writings,* translation, the Penguin Group, Penguin Books Ltd, 80 Strand, London WC2R 0R1, England

(3) Chen, Pauline W., 2007, *Final Exam, A Surgeon's Reflections on Mortality,* Alfred A. Knopf, a division of Random House, Inc., New York, NY.

(4) Krauss, Lawrence M. and Dawkins, Richard, July, 2007, "Should Science Speak to Faith?," *Scientific American,* New York, NY.

CHAPTER 17

Spiritual Awakening

The Battle Hymn of the Republic (Excerpts)

Mine eyes have seen the glory of the coming of the Lord;
He is trampling out the vintage where the grapes of wrath are stored;

. . .

Glory, glory, hallelujah!
Glory, glory, hallelujah!
Glory, glory, hallelujah!
His truth is marching on.

The Atlantic Monthly, 1862

The atom and the universe are based upon uncertainty. Life, the universe, and even God, have no purpose without uncertainty. If we always knew what will happen in the future, we would be predestined without options or judgments in life. Competitions have little purpose with certain of results.

At times, I awaken with wordless inner excitement knowing I am aware of life and God. If anyone would abruptly experience the sensations I experience without the years of manic and spiritual experiences they would become insane with uncertainties. My mind and soul briefly become free of earthly worries, filled with hope.

Difficulties in the world are often caused by assuming beliefs are facts.

Including science facts and reason in religion promotes true beliefs.

We have spiritual knowledge within us that we can recall and share. Reading science and spiritual books and activating inner abilities expand mind and soul. Hopefully, our souls will be as inspiring at eighty years old as they were at eighty days old.

It is not difficult to understand why Mohammad developed Islam exclusiveness in the Koran. End of times prophecy is a major theme in the Bible. Prophecies predicted that only Christians believing in, and the redeemed dead that believed in, Jesus will be eternally saved at the end of times. All others will suffer long, severe deaths without hope of heavenly existence.

No one wants to feel inferior or spiritually inferior. Christian exclusiveness may have caused Mohammad to build an exclusive "superior" religion to give hope to his people. His Koran gives spiritual value to Muslims above all others – similar to Christianity. Mohammad even gives Muslims the right to kill anyone refusing to convert to Islam.

Religions perpetuate control over people in many ways. My hope is that world spiritual leaders will unite the best of all religions to include everyone in peace. Think what can be accomplished if all peoples of the world work together to enhance quality of life and life after death for all. As a world ling, I love the human race holistically and pray for human spiritual advancement.

True spiritual leaders promote diverse spiritual opportunities for all. Christians believe God, through Jesus, gives spiritual certainty to all who believe in Jesus.

If a doctor developed healing technology and saved many lives, we would praise him for his work. If he did not share his healing technology and died, we would blame him for not sharing his life saving technology.

Jesus developed healing and spiritual technology. He did not record His technology for future generations. Eventually, much of

Jesus' healing technology was lost. Christians do not blame Jesus for not recording His work and technology.

Humans are limited with little concept of perfect. We describe God as perfect. If we learn, God learns and will become more perfect tomorrow! If God is perfect, He can improve perfection. God is always the "current" definition of perfection.

If Jesus is alive, or spiritually alive, as we Christians believe, certainly, His thinking, knowledge, and abilities have progressed over the last two thousand years. Jesus and God are beyond the Jesus and God of two thousand years ago.

God and human minds construct virtual holograms in spiritual dimensions by interacting with and integrating sensations from three spatial, and one time, dimensions. All atomic activities in the universe create electromagnetic radiation and other field forces that extend throughout the universe, as God, with each nearby point in space having slightly different hologram perspectives.

The idea of God being everywhere is understandable. For example, I can take my cell phone many places and send and receive information. God and our minds are universal cell phones sensitive to spiritual frequencies throughout the universe.

In uncertain times, Jesus spoke with certainty. Characters in the Old Testament went to heaven. Jesus said no one goes to heaven except through Him. I must interpret that Jesus was referring to those present.

We develop mind models for navigating our environments. Many of us believe in Jesus' model that guided His life and sometimes guides ours. Good Christian leaders reasonably extend Jesus' model to meet today's complexities. Scientists must have confidence in their instruments and models to understand God's universe for the benefit of God and man.

Organizing and uniting science, Christian, and manic experiences present new spiritual concepts. This work reveals inner mental and spiritual processes.

There was a brief record of Jesus when He was twelve. Then there was no record until He began preaching at the age of thirty. With such expected responsibilities and stress, Jesus probably became a manic-depressive. When He lived, anyone being out of control would have been stigmatized and hidden from the public. It takes years to overcome manic depression. Manic-depressives are stigmatized today.

Jesus later developed an amazing ability to communicate with God and fulfilled prophecy. It was never recorded that Jesus was a well read scholar. He simply learned to communicate with and listen to God. Manic-depressives receive strong messages from God, today.

I give spiritual importance to scientists who discover physical architecture of God's universe. From spiritual experiences, I believe God revealed His architecture to Einstein for him to develop such abstract theories. A key to spiritual discovery is to concentrate in one arena of interest over a long period of time. Jesus also did this.

As an engineer, I marvel at the universe and human designs. Humans are God's design. DNA is God's framework for designing and updating the human family.

We cannot improve spiritual communication abilities and attain God consciousness if trying to think like someone else. We must mentally reconstruct to develop reasoning to complete our souls. The first part of mental reconstruction is unlearning indoctrination, fears, and effects of traumas. Christians believe they must develop a personal relationship with Jesus, now integrated within God, to attain eternal life. Many religions are rigid, do not allow compromise, and encourage worship with ritualistic, primal awe.

Some of the Bible was revealed through dreams and visions. With resonating electromagnetic and spiritual waves, God can be received and interpreted by human minds. Spiritual waves have not been detected by scientists with their instruments. Many of us receive dreams, visions, and revelations from God. Spiritual communications remain private between God and each of us.

In England in the 1500s and 1600s, people were forced "to believe" as the king or queen dictated or face death. The King James Bible was written in this environment. Differing believers had to hide their beliefs or face death. Similarly, today, Christian followers are taught that they can only receive significant spiritual messages through traditional spiritual leaders or face stigmatism. Traditional religious leaders continue their power and control.

Business, political, and spiritual leaders have falsified histories for centuries to continue their influence, policies, and successes. In our lifetimes we have seen businesses (Enron, Madoff) and religions (the catholic sex scandals) lie to continue their organizations. Religious dogma has been skewed to attract and indoctrinate followers. Today, religious leaders are rewarded by numbers of their followers, and money they take in.

Science is an increasingly organized model to discover and document repeatable facts about man, the earth, the universe, and possibly God. Fundamental Christians ignore astronomical and carbon dating science, insisting the earth and universe are only 6000 years old. In traditional religious times, writers thought the world was flat and aggrandized their heroes' to increase their own importance. Early scientists were jailed for expressing views opposing established religions.

Science supports creation and evolution. Astronomy, physics, and nuclear science make it factual that the universe is billions of years old and not a few thousand years old. Without today's science and math, traditional religious writers would think six thousand years was a long time. They interpreted God's analog message the best they could. Religions have resisted scientific discovery for centuries.

The Catholic meltdown is an example of spiritual fraud. When catholic priests were exposed, catholic leaders transferred priests to other dioceses to maintain the church's power rather than caring for the abused.

It is simplistic to believe traditional religious leaders have perfectly interpreted, translated, and updated God's words over thousands of years. With each interpretation and translation, spiritual leaders have altered messages to appeal to current generations.

From traditional religions, miracle implies a spiritual event beyond reasoning that should not be reasoned about. Miracles are influenced by a higher power for human benefit. With new science, medical, and spiritual technologies, miracles may be understood.

God has complete up-to-date awareness of all events in the universe up to the current point in time. Integrating light over three spatial and one time dimensions for historical awareness, independent of space and time, requires six additional degrees of freedom. God and man predict the future in a virtual time dimension. God's additional awareness during our lifetimes are nearly negligible compared to His virtual awareness over 13.7 billion years. God is so very nearly constant.

Humans are mental and, sometimes, physical modelers. We extend imagination to fit important things into our models of understanding. Fundamental Christians fit daily life and spiritual beliefs into ancient biblical models that have been updated over thousands of years. Christians have been brainwashed to give little importance to current spiritual messages. Most religions preach supreme importance of their dogma with blind belief and little reason.

All electromagnetic and other waves in the universe are created by uncertainties from instabilities. God's constant spiritual waves synchronize with brain waves to produce resonances within human minds. God's spiritual wave information is similar to computer binary that can be interpreted similarly into all languages.

God creates fundamental spiritual awareness upon conception that can exist beyond physical lives. God's complete knowledge of the universe resides in every point of the universe including within our brains. Human spiritual knowledge recedes into the subconscious mind as our free wills became dominant. If we surrender free will, and God influences our minds, He certainly influences new born babies without mental resistance to His guidance.

Jesus said, "In my father's house are many rooms (mansions)," (John 14:2). Jesus spoke to ancient audiences in a language they understood. I translate this sentence as: "There are many spiritual frequencies in heaven which will be home to saved souls and their spiritual thoughts for eternity." I have little belief there is a hotel in heaven for physical bodies. Our spiritual resonances expand into God's existence throughout the universe in relativistic spiritual time and space, forever. We know so little about forever. I doubt forever will last a trillion years.

Spiritual awareness resonates forever without requiring physical energy. Spiritual light may be visible in the form of bodies as it ascends to Eternity. Upon death, spiritual light was described in the Bible as:

". . . horses of fire, and separated the two of them; and Elijah went up by a whirlwind into heaven," (2 Kings 2:11.)

In the "flash of death," complete lifetime memories are read from holographic neural membranes and transformed into eternal dimensions independent of physical energy, space, and time for those passing the final bar.

During life, severe pain raises mental energy above free will levels. Thoughts, of helping others while in severe pain, demand God's attention. In severe pain, Jesus forgave those who tortured Him, and opened spiritual channels for believers to communicate with God.

Humans and the universe evolve. God's continuous spiritual analog message is perfect. Spiritual writers are not. Conservative Christians believe the Bible is perfect. We must judge spiritual writing. Conservatives resist change, science, and invention. Religious leaders and scientists must understand limitations of quantum uncertainties in the universe and in human beliefs.

God is constant. Everything made by man degrades over time.

Some spiritual leaders use religious terminology to intimidate. Asking others aggressively if they are saved is degrading. Many religious leaders hold their beliefs as equal to science facts. Religions and science are different paths for understanding God and His universe.

God consists of a "near" infinite number of spiritual waves and resonances. He is "Light" from every atom. Our unique spiritual resonances can receive spiritual messages from God in a personal, meaningful way. Our minds are waves in an ocean of spiritual waves.

We have little interest or excitement in "certain physical" things and events. Winning a game that is certain is of little excitement or pleasure. Winning tough competitions with uncertain outcomes is rewarding. Overcoming uncertainties are God's and Man's greatest achievements. However, as we get older, we have greater interest in justifying our lives for "spiritual certainty."

God or Light, traveling at the speed of light, integrates space, matter, and time awareness into holistic completeness, independent of physical dimensions. Including scientific facts within religions will increase believers' spiritual discovery and confidence. Philosophers and physicists, with mathematical, physical, and human insight, will enhance spiritual understanding. Physicists should not be reluctant to add to or dispute "spiritual" beliefs and opinions. Responsibilities need abilities, and abilities need responsibilities. Scientists will eventually understand spiritual dimensions. Whatever God "thinks" or does becomes reality.

Histories are factual. Futures are probabilistic and predictable with levels of uncertainty. Foundations of the universe are built upon quantum uncertainties. God has a probabilistic understanding of the future. He would have little purpose if He knew His, our, and, the universe's entire futures. He would be only a simple recorder as the universe and our lives progress. Our God is greater than that.

We and God make decisions. Decisions change the future. The universe is constructed with quantum uncertainty and probability. God integrates uncertainties to construct the next iteration of quantum time into a certain purpose for the universe. Iterations of quantum time are founded upon elementary particle uncertainties.

Even though God makes perfect integrations over, and decisions from, awareness of all universal quantum data, elementary particle uncertainties cause unpredictability. This process is like predicting the weather. With their iterative models of the earth's atmosphere, forecasters predict tomorrow's weather better than next month's weather.

God makes perfect quantum decisions to evolve the universe and, with our surrender to Him, nurtures our minds with His purposes. Would it not be great to scientifically prove God's guiding spiritual communications? Following His guidance would become scientific.

Can we prove the brain has subconscious processes? With electroencephalograms, microprobes, and repeated experiments we may correlate consistent subconscious brain activities with specific conscious ideas. In the same manner, can we scientifically prove God's existence?

God and mental processes integrate and record physical events into spiritual dimensions for awareness and memory. We should not limit God or our minds to physical dimensions. Scientists may become able to calculate integration properties of spiritual dimensions.

If scientists could measure very long electromagnetic and other field force waves from galaxies they may be able to decipher spiritual waves. Wave lengths might be long as galaxies. It would take sensitive instruments over long times to measure slight changes.

Man has always related things he does not understand to things he understands. We can relate only some aspects of God to our limited senses and mental abilities.

Field forces between the earth and sun may produce cognition similar to activities in the brain. The sun and earth are aware of each other. Analyzing electromagnetic and other field force activities between the sun, earth, and other planets might allow proof that God exists. Gravity provides constant information and a consistent force between the earth and sun.

We can only write with words we, and others before us, have defined. When asked for my spiritual references, my answer is: "I need only one reference – God." Most gentiles did not believe in Jesus until two to three hundred years after His death and resurrection. Today's spiritual innovations may not be recognized for centuries.

Exciting things, relationships, and methods are waiting to be invented, nurtured, and matured for God's and the universe's benefit. With spiritual freedom, together, we can benefit the universe and God.

Fundamentally, we are all God's children. If truly spiritual, we will recognize and nurture God within all others. Then the world would be truly blessed.

CHAPTER 18

Inventing the Future!

"I think; therefore, I am!"

Rene Descartes

Renew your mind to invent a spiritual future.

Hugh D. Fulcher

In the first half of the seventeenth century, Descartes added science and mathematics to the philosophy of the day for reasoning about the physical world, his own existence and life, and God's existence. Descartes claimed to be the first to separate the mind from physical things.

Without energy to relate physical things, humans could not think of, or control, the physical world or emotional relationships. Without an emotional God, the physical universe would not exist. At the beginning of time before He created the physical universe, God was initially "all powerful" but had little to think about or control.

Without uncertainty, God would not need to control anything. A simple analogy of God controlling the universe might be continuously juggling three balls. There is uncertainty when controlling three balls with two hands. One has to predict future tosses and catches.

New thoughts, words, and actions are built upon "once new" thoughts, words, and actions, including those of parents, teachers, and famous thinkers and doers.

Thinking holistically without subjects or objects is spiritual thinking: "Rain, shine, sooth, see, care, love, heal, compassion, guide, pleasant, aware, complete, joy, slow, fast." Imagine each action or feeling being constructed throughout the universe equally influencing the entire universe. With more global thinking, we will invent a spiritual future.

Good speakers use repetition, logic or deception, and vary volume and gestures to captivate and indoctrinate audiences. Writers became important in traditional religious times by writing about important, emotional things. This is still true today.

Church services unite congregations emotionally with spiritual songs. Preachers present ideas, which are easily accepted by congregations. Some repeat and add to these ideas – elevating emotional importance with high energy words and gestures for indoctrination beyond reason. Religion is big business in America. Ministers become wealthy, are well respected, and attract beautiful wives.

Children are more emotional than adults. High energy implies greater importance. Elevating voices and gestures raises congregation excitement to vulnerable childhood learning and indoctrination levels for spiritual, or evil, purposes. The unthinking public is attracted to strength and power without reasoning.

Inner mental processes occur at much faster frequencies than processes constructing slow-frequency, high-energy, conscious words, necessary for communication. At the beginning of severe, or life threatening, trauma, the mind flashes beyond attachment to physical time processing into spiritual time processing with unusual awareness of inner, spiritual thoughts. Minds are entirely spiritual, momentarily, during "flashes," and for longer times with practice.

Humans experience greater "reality" when seeing things in color rather than in black and white. Our eyes are sensitive only to a small spectrum of electromagnetic radiation – light.

God sees His, or true, reality through all electromagnetic and gravity waves – "God's Light." He is aware of our fast subconscious thought waves in spiritual time before we are conscious of our own thoughts constrained to physical time. If color gives humans a higher awareness of reality, imagine God's reality. His understanding of Light, Himself, is very different from shallow human understanding.

Christians must believe God exists in a very different time and structure existence than humans if He is omniscient and hears all prayers from every point in the universe. With advances in understanding relativity limits, scientists will develop spiritual communication technology, beyond current imagination.

Through all electromagnetic and gravity waves, God "sees" and "sees through" us in spiritual depth with complete awareness of our, and the universe's, entire history. From God's perspective, the current configuration of the universe is a higher dimensional mirror reflection of its and His entire history.

If we knew our entire futures, we could not make decisions or have anything to look forward to. Our lives, the universe, and God are based upon fundamental particle uncertainties as understood by quantum mechanics. If God knew the entire future of the universe, He could make no decisions.

God would have awareness of only a predestined universe processing alone a continuous blue print containing its history, present, and future. God would have nothing, or no uncertainties, to look forward to.

Humans would be predestined also with no individual purpose. Prayer would have no purpose. Human purpose would only be to complete God's and the universe's holistic, or holy, defined history.

In the beginning, there were uncertainties of nothing before time. God transformed uncertainties of nothing into increasing universal disorder in order to construct higher spiritual (and mental) order. Life is based upon uncertainties. The uncertainties of gambling, or getting much for little, can become all encompassing and ruin lives. Anyone who thinks he/she is certain about how to control other's lives destroys minds, and is a disgrace to God.

The brain and mind have uncertainties each moment. Billions of brain cells are disorganized without a united purpose. However, an internal or external stimulus can activate nerve cells to unite for one holistic purpose. More complex things can be more spiritual then the sum of individual things. We cannot imagine God's complexities.

We may relate brain cells to human awareness. When stimulated, individual brain cell awareness synchronizes to form the unified awareness of the human mind. Synchronized atoms within the universe construct God.

Since caveman times, men have felt the need to be in control. In some ways, women handle uncertainty better than men. Women accept uncertainties of finding things in a variety of stores. Men look like deer caught in headlights. However, women have been genetically indoctrinated to look for certainty in husbands. They are attracted to confident men. Unfortunately, many confident men have confidence in deception and drunken lies.

We study great art to understand great artists. We study the universe to understand God's perfect combination of physical uncertainties and spiritual certainties.

I believe early Christian writers wrote as truthfully as they could but having human biases and uncertainties. Several writers corroborated Jesus' three years of teaching. Jesus must have been logical and truthful to have excited so many people into following, and writing about, Him.

Jesus did not use threats or force. People discover deceit unless indoctrinated by life threats or existence after life threats.

Nuclear, chemical, physical, and mental activities have different uncertainties. Electromagnetic radiation and gravity have uncertainties. Paranormal activities, apparently, caused by extreme, or once extreme, emotions override "established" physical laws at times. God is consistent with His unemotional probability and mathematics laws, and His emotional paranormal laws. We have little knowledge God's emotional or paranormal laws. We must expand thinking beyond sense-initiated thoughts to understand God, and His universe.

Physicists are beginning to study the nature of paranormal occurrences beyond current physics laws. God dwells within spiritual space and time, or heaven, which is integrated within, and surrounds, physical space and time. Incomplete transitions of the mind from physical time and existence into spiritual time and existence may cause paranormal incompleteness.

Was and is Jesus God? Certainly His localized physical body was not. If Jesus' Mind was God, It was integrated throughout the universe with God in spiritual time in prayer, and in spiritual space beyond physical space. Jesus did and does paranormal miracles. We pray to integrate our minds with Jesus' mind and God in hopes of receiving love, guidance, and compassion; and sometimes, giving praises, and expecting miracles.

Paranormal events seem to be initiated by extremely emotional and painful events, or death. Jesus' death was extremely emotional and painful. I, like many, have experienced paranormal events.

On September 22, 2009, I was waiting for my son with normal parental concern when a child is driving at night in the rain. Suddenly, I received unexpected, frightening inner words: "What in the world will I do if Keston dies?" A few minutes later Keston calls on his mobile phone saying he has had a car accident, but was all right.

He hydroplaned on water in the road and spun several yards into a field. Momentarily thinking he might die.

He was about 45 miles away at 10:00 PM and unhurt. A wrecker pulled his car back to the road. There was considerable damage, but he was able to drive to my home that night.

This incident confirms high-energy paranormal, extrasensory, or spiritual communication. During high-energy emotions beyond free will limits, humans, with strong bonds, can experience paranormal, spiritual communications. Can loved ones with strong bonds invent their own spiritual communication language for normal situations?

A traumatized mind extends beyond free will thinking to communicate spiritually over long distances. God is aware when we suffer and hurt. We do not suffer alone but for everyone in the universe. Suffering for good causes is spiritual. Jesus suffered.

I should note the paranormal translation. My son's emotional thought was: "I have no control. I am going to die." The spiritual translation to me was, "What in the world will I do if Keston dies?" The message was translated for my perspective. This translation confirms that God understands the needs of His people.

Scholars have studied Jesus' paranormal resurrection. God suffered during Jesus' severe physical and emotional pain, and death. A supporter or supporters may have stolen Jesus' body and secretly buried it to keep it from being desecrated. God may have given Jesus' mind or spirit a paranormal body through spiritual forces, or supernaturally healed Jesus' physical body extremely fast.

I do not worry about details of Jesus' resurrection. After the resurrection, He was seen by many. God accepted Jesus within Himself to create His spiritual Trinity: Father, Son, and Holy Spirit.

Computers, mobile phones, other electronic devices, and the brain, work efficiently and faster using less energy. As electronics get smaller, I envision electronic brain implants for a variety of communication and security purposes:

- Communications between brains and minds of emotionally related people would not need words but consist of continuous waves or resonances. Communications would be faster, more truthful, and complete or holy – God-like. Thought "passwords" and encryptions would protect spiritual communications. Brainwaves are unique.
- Persistent brainwaves, preparing for threatening actions, would be electronically monitored and documented by law enforcement computers. Law enforcement officers would be frequently tested for truth in their policing activities. Societies could track, document, and mentally heal, perpetrators, to prevent pain, agony, murders, and expenses. Technology would prevent "Big Brother" government control. Costs of crime prevention and prisons would be less. Court processes and trials would be quicker and efficient with less expense. Convicted felons would be required to have brain electronic implants to prevent repeated offences.
- Normal, law abiding brain waves would be transmitted to addressees, only.
- Business communications would be faster, precise, and truthful.
- Continuous waves would improve communications to and from God. Humans would learn to serve God and receive blessings, including paranormal miracles.
- Micro-electronic devices could monitor and transmit health analyses to consciousness, and to health care computers. Medical care would be given early, precisely, and without unnecessary medical procedures, to save expenses.
- Under a psychiatrist's guidance, perhaps Dr. FEE's, embedded microprocessors will recognize high frequency,

repressed trauma memories, and send precise frequencies to activate and reduce their energy transforming them into more normal, conscious memories. In the future, mental reconstruction, and the clear mind, will be achieved in weeks rather than in decades.

- Spiritual communications and inner knowledge will be developed more through continuous waves, not discrete words. Microprocessors could notify individuals if not being spiritual.
- Micro-electronic computer/transmitter/receiver implants could be charged by specific brain wave thoughts, or by remote electromagnetic charging devices.

Lies and deception infest so many human communications and have made so many unworthy people wealthy and arrogant. Look at drug cartel atrocities. An increasingly connected world cannot continue for long based upon special interest lies. Open, honest societies are the solution to world prosperity and peace.

Humans need to mentally reconstruct for less self-centered, and more worldly, orientation. However, giving should go only so far. All able individuals must be educated and motivated to care for themselves, love others, and give to the needy. Repressed love and anger emotions should be stimulated to release energy and culture more normal, conscious feelings and emotions.

Repeated abuse ingrains rigid repressed feelings and thoughts in the brain. When abuse memories are stimulated, the mind reacts with childish out of control, sporadic, and illogical defenses. In expanding human free will toward global benefits, we will become more God-like, and receive His love, wisdom, and blessings beyond imagination.

We must reason about, and strive against prejudice and deception in religion, government, and business, or life on this planet is doomed. With technology innovations in communication and with increased human abilities and complexities, the future is the "clear mind!" Confident minds do not need to lie or deceive.

Complex American businesses force employees to work together and communicate with interdependence to accomplish complex goals and products. We learn from one another. Unfortunately, families today have little interdependence, respect for one another, or common purpose. America's foundation is crumbling.

American politics has become goofy. Rather than solving problems, politicians are more interested in showing their party they can get reelected and help reelect other members of their party. Both parties present half-truths in speeches and advertisements. Americans are influenced by emotional sound bites. Americans must demand that politicians present logical steps for accomplishing promised goals.

Companies are friendly and promising when selling health insurance. They pay only a small percentage of their overall premiums for actual health care expenses. Salaries and profits are excessive. However, if we become injured or sick, many insurance companies lie and do every thing they can to minimize payments, and discontinue coverage. Easy wealth has corrupted health insurance companies (and Wall Street) to the level of drug cartel corruption and atrocities. Neither cares about, or has compassion for, human suffering or life.

My initial intentions were to write about my personal suffering from, and healing of, bipolar disorder, and help protect my children from, or heal their, bipolar disorder. God commanded: "Don't Leave God Out!" These words meant for me to listen to God and His universe, and obey. In a small way my healing scope extended into the universe. I have more understanding that Jesus' severe suffering influenced the world, and universe. With work toward understanding and praising God, readers can, to some extent, influence the universe.

Did Jesus "save" the world and universe? I think this means that Jesus gave believers a path to be accepted in heaven by God: praising God, believing in Jesus, and asking for forgiveness of wrong doings. My path to heaven has extended into more involvement toward understanding God and His universe. There are spiritual people who do not know, or accept, Jesus as their Savior for their path to heaven. I think all humble believers who surrender to God can find or construct their own path to heaven, possibly with greater difficulty. Jesus is the basic foundation for my path.

Traditional religious leaders will disavow my philosophy and spiritual work. They will do anything to maintain and increase their power over everyone who will listen to them. For centuries religious leaders and kings tortured and killed anyone daring to believe differently than they did. People with different spiritual beliefs were prosecuted or executed as heretics. They continued to convince everyone they could control that only they knew the perfect way to communicate with, and worship, God.

I am a simple scribe trying to listen to, communicate with, and write about, God – for my children's and my healing and spiritual reasoning. I try to be honest, make mistakes, and do not preach or indoctrinate. My processes are not the only way to communicate with, and worship, God. There are many paths. Readers should develop their own reason through study and prayer.

I work to understand God's logic and His universe, discovered through science. My hope is to inspire scientists, open minded spiritual leaders, and readers to continue, improve, and expand my models for spiritual truth. Being a heretic today may be a good thing. My path has not been easy. My predictions may also be predicted by others.

I have been sprinting toward the clear mind for over seventeen years without knowing the finish line, or life after the race is run. However, this amazing journey has been filled with such unusual and wonderful sensations and ideas!

The years required for my mental reconstruction reveals the complicated structure of the brain. Unless reconstructing, individuals know little of the importance that countenance and attitude have on building the physical structure of the brain for a creative mind. Before mental reconstruction, thoughts felt as if submerged and swimming in water. After mental reconstruction, thoughts feel as if flying through air.

For anyone to acquire spiritual healing powers, he must develop his own healing resonances and cure before sharing healing resonances with, and healing, others. Jesus must have healed His own inner stresses.

We must learn to enjoy our lives, the lives of others, and God. Otherwise, the American dream will invent a less certain future.

CHAPTER 19

Clinical Trials and Implementation

This chapter presents suggestions to assist research institutions develop clinical procedures from *God, the Universe, and You* and *Bipolar Blessings & Mind Expansion.* A goal is to partner with a Research University or Laboratory to attain NIMH grants to develop clinical trails of suggested methods. Research institutions should refine processes into accepted clinical procedures. First volunteers selected should include children and adults having frequently reoccurring manic episodes, manic symptoms, or adverse reactions to psychiatric medications.

Volunteer patients need abilities to perform exercises regularly and understand modeling to help the subconscious mind understand and heal its self. Over time, many patients may become freed of depression, manic episodes, other disorders, and even institutions.

The author has developed innovative mind technology that has demonstrated successful results in curing his own bipolar disorder. Research given here should complement mind/body/spirit research at NIMH. Restructuring the fabric of the brain is a solution for curing bipolar disorder. Unique physical exercises stimulate energy releases from traumatized neural networks, and mind models guide healing.

An instruction manual should be developed based on this book and *Bipolar Blessings & Mind Expansion* for use by researchers to guide patient healing. Research is suggested for correlating neck energy release sensations, SCAPS, with childhood and adult trauma experiences, and lifetime stresses. Child trauma scars are less established and should be easier to release.

Image analyses from throat, neck, and brain scans are needed to record restructuring as a result of psychiatric exercises and other methods. Scans should be made for beginning patients, and repeated on a yearly basis as practice progresses. Hopefully, clinical procedures will develop quicker paths for mental healing. Freedom from manic worry is life changing and allows long-range planning.

The author has not had manic episodes for fifteen years. Performing psychiatric exercises has helped develop criteria for the clear mind. Manic-depressives and all of society will benefit from attaining clear minds. Imaging scans should register very different brain, throat, and neck activities when clear mind criteria are met. The author works to make mental reconstruction easier and quicker for manic-depressives and patients with other stress disorders.

In recent years, researchers have found that exercise is more effective in curing depression than current antidepressants. Unique psychiatric exercises should also be significant for healing depression.

Advanced throat, neck, and brain scan results should be correlated to SCAP releases and behavior changes. Medications may be needed to provide stability and enhance results. Bipolar and other stress-related disorders, and reactions to trauma, will become better understood.

Some research institutions may have prospective patients and equipment already available from current projects. The more a patient learns about his own mind, the better his chances are of controlling moods and emotions. The mind is good at thinking about outward things, but needs training in thinking inwardly into its own processes.

Unique exercise effects on the brain are not unlike effects of body building exercises. Consistent body building exercises at limits over time can be spectacular for developing the body. Psychiatric exercises at limits can also be spectacular for developing the brain.

Psychiatric medications often produce unusual feelings and zombie slowness that adversely affect daily functions and quality of life. Cultivating physical changes within the fabric of the brain makes permanent psychiatric changes for curing bipolar disorder.

Institutional research needs to extend five years or longer to analyze results. The mind heals slowly. The prospect of the brain and mind developing its own permanent cure of bipolar disorder is significant and proven with one individual.

The author is available to institutions for assisting research applications. Together potential partners and the author will determine the scope of projects. This research should develop cures for stress related disorders and free some from institutions. The author is requesting feedback to improve models and effects of models.

With years of meditation and mental discipline, the Dali Lama's brain scans showed high levels of activity in the pleasure centers of the brain. The author also expects to have high activity in the pleasure and other centers of the brain.

A goal is to share information and document successes so everyone can benefit health wise and financially. Manic episodes and their uncertainties are costly to individuals and families.

Therapists should encourage their patients to use advanced psychiatric guidelines and develop their own self-healing methods. Living on the edge for self-healing will become more accepted by psychiatrists. To improve in sports, we have to live on the edge at times. We need to know, and then gently extend, our limits in competitions and in mental reconstruction and healing.

Care should be taken to develop comprehensive questions to correlate SCAP sensations and trauma experiences. Initial interviews should include brief analysis of patient SCAP releases. Plans are for a psychology researcher to assist in developing questions.

The author plans to help establish criteria as to when manic-depressives are considered cured. This designation will be helpful in reducing medical insurance costs and assist in career stability.

Neuron and glia membranes are stable components of brain cells and should be analyzed microscopically. To some lesser extent, analyzing brain cell bodies may also be helpful.

Brain cell membranes should be analyzed for electromagnetic absorption, transmission, and reflective properties. Supplements may be developed to enhance membrane properties and mental abilities. Neuron and glia membranes contain the fabric of our memories. Evolving life experiences add structure to membrane fabric and DNA.

We cannot determine where each photon is absorbed in membranes but we can measure their integrated effects on neural membranes. Human histories are stored on brain, neck, throat, and, to some extent, other cell membranes.

Implementation of new methods will take time. NIMH, psychologists, physicians, and politicians will refine and implement processes. The general public will be introduced to processes after experimentation and refinement by medical professionals. Seeds have been sown. Let us begin.

Implementation of methods should be a reality. Today's ideas are tomorrow's reality. The author is available for presentations to interested groups.

CHAPTER 20

Conclusion

Crossing the Bar

"Sunset and evening star,
And one clear call for me.
And may there be no moaning of the bar
When I put out to sea.

But such a tide as moving seems asleep,
Too full for sound or foam.
When that which drew from out the boundless deep
Turns again home.

Twilight and evening bell,
And after that the dark!
And may there be no sadness of farewell
When I embark.

For though from out our bourne of time and place
The flood may bear me far,
I hope to see my Pilot face to face
When I have crossed the bar...."

Alfred Tennyson

Subconsciously and consciously, we search for completion in things we do. We must talk and write in complete sentences. The author's amazing bipolar disorder cure is by discovering and reducing neural network tensions to build a complete mind.

It is difficult to conclude such an unusual work. The author is grateful for spiritual healing, insightful feelings, and words from God. He has strived to present creative ideas truthfully. If he has paid careful attention to messages received from God, healing and spiritual processes presented will benefit the overstressed and readers.

Coping with severe bipolar disorder, the author has endured unimaginable horrors of insanity and near-death. At one point in depression, he could not think of a single word. During that period, the author had devastating uncertainties of whether thoughts were reasonable or believable. At other times, he has had brief unbelievable highs and felt he could think through and solve any problem.

The author has been blessed in developing a cure for his bipolar disorder. Constructing creative processes from manic uncertainties became spiritual. He fought an inner war and survived.

In the beginning of lonely struggles, goals were only a faraway dream. After years of psychiatric exercises, mental processes have converged for a relaxed, efficient brain. Stability, sanity, creativity, and spiritual confidence have been worth the author's long struggle. Thinking is a continuous, recursive process, which expands with meditation, study, imagination and challenges; otherwise, it shrinks.

Manic episodes occurred from 1977 to 1994. Mind models and psychiatric exercises began in 1993. Mental reconstruction excitement increased over the next ten years and accelerated over the last five years with science, mental, and spiritual integration. The author has successfully developed exercises and mind models to clear the brain of trauma effects and improve mental processes.

Being cured of bipolar disorder enhances creatively and spirituality. Mental pain and emotional tragedies may be reduced by having children practice mental reconstruction early in life. More children and adults will be affected by bipolar disorder as they exercise less and are exposed to more frequent reasoning challenges. Grownups who repeatedly fail to meet reasoning challenges rupture their childhood emotional thinking limits that cause bipolar disorder.

As with other scientific discoveries, the author made an educated guess to cure his bipolar disorder. He predicted that slight sounds, or SCAPS, resulting from neck exercises were releases of high-energy from localized repressed trauma memories. Confirmation of his theory was that SCAP sensations would change in character and position over time with exercises. SCAP sensations have dramatically evolved from sharp spikes to flowing, over fifteen years of exercises.

SCAP energy release sensations have become increasingly exciting and pleasant throughout the years. After years of experiments, the mind feels the excitement of a pure waterfall after exercises. Healing processes for curing bipolar disorder are physics based, experimental, and extend into metaphysics.

Mind models should be bases for research to understand activations within the brain. We are just beginning to understand processes within the human mind.

With internet searches, electricity is used to search millions of servers to find millions of matches on selected topics in seconds. Our brains are just as amazing. They can also search millions of memories in fractions of a second for matches to support current thoughts and experiences. Both are unbelievably fast and amazing.

Working with laboratory mice, Joe Z. Tsien in the "The Memory Code," (1) Scientific American, July, 2007, has developed methods of digitizing brain responses to traumas. It has been known for some time that the hippocampus is instrumental in developing memory. Experimental methods included placing over 200 electrodes in CAI neurons within the hippocampus. Monitored neurons are divided into "cliques" that are activated by similar event categories. Staging traumatic events for mice and recording their neuron clique responses allows digitizing of mental processes for computer analyses.

Clique activations and their follow-up harmonic activations support my theory that subconscious activities and consciousness are developed by resonances throughout the brain. Hippocampus activities may initiate many resonances within the brain at any one time. Integration of electromagnetic radiation from clique activations, throughout the brain, creates mental holograms which are foundations of subconscious and conscious processes, including memory.

Dr. Tsien's work may have far reaching importance. Near the end of future generation's lives, they may have their neuron activities monitored and digitally stored as "personal" server memories. Physical bodies will die but minds may live forever as simulated mental processes within "personal" servers. "Computerized" minds may provide guidance for their great . . . great grandchildren and continue to learn with original personalities and skills.

In a distant future a parent might say, "I don't know, log on and ask your great . . . great grandmother. When you are through, don't forget to turn her off."

Nothing happens in the brain or universe or without energy transfer. Memory requires precise energy to activate specific resonances. It takes repeated exercises to reduce excess emotional energy from localized trauma memories and spread their excess energy throughout the brain as normal memories.

During the years of trauma energy releases followed by mental reconstruction, sensations activated by psychiatric exercises have spread to wider areas with less dense energy. Long years of psychiatric exercises, required to reconstruct the brain, confirm the intricacy of the fabric of the brain.

Repressed conflicting memories produce anxieties that children and adolescents do not know how to express. They feel inadequate to express them selves or to reduce their uncertainties. Feelings of failure become so overwhelming that some have seizures and others attempt to, or commit, suicide. Mental reconstruction should include processes for children and adolescents to express feelings and reduce tensions.

Children can be healed from bipolar disorder with less work than adults. Trauma energy potentials are less set and can be purged more easily. Along with a normal exercise program, children need to perform psychiatric neck resistance exercises to reduce trauma action potentials. With lowered trauma action potentials, the mind will become more confident, reasonable, and spiritual.

All activities within the brain create the mind, and the mind recursively controls the brain. Without the mind the brain has no purpose. Without activities of the brain, the mind does not exist. All physical activities within the universe create God. God controls the universe. Without God the universe has no purpose. Without the activities within the universe, God does not exist. Our brains are part of the universe, and our minds are part of God.

Beliefs and spirituality are an important part of mental health. We hold on to early emotional and spiritual beliefs until we have a significant emotional event. This event may be a spiritual relationship.

Mental and spiritual processes are iterative. There are no permanent mathematical solutions in the universe. Thinking processes iterate as they search to converge toward solutions. Man's best accomplishments dissolve in time. God continually iterates toward higher spiritual completeness as the universe evolves into greater physical disorder. God becomes more complete each day.

God created constant physical and spiritual laws as reactions to constant uncertainty and chaos. "Nothing before time" was complete uncertainty with no space and no references. God is referenced to the universe, and the universe is recursively referenced to God.

Spiritual Healing

Writing is an adventure into the inner mind. With persistent work in the same arena, God provides amazing ideas never thought possible. We should evaluate traditional tenets, and current spiritual ideas received by others. Inner thoughts received directly from God should frame the founding purpose for our lives.

Living on a mental edge with uncertainties beyond normal mental confinements is our choice. Once beginning an inner search, you will have a new self-image and goals. Take your mind to limits briefly, at times, to experience new mental and spiritual abilities and freedoms. God speaks to us softly, but sometimes astonishingly.

Creativity attracts spirituality, and recursively spirituality is the foundation of creativity. Constructing certain thinking from manic uncertainties is spiritual. A grateful attitude develops creative ideas.

Learning from trials and errors, the author hopes to help readers experience their minds more fully. He stresses his methods and models are not the only paths to heal the mind or experience God. Through personal relationships with God and your own experiments, construct your own spiritual reasoning. You were born with free will to develop your own thoughts and decisions.

Imagination creates exciting lives. Work to make thought patterns creative until they become part of you. With practice and patience, we can slowly restructure fundamental inner processes to accomplish amazing goals. Imagine goals being accomplished until they are realized. Be grateful for what you already have. Being consistently grateful refines mental resonances to attract spiritual frequencies and blessings. Visualize spiritual goals being true to guide your future. Positive thinking beyond self attracts God into our lives.

Much of life consists of repetitive and iterative experiences. However, we overcome uncertainties and challenges each day to prepare for exciting challenges in Heaven. Heaven with absolute certainty and no spiritual challenges or uncertainties would be Hell. There would be no reason for eternal life without continually looking forward to exciting heavenly challenges. Heavenly adventures may include assisting God in integrating uncertainties throughout the universe into spiritual certainty with perfect purpose.

People generally have expectations or models of faith to guide them in everyday life. Expectations help us predict how coworkers and family members will react to and accept us.

In depression or mania, the afflicted go beyond normal thinking limits with opportunities to refine spiritual understanding. Free will thinking is independent of God's guidance. Surrendering free will of truthful lives attracts God's guidance.

Take your mind to limits briefly, at times, to expand mental freedoms and receive spiritual messages! God normally speaks to us softly, but sometimes astonishingly with disappointment.

A clear mind freed of trauma effects will be more aware of inner processes for solving emotional and complex problems. We will have deeper purpose. A clear mind will have three improvements:

1. Relaxed emotional thinking limits for expanded reason developed by mental reconstruction and adult reasoning rather than by disorganized infant and childhood helter-skelter traumas and emotional experiences;

2. Faster analytical processes separated from sensing and muscle controlling processes - may attain the speed of dreams;

3. In-depth God consciousness for receiving spiritual communication directly in "words."

What may happen in the third level? God Consciousness could be attained whenever lowering or raising emotional energy levels beyond free-will frequencies. Spiritual communications would be received more as discrete words rather than difficult to define feelings. Higher spiritual reasoning and purpose will be shared throughout the world. The author's prayers are that readers will use their most precious gifts, their minds, to their fullest extent.

Spiritual Science

The author's religion is like his approach to science. Small individual things or statements have uncertainty, but the entire fabric throughout the universe integrates into a certain belief in an omnipresent and omnipotent God. Integration of science with Christianity, spiritual words received, and a holistic view of life with its wonder, confirms certainty of an all knowing God in this universe.

On a small scale, thinking begins with uncertainty. Molecules have uncertainties of passing through neuron membranes to create action potentials. Thinking is based upon probability of billions of brain cells firing in symphony to create one focused thought at a time.

Humans must have faith in predicting their abilities within environments in order to survive. In nature, larger things are generally more predictable than smaller things. Even space itself appears to be unpredictable and unstable on very, very small scales. Galaxies are more predictable than human sized things and humans are more predictable than atomic sized things.

Conflicts continue between science discoveries and beliefs of traditional religions. Both give generations abilities to predict the future. The author's research has resolved many conflicts between Intelligent Design and evolution.

Statistically evaluating current traditional believers' minds may scientifically confirm the truthfulness of traditional religions. Truthful religions nurture and expand the minds of followers.

With gentle spiritual messages shared, we can create a utopia on earth. There are no outsiders in a utopia. "Clear" religious leaders from all over the world will integrate certified messages from God as a basis for spiritual reasoning.

God responds to action potentials within prayers. He reflects symmetric resonating waves from our minds and souls as spiritual frequencies throughout the universe. Messages from God have a dual nature like that of light. Messages are holistic and flowing or are probabilistic and discrete. Before prayer, think of the happy times in your life and praise God for those times, feelings, and successes.

As well as listening to individual prayers, God statistically evaluates and integrates and all prayers from within the universe. God nurtures all humans holistically and individually as a choir director nurtures the integrated choir and its individuals.

Chemical and electromagnetic energy within the brain creates man's awareness. Nuclear, chemical, and electromagnetic energy throughout the universe creates God's awareness. Nuclear energy within stars creates much of God's power.

What does God look like? He is Light and looks like you. He is our spiritual reflection in an infinite mirror. He reflects more about us than we know about ourselves. He reflects our images as multidimensional holograms in all spiritual dimensions throughout the universe. God is the reflection of all atoms and physical things in the universe. He is an infinite Hologram with knowledge of each point within the universe from slightly different perspectives. God's time is relativistic to our time. He is aware of our thoughts before we are.

Eventually, cosmologists may indirectly discover the very low energy, very low frequency "constant" EMR waves of God's spiritual structure. Very low frequency waves have higher spiritual value. Spiritual waves allow very high density modulation. Are spiritual waves the long sought after ether physicists pursued in earlier years? Scientists may discover breakout spiritual communication technology. Can science reconnect Adam and Eve with God?

God's symmetric low frequency, low energy spiritual waves extend along all diameters of the universe in all true directions. Mental waves at each point in the universe and in all local directions can interact with God's waves.

Traditional religions should have a structured approach to accept science understanding of the brain and universe, and the physical brain's relationship to its spiritual mind. Spiritual leaders may inspire scientists to discover God. They should study and respect science as a method for understanding God's universe, and in turn, God. With attention on God, anything is possible. We need progress in science and in spiritual discovery in order to integrate the two.

Throughout history, the wealthy and powerful have tried to live forever. Prophets have tried to extend their influence forever. With advances and fast paced changes today, traditional religions seem less valid for some. Traditional religions have kept spiritual advancements in a time warp. Integrating current and traditional messages from God should make religions more valid.

The physical universe and God, separated by the speed of light, when in synergy construct one entity. Man and living beings are bridges between the physical and the spiritual.

Models of faith are developed by spiritual meditation, praying, reading the Bible and other religious books, physics, other sciences, and writing for understanding God. Each of us experiences struggles along unique spiritual paths.

What is the difference between mental or spiritual holograms and God, the Infinite Hologram? They are alike in that they coexist in the same spiritual space. The difference is that God is 10^{100} times more detailed, dense, and reflective, in spiritual space than our mental holograms. We need to purge all conflicting trauma scars for our minds to synchronize with God.

God wants us to experience heaven on earth as we would want for our children. Humans must do their part as God's children to synchronize our mental resonances with God's perfect resonance for Him to help us advance toward His perfect spiritual awareness.

We must learn about God in every way we can. With our current language, spiritual communications, and abilities we can expand the frontiers of spiritual wisdom beyond historical levels.

We can synchronize our minds for God Consciousness. Our duty is to rediscover our infant spiritual communication to receive God's guidance. God learns from us. If we make Him more aware of human lives, He can help us reduce pain and harm.

God breaking his (holistic) physical laws to do miracles is much like us breaking out of right-brained holistic baby thinking into left-brained specific up-close physical abilities and activities.

God gives us free will, but expects recursive, reflective relationships with us, as a father expects from a child. If we surrender to God's Will, our spirits resound throughout the universe independent of time into Eternity.

We should lose our wills within God's Will often. Human spiritual dimensions are independent of, and expand beyond, spatial dimensions. God's up-to-date awareness of our prayers exists on the far side of the universe.

A goal is to inspire the physics community to develop models of the mind and God, and communication methods between the two. Scientists may develop models demonstrating physical and spiritual synergy. If electromagnetic and chemical activities within our brains develop intelligence, these same activities throughout the universe must certainly develop a higher intelligence, God.

I love thinking about science, God's universe, and God. I do not pretend to be a Biblical scholar. If you have questions about the Bible, ask a minister or a priest. They can explain traditional beliefs.

Spiritual

With bipolar disorder, my spiritual path became involved. I needed to cast out sins or trauma scars, with a long mental reconstruction process, for attaining a clear mind to be spiritually "saved." Others have found spiritual rebirth easier with faith alone. Certainly every path to heaven is wonderful.

Our purpose is to extend knowledge into spiritual frontiers for us and for God. Moses, Jesus, and other true spiritual leaders were tightly bound to God's purposes. Will a new spiritual leader begin a spiritual revolution or will scientific discoveries understand God as an intricate part within our universe for guiding our lives?

An important part of faith in America is respect for ideas and freedoms of others. This is a social and spiritual miracle in America today. However, there are religious zealots who think their way is the only way to salvation.

Each life is precious to God and should be precious to us. God created each and every life with purpose. The worst sin is falsely referencing God as the reason for harming or killing others for selfish purposes. The meek shall inherent the earth. My prayer is that the meek will eventually include all of God's people in our world.

Religions, that preach their methods of worshipping and beliefs are superior, do God a disservice and condemn all others. Superior "religions" spawn ruthless dictators and terrorists. These historical mistakes have caused so much suffering and so many deaths. Self-aggrandizement destroys, divides, and does not unite.

Claiming spiritual superiority is the worst of sins. Spiritual superiority does not exist. We were all perfectly spiritual upon conception. God evaluates our souls at the moment of death as our final judgment. Many claiming to be saved do the worst of things. God has chosen many of us to interpret and write for Him. With limited skills, I write truthfully.

God and humans seek completeness. "Nothing" was a simple yet complete existence before space and time without any frame of reference. Through gravity, God strives to return the universe to this completeness before time.

There are models of faith in the Bible. Noah had faith he had received a message from God. He followed God's commands, built an ark, and saved his righteous family from the flood. Moses had faith, followed God's commands, and freed the Israelites from slavery. Jesus frequently received and spoke the "Word of God" as He preached and performed miracles. Jesus' works formed a model of faith and a religion that many of us believe in and follow today.

Many of us believe God is infinite from our perspective. However, humans have little idea what infinite really means. God challenges us to expand our minds into the universe. As He enriches our lives, we have some ability to enrich God and the universe.

Spiritual words mean very little unless we explain attitudes, emotions, and circumstances when receiving God's words. We must increasingly update our models of God to understand and serve Him.

The author has studied the nature of his inner voices and sensations he has received and strongly assigns them as blessings from God. Patiently interpreting messages from God is like interpreting dreams. Once understood, the meaning becomes crystal clear.

In storm filled minds, God comes to us as a tornado abruptly blowing us in His spiritual direction. This book is the author's summer breeze and his storm.

It is impossible to reduce distrust and hatred with traditional religions claiming spiritual superiority. Spiritual superiority practices bring damnation to their followers and to all others. Power hungry leaders dishonor God, their followers, and all of humanity. With global communications of today, we have an opportunity to build bridges for an inclusive integrated world religion.

God's family unit is all living beings with resonating spiritual characteristics. This definition of universal spiritual identity is vague but difficult to make more precise. The author is beginning his spiritual identity. Many, who are humble, surely have well defined spiritual identities.

Many of us believe God answers our prayers. At times, we feel God's closeness as He responds to us. Let's make an analogy. A good earthly father has ten children. He loves them all but has to spend time and energy working. He spends time with each child and teaches them as their abilities and his time allows. When all are healthy, he spends more time with those showing more promise. God may do the same.

God keeps track of and guides all living beings throughout the universe. His arena of influence is astronomical compared to our own.

God has love or integration responsibilities throughout the universe. The more similar spiritual messages He receives from earth, the more important their action potentials become. The author has received many emotional and spiritual feelings before receiving his full blown amazing messages in words.

His "forgotten" highly emotional, spiritual word message was initiated by anger and disappointment. Emotional disappointment may justify anger that opens spiritual channels. If attaining eternal life, we will look up to all we have looked down on in earthly life.

If man were to reason about and integrate spiritual messages, God will guide us to a united future. We should learn about God with the science logic and reason we apply to learn about the universe.

Most of us are biased or prejudiced. In some ways, we think we are better than others. When some people receive spiritual messages, they think they should declare themselves a spiritual leader or prophet. This has not been the author's calling. Self-centeredness and power seeking corrupt spiritual messages.

My goal is to have patience and write for assisting believers in receiving messages from God. We do not need only one spiritual leader, but need to work together on an equal basis to understand God.

We must recognize that man can only translate God's perfect flowing language into imperfect "manmade" words. All religions and religious leaders are imperfect. Priests, ministers, and missionaries receive callings to become humble servants of God as models of faith in traditional ways. They accept challenges to understand and nurture their followers and meet their spiritual and worldly needs.

With new knowledge, science models are updated or replaced. Spiritual models also need to be analyzed and updated with reason and not perpetuated with memorized emotions.

With only historical words and understanding, scholars could only translate God's spiritual abilities as omnipotent, omnipresent, and omniscient. With science and relativity, we understand that we and God observe the universe from different perspectives. Learning more of God's perspective may help us spiritually and prevent catastrophes.

From God's perspective, pain and death may be burdens or opportunities to become free of the physical body for blessed eternal life or as punishment toward eternal damnation. We have a choice.

God must maintain holistic awareness of the universe to manage and control its evolution. This may be the reason prayers are not answered right away. We need to pray holistic prayers to attract

God's attention for Him to override physical laws and focus on our individual needs and bless us with miracles. God manages the universe and all forces as the all powerful CEO of the universe. All forces maintain their directives given at Creation unless God intervenes.

The Spiritual CEO

There are many questions as to why bad things and even death happen to wonderfully spiritual people. The author's near death experiences and bipolar disorder have given deeper perspectives toward life, death, and God. He thinks of God in science terms which include predicted additional dimensions that exist within God's realm, not normally sensed by man.

God traveling at the speed of light relative to all matter is a holistic spiritual reflection of our universe. God, His angels, and the redeemed exist within a different realm. The current configuration of the universe is the warehouse of God's spiritual memory. All minds and force fields construct spiritual software for spiritual relationships.

As God manages the universe and heaven, He asks for our loyalty. Holy relationships exist between God and His heavenly beings and between God and human beings. Only with unselfish intentions do we develop spiritual relationships. God cherishes attention from His children throughout the universe.

God's heavenly duties take precedence over His physical laws and relationships, and maintaining His physical laws takes precedence over man's emotional lives. From emotional communications with living beings and man, God overrides physical laws when their needs become synchronized with His.

Humans have only vague concepts of what being all-powerful really means. Except that God's power is beyond our imagination. From God's viewpoint, He may not think He is all powerful. Some of us may think the same since evil things continue to happen on earth.

We also have vague ideas of what God's omniscience of the universe and heaven might be. We have little idea of God's true scope. Does our God know everything about all other universes? Let's look at God from a new perspective.

One view of omniscience may be that of a perfect Chief Executive Officer, CEO. God receives and understands all knowledge to make perfect management decisions for an evolving and increasingly disorganized universe and an increasingly organized heaven. Heaven continually increases perfect organization. Relative to their 13.7 billion year history, the universe and heaven change very slowly and are essentially constant over our lifetimes.

God knows the universe's statistical structure, organization, and important problems, in order to make decisions for heaven and the universe. Like a CEO, He may rely on "spiritual managers, or angels" to provide Him data and support His efforts. Angels, and earthly spiritual leaders who believe in God's purposes, have direct access to God. Jesus reached this level.

God knows mental frequencies and resonances that construct our words. Our strongest communications to God may not be words. In solitude with eyes closed, we can construct scenarios of spiritual events we wish to happen. Mental visualizations for God may be more powerful spiritual communications than words. God is most interested in deeds that unite people and reflect His integration purposes.

This spiritual CEO model may help us understand why things on earth happen as they do. God looks for talent and obedience to meet His goals. Our goals should be God's goals. God's decisions, as our spiritual CEO, are always in the overall best interest of heaven and the universe. God ensures heaven remains constant and that all changes are consistent in complete or quantum steps. Our work to help complete God's goals elevates our purpose.

Humans have little idea of what is in the best interest for heaven or the overall universe. We may have some idea of what is best for the human race but should expand prayers to reflect blessings to God, heaven, and the universe.

To attract the attention of a CEO or God, we must provide Him with suggestions or action potentials for meeting His goals. Excellent supervisors and workers, when bringing problems to their managers or CEOs, present options for solving problems and ask for insight and permission for pursuing solutions. Too many of us are near sighted and only care about our own work, families, and communities. Caring for God is caring for everyone equally throughout the universe. We must think beyond self interest to be spiritual. Our efforts to unite all people on earth helps God unite all spiritual beings throughout the universe.

For key decisions, CEOs gather and integrate information on company goals, customer needs, laws, company abilities, and their competition to develop strategic plans. God gathers all spiritual and physical histories, current emotional, and relationship information, and relates them to His spiritual needs and goals for heaven and the universe. Secondly, He takes care of all spiritual beings needs. We must recognize our position in the universe to increase our spiritual status. All heavenly beings have already proven themselves to God.

Jesus, and probably other beings throughout the universe, has developed direct access to God. God and our brains are like radio stations, for sending out spiritual waves, and like radios, for receiving spiritual waves. Overstressed minds increase ability to become more attuned with God's wavelengths out of greater need.

Many, not having experienced near death, think everyone is similar to them selves and dismiss spiritual messages received by others. Everyone is free to believe or not believe in spiritual messages.

God creates frequencies that affect minds holistically. At times, some frequencies create discrete resonances for images and abilities of angels even in the minds of crowds as miracles. Angels do God's discrete work.

If God is constant, what is the difference between spiritual messages received today and those received in traditional religious times? There is none! Arrogant minds do not receive spiritual messages. They are too arrogant and busy with their rituals and dogma to listen for God today.

We have equal opportunities to serve God. He loves children, with open spiritual channels. God judges by perfect spiritual laws.

The author writes about His spiritual communications. One does not need to be a scholar to receive God's messages. Traditional religions promote their histories of serving God. Historical traditions are more important than current messages from God.

Religions encourage us to pray and receive spiritual messages and learn about God. If we receive strong spiritual messages beyond their dogma, they discredit anything that reduces their spiritual status. To maintain status, some religions develop complex dogma and rituals to elevate their leaders' status and beliefs. Jesus did not teach as the high priests of His time did.

There must have been a reason for such a little record of Jesus' life until He was thirty years old. The stress on His early life must have been unbearable. He probably became bipolar including near death experiences. It took years to heal and culture His spiritual abilities. If true, writers did not do us a favor by hiding His difficult emotional history. Others throughout history may have acquired similar spiritual talents, but not have been bold or organized enough to confront beliefs of the time.

Even today manic-depressives and believers of dissimilar religions are stigmatized without compassion or understanding. In Jesus' era, stigmas against bipolar disorder and new religions were certainly more severe. Today, comments show lack of compassion for or understanding of manic-depressives or dissimilar religions.

God is the CEO of the universe. The conscious mind is the CEO of the body. Our minds are to God as individual awareness of each cell in our bodies is to our minds. Each cell has some input in constructing our minds.

We develop a general or holistic thought with a specific purpose when we want to move an arm. Since birth, we have developed subconscious macros to organize and integrate millions of nerve and muscle cells to respond to each arm command.

We are concerned about abilities and responses of our arms, and, of course, about pain in our arms. However, consciously, we are not concerned about individual muscle or nerve cells unless they cause pain. If muscle or nerve cells are not helpful in overall body tasks, they are not as important to us. God has an overall purpose for the universe. It is important to be a part of that purpose.

Think about God's creativity and record thoughts and feelings during spiritual experiments. Choose a path with confident spiritual feelings. Think holistically of assisting the world, the universe, and God. We have diverse minds to worship differently. Many readers find comfort in traditional religions. That is fine as long as they do not feel or act superior to, or degrade, any humble person or religion. Humbleness before God means humbleness toward all people.

Concluding Spiritual Model

God and His perfect, complete record of every event in the 13.7 billion year history of the universe exist in spiritual space independent of physical space. Physical space, a freedom we sense and can sometimes measure, is enmeshed in higher dimensions within spiritual space. Humans cannot imagine God's freedoms, and that of the redeemed, in higher spiritual space.

In quiet, or in emotional times, beyond free will thinking limits, we may receive glimpses into spiritual space. With emotions, sincerity, truthfulness, dedication, mental refinement, or during traumas, we may receive spiritual feelings, images, or words at times. Spiritual feelings may be of higher dimensional activities we cannot imagine, understand, or express.

God's message is identical everywhere in space with slightly different perspectives and nearly the same over our lifetimes. Our lives are so very short compared to 13.7 billion years. Spiritual receivers must remain humble or will immediately corrupt spiritual messages with self-centered selfishness. God's message applies to all responsive beings in the universe. Receivers must interpret holy or complete messages to benefit all humans.

Humans should not be short-sighted with corrupt spiritual translations to aggrandize themselves, or their gang, cult, or country. From human perspectives, the universe is so large that our one God must have higher dimensions to nurture life throughout its entirety.

The spiritual words the author received: "Don't Leave God Out!" applies to all reflective and responsive beings throughout the universe. The author's mind resonated briefly into a glimpse of God's spiritual space. The author's spiritual writing is for the benefit of everyone. God's true warriors provide opportunities for everyone to expand their minds and freedoms. False leaders or impersonators rule through power and brainwashing to control.

Dictators do not help their subjects expand their minds. They are shamelessly afraid of losing their undeserved power and control. Controlling people are never spiritual. People guiding opportunities for others are spiritual. We should ponder who is spiritual in our lives.

God's perspective is very different from ours. Our thinking, actions, and perspectives can be helpful to Him. We can be supportive partners with God. Our minds are small dots, in a God's near infinite Hologram, but can make God's Hologram brighter.

A tragedy is that, with science, higher education, and reason, more people will reject "unreasonable" religions, and unfortunately, God. We need to receive spiritually and add science reason to our models of God. Religions should not remain in time warps. Traditional religions need to evaluate their origins, and progressions throughout the centuries, to distinguish between truth, aggrandizement, and corruption.

A concern is religion becomes an excuse for not reasoning. In a discussion on science and religion with a wonderful Christian lady, she asked why the author found it necessary to unite science and religion. The author asked her, "How do you think you are able to think?" After some thought, she responded, "God gave me a mind to think." The author suggested that God is often used as a crutch for not thinking in depth. We can learn more about ourselves through God.

Jesus must have had difficult early times to be truthful, humble, understanding, and even bold in His caring and spiritual leadership. From early training and inner study, the miracle of Jesus has been a foundation for the authors' life. However, there are reservations that faithful writers aggrandized Jesus' history by confusing parables with actual events.

Leaving Jesus' early struggles out of the Bible made Him less miraculous. The author believes Jesus, upon resurrection, became part of a Holy Trinity with God and the Holy Spirit to resonate forever in spiritual space. We may also form Holy Trinities in heaven.

Cognitive science establishes reasoning theories. Ideas are accepted according to metaphors learned mostly in childhood frames. For example, God is traditionally thought of as being "on high or above us" rather than permeating the universe since with the earth's gravity it is an advantage for man to be high rather than low.

Jesus championed the poor. Where is the empathy today that Jesus displayed toward the poor? Some Christians aggressively taunt others they meet by asking if they have been saved by Jesus Christ. This question controls by challenging strangers into a two thousand year historical frame.

We must not fear the future. Using science, spiritual reasoning, and all true religions, we must invent an integrated spiritual future.

Temporary Ending

We have constructed a spiritual hologram - an approach toward healing and expanding the mind for attaining God Consciousness. We wish to construct many successful paths to heaven.

With free will choices, develop spiritual reasoning through your own inner journey. Spiritual thoughts resonate throughout the universe independent of physical time and energy.

Long range hopes and direction include:

- Mental healing research and practice for young and old by NIMH and other research organizations;
- All new and traditional religions culturing minds to love, care, and share globally, for peace;
- Research to enhance spiritual communication and healing for God Consciousness.

Science and spiritual wisdom will become integrated in one arena. Manmade boundaries between disciplines of study will become obsolete. God integrates all good things into spiritual oneness.

This book was written independent of time constraints. Work continued until having attained feelings of completion. Written ideas continue until the last reader finishes reading. If I have done my job well, ideas will seem like having been known for a long time.

Additional mental reconstruction details are given in a "*Mental Reconstruction Log*" for researchers under separate cover by the author. This log contains sequences of psychiatric and spiritual events that may be useful for researchers in developing experiments.

People, who destroy innocent minds or bodies, are lost souls without a conscience. We must recognize, understand, and possibly help them, but protect ourselves and the abused.

Alcoholics destroy spouses' minds to convince them and others of their "perfection" without needing to stop their excessive drinking. Also, easy money enables the "false rich" to destroy others threatening their ill begotten "superiority."

Selfish people psychologically damage. Forgiveness is not easy, but releases stress burdens from negative judgments. Our brains, minds, thoughts, and actions are structured by our and our ancestors' experiences. We cannot judge spiritually without knowing lifetime and genetic histories. God integrates entire histories for final judgments.

When the body wears out, including from disease or tragedy, the mind sheds the body and transcends to a higher relativistic existence, awareness, and reality, assuming a loving, giving, and sharing mind. The spiritual is more real than the physical.

While exciting, encouraging, and sometimes profound, healing processes require effort and time. The brain is complex. Research should refine processes for a faster cure. This challenge fits into the relatively new category, "mind/body/spirit," established by the National Institutes of Mental Health, NIMH.

Ideas can be flighty and meaningless or foundations of a new skyscraper, airplane, or spiritual communication technology. When writing this book you were imaginary. Now, within an infinite time, we have a flighty moment of reality.

A Heavenly Glimpse

After receiving spiritual communication just before printing this book, I felt compelled to describe a glimpse into heaven. I have translated this higher dimensional spiritual message into the English language. Human ideas and writing can always be improved.

I am only able to use words, previously defined by others, for communicating human endeavors. Humans do not have the ability to perfectly translate God's, or heavenly spirits', messages.

From an earthly perspective, heaven consists of everlasting spiritual waves, independent of time, without needing physical energy, even though physical energy may have reflected spiritual waves into heavenly existence.

In heavenly existence, all thoughts are exciting, perfect, quantum or complete, and relate to the entire universe, heaven, and, possibly, existence. This gives some definition of what Holy, omniscient, omnipotent, and omnipresent mean.

Our beloved spirits, now in heaven within quantum waves, understand all earthly and spiritual things. Spiritual "imaginations" develop higher realities than earthly relationships and experiences.

Spiritual joy in heaven between loved ones is beyond our imaginations. All heavenly spirits will be better to us than trusted, best friends on earth. If heavenly spirits "imagine" celebrating spiritual relationships in heavenly mansions, it becomes true.

Heavenly spirits experience joy individually, and with all heavenly and earthly loved ones, independent of time, with omnipresence. Everyone in heaven is perfectly truthful with unlimited multitasking abilities.

You will recognize loved ones in heaven, but as more beautiful than imaginable when they were on earth. Their reflections magnify the love they had for you on earth.

You will see, and see through, God in all clear spiritual dimensions, with all frequencies, to become completely aware of the universe, heaven, and, possibly, all of existence in humanly unimaginable dimensions.

Humans have freedom in three dimensions of variable space experienced in one variable time dimension. In heaven, there are no boundaries but freedoms within many constant spatial dimensions and, possibly, several dimensions of constant time. Humans cannot imagine spiritual freedoms in heaven.

On earth atoms and matter constrain time to one rather constant dimension. In heaven, there is no matter to constrain time to one dimension.

God and heavenly spirits exist as a Holy Trinity. All heavenly spirits are holistically integrated within God into oneness. However, they also retain dual existence as individual heavenly free wills to guide loved ones on earth, who have learned to listen and receive.

Jesus' Spirit has broad heavenly free will and abilities to guide mankind, and, possibly, all reflective beings in the universe, to heaven. The Holy Spirit develops God's communication technology for influencing humans, and reflective, responsive beings throughout the universe.

Awareness in heaven includes knowledge of Hell. For every existence there is an opposite existence. There is no sorrow for insignificant lost souls. They have made their own choices on earth.

Lost souls are confined negative energy in individual elementary anti-particles with negative quantum reflections in total seclusion. Negative reflections mean evils and pain inflicted upon others is continually reflected back, and forced upon, perpetrators, in parallel, independent of time. Unbearable shame, with respect to life on earth, completes their just punishment.

To an earthly observer, physical things seem to remain stationary or flow rather consistently in time. However, the mind can see and think of something currently happening in one moment and then remember, and visualize, something that happened fifty years ago in the next moment. The current thought or the historical memory can promote the next thought and action.

From human perspectives, God has infinite freedoms of thoughts and actions in higher spiritual dimensions beyond human imaginations.

Upon death, redeemed souls remain in bodies but are also reflected evenly throughout spiritual dimensions. Cremation may not be good for human souls.

Where is God? He and His complete cognition are distributed evenly throughout heaven and the universe, in higher relativistic dimensions. God exists all around, and through, us. That is what omnipresence means. God nurtures the good we do, and shares it evenly throughout heaven and the universe.

Hopefully, this model will encourage readers to care for, and be truthful and share with, one another. Some readers may receive spiritual messages and construct advanced models of heaven. Reconstructing the brain and "renewing" the mind improves spiritual communication technology.

I will never be able to repay my debt to God and my parents, integrated within God, for my life and their love, first given, to me. Their love saved me when depressed and in despair. All I have to offer them are praises within fragile prayers.

Thank you for being a part of this mind healing and spiritual adventure. An easier path would have been to continue to follow the author's traditional religion. The author has taken a path less traveled. We can improve spiritual communication skills to attract attention, love, and action from a very busy God. The author's prayers are with readers and their interpretations for improving this work.

We spend a lifetime building minds, which show on our faces as we age. Does your face show love and concern for others? In this world with so much hate, please keep love alive. May God bless you!

Hopefully, this work provides direction for developing a clear mind. The author's next book, *The Clear Mind,* is expected to include hope, challenges, and spiritual reasoning from readers.

During childhood, his mother's, (a first grade teacher,) frequent words were: "Can't you just try to get along?" These words have become the author's philosophy for world peace.

His mother passed away years ago, but I still hear her voice:

["Hugh?"]

"No mother, I did not leave God out! I no longer conform to current patterns of this world."

["Your soul?"]

"When insane and near death, your and dad's love saved my life! My soul has been restored with spiritual excitement! My soul is well! My soul is well!"

["This is our story; this is our song, praising our Savior all the day long. Good Night, Dear!"]

"Good Night, MOM and DAD."

REFERENCE:

(I) Joe Z. Tsien, July, 2007, "The Memory Code," Scientific American, New York, NY.

Epilogue

Create universal love that binds,
With caring and refined minds.
Writing with love for the Lord;
The pen is mightier than the sword.

Hugh Fulcher (1995)

E*motional Mind Modeling* and *The Clear Mind Procedure* are foundations of *God, the Universe, and You! 2nd Edition.* Updates and refinements focus on spiritual aspects. However, it was necessary to build some understanding of the mind to develop spiritual models. Another project entitled: *The Clear Mind,* will be written only after several years of experience with the clear mind.

Humans are free to follow science procedures and develop logical discoveries without offending anyone. If we use our free will and apply science toward spiritual models of God, people of tradition religions will not believe we can receive significant spiritual messages today. Fundamental religions force followers to believe only what they say. They want followers to learn and memorize only their doctrine.

Historically, kings forced subjects to believe as they believed. Religion has long been used to control societies. Sometimes it is difficult to distinguish between spiritual leaders and tyrants.

Current spiritual messages received from God are very important. I am requesting feedback from readers who have received life-changing spiritual words or visions. One does not need to be a spiritual leader to receive spiritual messages in words. Please, include exact words of your messages from God. Include experiences that help prove God exists. What were dates, locations, your age, and circumstances? What were feelings, emotions, and conflicts before and after spiritual messages? What life changes occurred? Why are you sure you received a message from God?

Significant spiritual research and advances are also requested. Don't be afraid to let your inner self out. Be absolutely truthful or you may hurt others. If you wish, give your religion. Spiritual messages from all faiths are welcome. The goal is to integrate spiritual messages received by readers to develop spiritual communication technology and spiritual reason.

Feedback from significant emotional events, extreme traumas, and their spiritual effects will add to analyses. Also, please provide effects of unique exercises and mental reconstruction on mental disorders and challenged minds. Send information only in which you give permission for the author to integrate into a spiritual log. Designate if you want material to be anonymous. The author cannot guarantee using submissions or timing for another book. Be truthful about your experiences and work, and they may help many people. I am interested in new creative spiritual experiences and ideas. Please do not simply repeat traditional religious doctrines.

Please make submissions concise. Let God be your guide. Have a friend edit and comment on your writing. It may seem difficult, but allow a month of refinement before sending in submissions. Indicate number of refinements. Compositions must be **three** pages or less in **12pt. font**. Submissions may be condensed for integration and publishing. If your work is extensive, publish your own article or book. Sorry, I cannot spend time deciphering poor writing.

Include your email address. Work must be in English. Acknowledgments depend on time available. Have a spiritual brain day, and pass the "biscuits" please!

Send submissions to: *The Clear Mind*
P.O Box 1278
Forest, Virginia 24551

Appendix A: *Dark Energy and Matter*

In 1998 astronomers discovered that an additional three quarters of the universe's energy exists as dark energy. Dark energy is predicted to be consistent everywhere. This enhances my earlier position that dark energy is spiritual energy since from a biblical standpoint God is Holy or the same everywhere. The dark energy density is calculated as 10^{-26} kilograms per cubic meter. This mass is similar to that of a few atoms per cubic meter. This information was taken from Scientific American, February, 2007, *The Universe's Invisible Hand* [(1)], by Christopher J. Conselice. Here are brief quotes:

- "Dark energy is best known as the putative agent of cosmic acceleration- an unidentified substance that exerts a kind of antigravity force on the universe as a whole.
- "Less well known is that dark energy also has secondary effects on material within the universe. It helped to imprint the characteristic filigree pattern of matter on large scales. On a smaller scale, it appears to have choked off the growth of galaxy clusters some six billion years ago.
- "On a still smaller scale, dark energy has reduced the rate at which galaxies yank on, bang into and merge with one another. Such interactions shape galaxies. Had dark energy been weaker of stronger, the Milky Way might have had a lower star formation rate, so the heavy elements that constitute our planet might never have been synthesized."

The interesting aspects of the above theories fit astronomical observations that dark matter appears to be the same throughout the universe, but has influence on individual structures. Galaxies have overall, integrated resonances. Dark energy has wide influence on these integrated resonances within galaxies. Scientists may not have discovered or recognized these galactic resonances.

The above astronomical observations and theories on dark energy fit Christian models of God being everywhere equally and influencing atoms, galaxies, and man. Each action, within the universe, influences dark energy equally. Spiritual space and time are different than physical space and time. One would expect spiritual or dark energy to have very a low, refined energy density. Energy within the brain is small, but controls higher energy throughout the body.

Dark matter makes up 85 percent of all matter. A dark matter property is that it does not emit or absorb radiation like observable elementary particles. This property has kept dark matter from being detected directly. Dark matter seems to have the same gravitational properties as matter. Cosmological theories suggest that low-mass dark matter halos were formed at the beginning of the universe. Dark matter halos influenced the formation and configuration of galaxies.

God influences each atom, our minds, and galaxies differently but maintains His constant spiritual fabric throughout space. We can pray to God wherever we are in space. God is all field forces, including dark energy. My models of heaven consist of quantum vibrations to and from the point of the Big Bang every 10^{-106} seconds to maintain a consistently updated fabric throughout the universe.

Galaxies and atoms affect dark or spiritual energy holistically throughout the universe, independent of space. Quantum mechanics, relativity, my spiritual models, and God listening to and understanding prayers from wherever we are, does not make everyday or worldly sense. Scientists and we must learn of God's perspective.

Einstein proved that energy and matter are interchangeable. At relativistic speeds, matter itself increases relative to an observer. Electromagnetic energy created within a stationary brain travels at the speed of light and is interchangeable with spiritual energy independent of space throughout the universe.

Science continues to discover how God mathematically designed the architecture of, and physically constructed, the universe. Even though God remains constant throughout time and space, He influences galaxies differently and us personally.

REFERENCE:

(1) Conselice, Christopher J., 2007, February, *The Universe's Invisible Hand*, Scientific American, New York, NY.

Bibliography

The Holy Bible -New International Version - Disciples' Study Bible, 1984, Holman Bible Publishers, Nashville, Tennessee

Ariniello, Leah, Science Writer
2001- October. *Depression and Stress Hormones,* Society for Neuroscience, Washington DC

Armstrong, Karen
1993. A History of God, Ballantine Books, New York, NY.

Babyak, Michael, et al.
September/October 2000. *Exercise Treatment for Major Depression: Maintenance of Therapeutic Benefit at 10 Months. Psychosomatic Medicine,* Hagerstown, Md.

Byrne, Rhonda
2006. *The Secret* by, Atria Books, NY

Cary, Henry F.
1909 – 14. *The divine comedy of Dante Alighieri: Hell, Purgatory, Paradise,* The Harvard Classics, Vol. 20 of 51, edited by Charles W. Eliot, P.F. Collier & Son, New York, NY.

Chen, Pauline W.,
2007, *Final Exam, A Surgeon's Reflections on Mortality,* Alfred A. Knopf, a division of Random House, Inc., New York, NY.

Conselice, Christopher J.
2007, February, *The Universe's Invisible Hand,* Scientific American, 415 Madison Ave., New York, NY.

Darwin, Charles

1909, *The Origin of Species*, P. F. Collier & Son Company, New York, NY

Freud, Sigmund

1899. The Interpretation of Dreams, translated by James Strachey as: *Sigmund Freud: The Interpretation of Dreams*, Avon Books, 1965.

Fulcher, Hugh Drummond

1995. *Emotional Mind Modeling*, H D Fulcher Publishers, Inc., Lynchburg, VA

2007. *The Clear Mind Procedure*, H Fulcher Publishers, a Division of Wide Acceptance Financial, Inc., Lynchburg, VA

2008. *Bipolar Blessing & Mind Expansion*, H Fulcher Publishers, a Division of Wide Acceptance Financial, Inc., Lynchburg, VA

Greene, Brian;

2004. *The Fabric of the Cosmos, Space, Time, and the Texture of Reality*, Vintage Books, A Division of Random House, Inc.

Kentish, Jane

1987,_*Leo Tolstoy - A Confession and Other Religious Writings*, translation, the Penquin Group, Penguin Books Ltd, 80 Strand, London WC2R 0R1, England

Krauss, Lawrence M. and Dawkins, Richard

July 2007, "Should Science Speak to Faith?" Scientific American, New York, NY.

Tipler, Paul A.

1991. *Physics for Scientists and Engineers*, Extended Version, Worth Publishers

Tsien, Joe Z.

July, 2007, "The Memory Code," Scientific American, New York, NY

White, Peter T.

1986, June, *The World of Tolstoy*, National Geographic, Vol. 169, No. 6, 17th and M Sts. N. W., Washington, D.C. 20036

Wikipedia, the free (internet) encyclopedia, http://en.wikipedia.org/wiki/Biochemistry

Glossary

10^{-35} seconds = 0.00000000000000000000000000000000001 seconds; a very, very small fraction of a second

Angels – spiritual beings superior to man in power and intelligence, who, sometimes, are messengers from God to Man

antidepressant – a prescription drug that relieves negative thinking and can "force" positive thoughts

autocorrelation – statistical measure of the tendency of neurons to fire in volleys

axon – a long stringy extension of a neuron that sends electrical impulses and chemicals to other neurons and nerve cells through their dendrites

big bang – a scientific theory that all of the matter and laws of the universe came from a near point source; this theory is consistent with God's Creation of the universe

binary language – the language of digital computers; all data manipulations and calculations are performed using the binary number system – with ones and zeros.

bipolar disorder – manic-depressive illness; disorder in emotional communication

between left and right brains; a disorder of moods accompanied with loss of reasoning

Bohr Model – an early model of the atom with electrons revolving around the nucleus like planets revolving around the Sun

Born-again (spiritual rebirth) – the adult mind is cleared of all trauma and emotional scars and is able to experience God Consciousness

brain – the organ consisting of interconnected and coordinated neuron and nerve cells that create thoughts, judgment, and self-awareness

brainmind – an integrated concept of the brain and mind when physiology of the brain and psychology of the mind converge to form one integrated analysis.

brainstem – part of the brain at the top of the spinal cord that transmits body nerve signals and relays signals to and from the rest of the brain; coordinates and to some extent controls sleeping or waking states

brainstorming – a creative management process allowing only positive ideas and group decisions, the process includes a facilitator to ensure avoidance of negative ideas

Caveman – our ancestor communicating with sign language and coordinated grunts

censorship – activities of the subconscious mind to suppress dream "sub-thought" processes upon awakening, conscious mental process of reining in dream free will to conform the mind to conscious responsibilities

cerebral hemispheres – the two upper brain hemispheres; the latest evolved areas of the brain associated with human higher reasoning levels

chemistry – a science that deals with the composition and structure or materials and fluids and includes their abilities to interact and bind with other materials

Christian – religion based on Jesus' life and teachings and the Bible as sacred scripture

circular thinking – continually recalling the same old negative thoughts; negative thoughts revolve like a broken record with little success in finding solutions

"Clear, A" – a person with a clear mind free of all trauma effects

Clear Mind – A mind cleared of psychoses, neuroses, compulsions, repression, and psychosomatic ills, a brain free of all trauma and emotional memory scars or "engrams"

clique – a small group of people sharing selfish interest; a group of neurons reacting to the same stimuli.

cognition – mental processing including awareness and judgment

cognitive science – the science that studies processes of awareness and of being able to make judgments on that awareness, the study of how we and robots learn

communion – a Christian sacrament in commemoration of the death of Christ

consciousness – a state of being aware of one's body, mind, and environment including touch, emotions, and volition (the power of choosing); an integrated resonance of sensory nerve signals and subconscious mental processes amplified for evolving awareness

controlled conflict – forcing the mind to sense conflicting signals with conflicting exercises and mind experiments

coriolis force (or pseudo force) – a force perpendicular to a direction of motion. This force is evident in reference frames when masses like the earth are rotating. This force is referred to as a virtual force since it appears the way it does due to the earth's rotation.

cosmic sound – awareness of an inner mental sound during meditation and reduced mental energy, the inner sound is similar to cosmic noise

cosmic noise – celestial radio-frequency radiation from outside the Milky Way

cosmology – study of the origin, structure, and space-time relationships of the universe; relating high-energy properties of elementary particles to near the beginning of the universe

cosmos – an orderly self-inclusive harmonious and systematic universe

Creation – "The Big Bang;" fundamental change in existence with increasing spiritual order and decreasing physical order; God created the universe from nothing.

creative idea – an idea derived from subconscious and conscious processes that an individual has not seen or heard of earlier, an idea received from God

"deep structure language" – a part of any natural language that promotes self-reflection, inner awareness, and God-consciousness

dendrite – a long stringy extension of a neuron that receives electrical impulses and chemicals from axons of other neurons and nerve cells

depression – extremely negative thinking about oneself; a disorder of mood

dipole – an entity having only two distinct states

discrete – consisting of or studying separate identifiable entities or parts, not continuous

displacement – an object or image being removed from its normal place; a "remote" awareness viewing his own image in a dream or vision

DNA (deoxyribonucleic acid) – the molecular basis of heredity in living organisms

dream content – animated dream pictures, memories and hallucinations experienced in, and sometimes remembered after, dreaming. Dream animated image content referred here also as mental binary processes.

dream images – images within the dream content

dream thought – usually integration of recent and early childhood memories that instigate dreams and future wishes. Dream thought is the true meaning of the dream that must be revealed for psychiatry to be successful with healing stressed patients.

dream work – mental processing during dreaming; retrieving, comparing, organizing, and storing daily experiences within long range memory; integrating daily experiences into a unified set of emotional or logical life memories

dysfunctional – impaired or abnormal function

EEG (electroencephalogram) – display of brain electrical activity

ego – inner reflection of self and self-worth

Electromagnetic radiation (emr) – produced by moving or vibrating charges causing alternating electric and magnetic fields to be propagated outward at the speed of light;

electromagnetism – the physical science that deals with the relationship between electricity and magnetism; magnetic fields are caused by changing electric fields

elementary particles – the building blocks of atoms and nuclei; the "glue" that holds nuclei together

embryo – an implanted egg through the eighth week after conception

emotion – mental and bodily reaction marked by strong feelings that prepare the mind and body for action or reaction

emotional scar – a neural network injury caused by traumas or persistent emotional abuse developing inadequacies and slowly degrading mental processes

emr – short for electromagnetic radiation

enlightenment – a spiritual state marked by the absence of desire and suffering; rejection of social and material status

entropy – a thermodynamic function that is a measure of the disorder or state of a system, in closed systems such as the universe, entropy is continually increasing.

episode – an abnormal or unusual situation for some period of time that is separable from normal continuous life activities

evolution – slow creation (able to be perceived and understood by Man)

"fast thinking" – thinking as the manic mood evolves, includes "forced" and "strong" ideas that tend to intensify and compel thought patterns and actions

"Flash, The" – a near death experience in which important occurrences in one's life quickly flashes through the mind

"footprints" – God's discrete physical path as He created the universe

free will – God's most precious gift to Man; freedom of thought, choice, and emotions

"freeze" – a very depressed state in which an individual might stop all movement and remain in any position; a person experiencing only holistic thoughts

fMRI – functional magnetic resonance imaging, a method of imaging brain activity at higher resolution than PET without radioactive methods. The process uses differences in magnetic resonances of specific nuclei in active neural networks.

genetics – determined from the origin or from the genes, study of living building blocks

genre – a distinctive type or category of literary or musical composition

glia – structure or support cells within the brain that may also influence on long term memory processes and mental abilities

God – the supreme reality and awareness, being perfect in power, wisdom, and goodness, worshipped as creator and ruler of the universe, the infinite Mind; Light

googol – an extremely large number; 10^{+100}

harmonic vibrations – a periodic motion that has a fundamental frequency and amplitude and with lower level corresponding vibrations.

heart – emotional feelings and thinking as distinguished from the intellect; holistic thinking with body, mind, and soul; an organ of the body.

heaven – God's and the blessed Dead's sanctified, joyful structure or home; light and all field forces that are structures for God's Resonance; spiritual stability

Heaverse – term used when mentally integrating heaven and the universe as one entity

Heisenberg Uncertainty Principle – a well accepted theory in physics that characteristics of elementary particles can never be known precisely; for example, the energy level and the time of the level energy of an elementary particle cannot be known more precisely than a certain value

hell – all that is not heaven; spiritual instability

heuristic – involved in or serving as an aid to learning, discovery, or problem solving by experimental and trial-and-error methods, exploratory problem-solving that utilizes self-educating techniques and feedback to improve performance.

Higgs Particle – an elementary particle having symmetry-breaking mechanisms, and possibly having properties that will help scientists scientifically define God

hippocampus – part of the brain resembling a seahorse that is critical to long term memory formation in the cerebral cortex

holistic – relating to completeness and whole systems; in medicine attempting to heal the whole body; a feeling of wholeness and completeness by perceiving details equally by focusing long distance through visual details.

hologram – a three dimensional image using interference patterns between two coherent beams of light, the fundamental method of creating memories with electromagnetic interference patterns on brain cell membranes; see appendix A.

holographic film – film used to capture there dimensional hologram images

Holusion – a visual product of NVision Grafix, Inc. A two-dimensional image that can be interpreted by the subconscious mind to produce a conscious three-dimensional image

Holy – exalted and righteous completeness; worthy of humble devotion, continuous or analog thinking

Holy Trinity – the unity of Father, Son, and Holy Spirit as three persons in one Godhead according to Christian dogma; simply referred to as God in this book

imagination – a process of forming mental images not presently stimulated by the senses or never before wholly perceived by the senses

infinite – a concept, thought, time, or distance beyond limited human ability to understand or imagine. A number so big that it can be multiplied or divided by any number humans can write and still be the same unimaginably large number. (This may not hold true, only, if multiplying or dividing by zero.)

insanity – a deranged state of the mind, a mental disorder in which one is not able to cope within his "normal" social environment

integrate – to blend or incorporate into a unified or functioning whole

left brain – the left cerebral hemisphere containing discrete verbal and mathematical mental processes

Light – God; the visible spectrum of electromagnetic radiation frequencies

limbic system – a group of structures below the cortex of the brain that are concerned with emotion and motivation

limits – a boundary beyond which some system or process cannot safely exceed. System and mental processes degrade and may have unexpected operation beyond limits.

macro (mental) – a routine mental process that can be performed with minimal consciousness, a signature is a mental macro.

mania – mental hyperactivity including disorganization of thoughts and behavior and elevation of mood

manic-depressive illness – a mental disorder characterized by alternating psychotic depression and mania.

manic episode – the mind attains a "feeling good" or "high" mood with fast, forced thinking that if continued evolves into loss or reason and reality; thoughts include more and more dream processes, so many good ideas evolve that the manic often goes in circles not knowing which to act upon

mass – an intrinsic property of an object or a particle that is a measure of resistance to acceleration; quantity of matter; confined (or "dark") wave energy

meditate – to focus on or ponder ideas while the body is relaxed; to relax body, facial muscles, and eye focus (with eyes closed) to enhance calm holistic thinking; to reflect on inner thoughts of self and God

"mental binary" – the natural language of the subconscious mind; relates to binary language used by computers.

"mental limits" – subconscious processing limits governed by emotions developed mostly during early childhood; transformed to more logical limits through mental reconstruction

mental reconstruction – self healing and corrective action the brainmind performs after positive stimulation through psychotherapy and psychophysiotherapy

"Metallic Ping" – abrupt reverberating inner ("anvil strike") sound of a large internal energy spike being released

Methodist – a denomination of the Protestant Church that follows the doctrines and teaching of John Wesley in Christian worship

microelectrode – an electrical sensor small enough to be placed in, and monitor electromagnetic voltages from, a single nerve cell

mind – the function of the brain and nervous system; functional awareness

mind modeling – processes, patterns, similarities, descriptions, and analogies to visualize and understand mental processes

model – a pattern, similarity, description, or analogy used to visualize and understand some process or system; includes postulates and assumptions as to what is modeled and what is not modeled

modeling assumptions – precisely stated, assumed structure and boundaries surrounding model systems, conditions expected during operation and expected interactions with the environment

momentum – product of mass and velocity; mass increases near relativistic speeds

mood – predominant conscious emotion or orientation; contains reflections of self

MRI (magnetic resonance imaging) – a technology for developing images through the response of brain electrons, atoms, nuclei, or molecules to discrete radiation frequencies as a result of space quantization in magnetic fields

mysticism – direct communication with God as ultimate reality as reported by mystics; inducing a feeling or awe or wonder

narrow-minded – thinking of only old routine ways of doing things, responding to others, and solving problems; causes the face to narrow and the brain to stay tense

neuron – a grayish or reddish granular cell that develops fundamental electrical and chemical processes within the brain; neurons contain stringy appendages, axons and dendrites, that allow communication with many other neurons

neurosis – a nervous disorder marked by anxiety and the use of defense mechanisms to escape from the anxiety; especially when there is no defined cause

neurophysiology – study of the functions of the brain including neurons and nerve cells

neurotransmitter – a chemical substance that transmits nerve impulses across a synapse from one nerve cell to another

neutronics– calculations in nuclear engineering to design and manage the control of neutrons; power is produced by neutrons interacting with heavy atoms such as uranium

non-verbal communication – important communication using arms, legs, body, head, and eyes that may conflict with or support one's verbal communication

normal – typical behavior, actions, and reactions within an environment, conforming to and being accepted in an environment, characterized by average intelligence

nothing – a lonely point and its infinite reflection from which God created the heavens and the universe

NMR scan – nuclear magnetic resonance scans providing images of the brain and other parts of the body so anomalies can be discovered and studied

nuclear engineer – one who designs, and verifies safety and performance of, nuclear systems, one who interacts with (or as) regulatory authorities to comply with nuclear safety requirements

"Mental Nuclear Explosion" – extreme holistic mental energy release with perceived brilliant out-flowing of yellow light

nuclear reactor – a device for controlling nuclear reactions for experimentation or producing electricity, nuclear weapons, radiation, or commercial products

Nuclear Regulatory Commission (NRC) – US agency given authority to oversee and regulate operation and safety of nuclear reactors and nuclear products

omnipotent – all powerful or powerful beyond that which humans can imagine

omnipresence – being everywhere at the same time; God is everywhere at the same time and independent of space, considers man's limited knowledge of everywhere

omniscient – having infinite physical and spiritual awareness; God is omniscient of the entire history of the universe and heaven; may not apply to the entire future

out-of-body experience – an acute awareness of perceptions beyond the ability of normal senses.

paranormal – unexplained occurrences that violate currently understood scientific laws of nature.

perfect – a term to be used in referring to God or others but never referring to self, having properties that advance the entire universe and heaven.

PET (positron-emission tomography) – a diagnostic scan using images from emission of positrons in which shadows of structures beyond a narrow section under scrutiny are not shown. PET scans can show slices of the brain at various depths.

philosophy – all learning excluding technical, practical art, medicine, law, and theology

physics – the study of matter and its energy; includes mechanics, optics, heat, electricity, magnetism, atomic and nuclear structure, and motion energy.

physics mind model – awareness is constructed by resonances and interferences of electromagnetic radiation stored on membranes and outer surfaces of the brain; stored energy is a reflection of the continuous symphony of integrated neuron activations

physiology – part of biology dealing with the functions and activities of living things plasma – an extremely hot gas in which electrons are no longer chemically connected to any one individual atom and are free to travel from atom to atom much as a fluid.

Planck's Constant – a fundamental physics constant that defines elementary particle uncertainty and relates the wavelength of light or electromagnetic radiation to its energy; a part of deep structure language

primordial – a philosophical and simple fundamental existence before creation of the universe, existence before the expanse of the universe

Princess Karalla – an imaginary princess

process – a natural phenomenon with gradual changes that leads toward a particular result; includes subconscious neural activies that lead to conscious thoughts

prophet – one who proclaims divine revelations for the future

psychiatrist – a physician who specializes in psychiatry

psychiatry – a branch of medicine that deals with mental, emotional, or behavior disorders

psychoanalysis – method of explaining and treating emotional disorders that emphasizes the importance of talking freely about conflicts, childhood, and dreams

psychology – the science relating mental processes and behavior

psychophysiotherapy (PPT) – mental healing through physical exercising of neck, throat, facial, eye, and, to some extent, other muscles, and including forced, conflicting, or resistance exercises

psychophysioanalysis (PPA) – determining a logical selection of physical exercises to promote psychophysiotherapy and mental reconstruction

psychosis – severe personality disorder characterized by defective or lost contact with reality and often with delusions and hallucinations

pulse – a forced increase of a parameter or parameters of a system above normal levels

putative – commonly accepted or strongly supposed to exist.

quantum mechanics – a mathematical physics methodology of representing elementary particles as waves; particles are represented as standing or confined waves, and exist only as certain discrete qualities or quanta of energy

reactive mind – the course, rugged, fast-acting, mental response system, consisting of localized neural networks, that is naturally self-centered for self-protection

rebirth – freed from effects of trauma scars and of sin; surrendering one's life to God.

recursive – a procedure that can repeat itself indefinitely or until a specified condition is met; in computer programming, a program that calls itself, iterative

redeem – to free from what distresses or harms; to remove obligations and convert to something of value

reflect – to give or return back an image or outline with possible awareness of that image or outline, to ponder meaningful images or ideas

relativistic – an entity traveling relative to another entity near or at the speed of light

relativity – a theory based on two postulates, the speed of light in vacuum is constant and independent of the source or the observer, and laws of physics are invariant in all inertial systems, which leads to the physical equivalence of mass and energy; the relative variation of mass, spatial dimensions, and time with velocity variations near light speeds

religion – faith in and worship of God or the supernatural, a system of beliefs

repress – to prevent the natural or normal expression, activity, or development of; to exclude from consciousness; to inactivate recall of trauma memories

resistance (mental) – prevent from happening; trauma scars resisting normal mental processes; a hand resisting neck movements and stimulating trauma energy release.

resonance – large amplitude oscillations occurring when a driving frequency equals a systems natural frequency; conditions in which the maximum energy is absorbed by an oscillator (a device for producing alternating current), dominant frequencies from a system, including the brain.

resurrection – the rising of Jesus Christ and the sanctified dead from death

rhythm – a pleasing flow of sound and silence that includes music right brain – the right cerebral hemisphere containing spatial and holistic mental processes

safety analysis – modeling the operations of nuclear reactor systems to ensure that the overall system will operate and shut down as designed if design limits are approached or exceeded, verifies acceptable operation of redundant safety systems

salvation – methods of delivering or being saved from sin for everlasting life

sanity – being mentally sound and healthy and able to accomplish expected tasks and communications

saved – In Christian doctrine, being spiritually reborn by surrendering and committing lives to the spirit of Jesus Christ for everlasting life.

SCAPS (Snaps, Crackles, and Pops) – inner localized sounds of energy releases from neuron and glia cells within neural networks and from nerve cells mostly within the neck and throat

Schizophrenia – a psychosis characterized by abnormalities of thought; interactions and emotions inappropriate to the thoughts or behavior associated with them; delusions; hallucinations

science – systemic knowledge acquisition about occurrences and forces in nature using the scientific method

scientific method – principles and procedures for the systemic pursuit of knowledge involving the formulation and recognition of natural occurrences; formulation and testing of physical hypotheses

scientific notation – a short method of writing extremely large or small numbers; for example, 2000000. can be written as: $2. \times 10^{6}$; .00005 can be written as $5. \times 10^{-5}$.

Sierpinski Triangle – a continuous or fractal process of dividing larger triangles into smaller triangles

simile – a story comparing two dissimilar things

sin – a transgression of the Law of God – The Ten Commandments; a vitiated state of human nature in which the self is estranged from God; trauma scars within the brain caused by our or other's actions and our reactions to traumas and evils that divide us from God Consciousness.

singularity – an unusual or distinctive quality or state of being at one instance and place, possibly having extreme qualities, any number divided by zero causes a mathematical singularity and an infinite or indeterminate value.

soul – the spiritual foundation within human beings, a part of God that dwells within us, the inner most part of humans holistically distributed throughout the human mind

spinal cord – nervous tissue in the cavity of the spinal column that connects the nerves of the body to the brainstem and brain

spiritual – relating to God and loved ones holistically through worship, humility, and love, directed toward positively affecting the entire universe

standing light waves – large amplitude electromagnetic oscillations or reflections when a frequency equals a systems natural frequency; frequencies in which the maximum energy is produced by brain cells and absorbed by membranes throughout the brain; brain processes are recursive.

stigma – a mark of shame or discredit recognized by the unhelpful, uncaring narrow minded.

stimulus-response – analyzing responses when emotional or physical stimuli are applied

strata – roughly parallel layers of substance; or trauma scarred neurons with equal energy

subconsciousness – a wide variety of supporting neural processes in the mind below the threshold of consciousness

"sub-thoughts" – supporting subconscious components of conscious thought

sulci – grooves on the surface of the cerebral hemispheres

superego – the subconscious judge of drives from the id; only acceptable drives or processes reach consciousness

suppress – exclude trauma memories and dreams from consciousness

synapse – a joint or connector where nerve signals pass from one nerve cell to the other; connection between axon of one cell and dendrites of other nerve cells syntax – an orderly system of putting words together to form phrases, clauses, and sentences

Ten Commandments – Laws that God gave to Moses; the only laws that man needs

therapeutic – treatment of disease or disorders by remedial agents or methods

thought – a complete conscious awareness, a discrete entity within an ever flowing mental process; a mental process that has a distinct beginning and end

trance – a state of profound abstraction or absorption

transform – change in composition, structure, character, or spiritual belief

trauma – a disordered psyche or behavioral state resulting from mental or emotional stress, or physical injury; an injury to living tissue; an experience causing momentary unconsciousness

trauma scar – a localized (rigid) neural network injury caused by traumatic overload

two-and-one-half-dimensional vision – the ability of a two-eyed viewer to perceive some three-dimensional aspects of three-dimensional objects at one glance

Unified Field Theory – A predicted theory that will frame Man's understanding of gravity, electromagnetism, and weak and strong nuclear forces into one consistent theory; Unified force of creation before separation into separate field forces and all atoms; The unified field also includes the electroweak Higgs field.

virtual – having effects of reality but not being reality. Memory of an event is not the event itself.

wavelength – the distance between two successive wave crests

"what if" thinking – thinking leading into and during depression; the worried and depressed mind keeps mulling over things that could have been done differently with really little logical work toward to solutions

wholeness – completeness that is every where the same, that which is independent of time and space

wish-fulfillment – frequent cause of dreams about things we wish would occur

www.ingramcontent.com/pod-product-compliance
Lightning Source LLC
Chambersburg PA
CBHW052029090426
42739CB00010B/1834

9780979071058